D0276921

SECRET SERVICE

SECRET SERVICE

BY

SIR GEORGE ASTON
K.C.B.

LONDON
FABER & FABER LIMITED
24 RUSSELL SQUARE

FIRST PUBLISHED IN MCMXXX
BY FABER & FABER LIMITED
24 RUSSELL SQUARE LONDON W.C.
REPRINTED IN APRIL MCMXXXIII
BY KIMBLE & BRADFORD
LONDON, W.I
ALL RIGHTS RESERVED

CONTENTS

CONTENTS

8

CONTENTS

9

CONTENTS

PLANS, MAPS AND DIAGRAMS

AUTHOR'S PREFACE

ALL COUNTRIES, as long as war is possible, need to be acquainted with the nature of foreign armaments, their state of readiness, and their probable disposition in the case of war. In this book I have traced briefly the growth of the British Secret Service and have given some personal experiences before turning to my main subject— the part played by the Secret Service in the Great War 1914–18.

The personal notes, which will be found chiefly in the early chapters, have been inserted partly to explain the nature of the Author's experiences, which covered about forty years of Secret Service work, and partly to enable the reader to approach the climax of the Great War from the same angle as the author, in the light of these experiences.

In dealing with incidents of the War, the object has been to disclose, in so far as such disclosure is possible without injury to national interests, the information which was at the disposal of the leaders of the fighting forces in the principal operations on land and at sea, and the means by which that information was obtained.

For this reason reliance has been placed mainly upon contemporary evidence affecting the different incidents: 'wisdom after the event', based upon evidence subsequently available, has as far as possible been excluded.

The pages of some histories (and the writings of many arm-chair publicists) abound in criticisms of naval and military commanders, framed in the light of information which was not at the disposal of 'the men on the spot' who were responsible for the decisions at which they arrived. Hamley, in his *Operations of War*, recommends a serious student to place himself in the position of the military commander responsible for a plan of campaign or for dispositions for a battle; then to close his book and to decide what he (the student) would do if he were faced with a similar problem; then to read about what the commander concerned actually did. The recommendation is admirable as a counsel of perfection. It fails completely as an aid to critics who cannot discover what was known by the commander about his enemy's strength and intentions.

To compile a full account of the Secret Services during the eventful years of the Great War would involve writing a history of the war itself. In this volume it has been necessary to concentrate upon a few outstanding incidents, and upon the branches of secret service which definitely affected the issue. These accounts begin with British pre-war counter-espionage and its effect upon the successful retreat of the British Expeditionary Force from Mons in August 1914; they end with the principal events in which the British Empire armies were concerned in 1918.

For the information upon which the Great War chapters are based, reliance has been placed partly upon personal knowledge appertaining to official positions occupied, and partly upon first-hand information derived from personal friends in the Navy, Army and Air Force who were directly connected with the events described. To them grateful thanks are tendered. Chapters VII, VIII and XIII, which refer to the activities and to the fate of certain foreign spies, are based partly upon personal knowledge and also, to a greater extent, upon published material, especially—in the case of the German secret agents, Lody and Muller—upon Mr. Felstead's book, *German Spies at Bay*, which, as can be gathered from the title-page, has been read and passed at the War Office. The book is, unfortunately, out of print, and copies are difficult to obtain. Some personal details about skilled solvers of ciphers and codes, and the identity of the solvers who are referred to in Chapters

XIV and XV, have been deleted in the public interest, about which a high authority on secret service has been consulted.

Some of the Jutland secret signals, originally included in Chapters X and XI, have been omitted by request. A few notes on anti-British propaganda in Russia when under Lenin's influence will be found in the concluding chapter. They are based upon information provided by a brother officer who was employed on secret service while hostilities were still proceeding in the Middle East. He has since passed away.

I should like, in conclusion, to acknowledge my indebtedness to various high commanders who have been good enough to verify statements of matters within their personal knowledge, to my friend Captain B. H. Liddell Hart for his assistance in proof-reading, and finally to 'X', the Unknown Quantity, who has guarded the public interests.

September, 1930.   G. G. A.

CHAPTER I

THE STORY OF ARMY 'INTELLIGENCE'
1865–1914

THE REPUTATION for thick-headed and John-Bullish stupidity which was enjoyed by the British Army before the Great War was a useful asset to those who were engaged in collecting military intelligence. From subsequent pages something will be gathered of the organization for obtaining information which was in existence in August 1914. The War Office Intelligence Department had grown very slowly. I first made its acquaintance in 1886, when the various departments now collected in the great building in Whitehall were divided between the War Office in Pall Mall, opposite to where the Army and Navy Club ('The Rag') building stands, and the Horse Guards in Whitehall. The Intelligence Department was installed as an offshoot in Queen Anne's Gate.

The history of its origin is illuminating in connection with the origin of the 'stupid John Bull' legends. Between the Battle of Waterloo and the Crimean War very little interest was taken by the British public in the efficiency of its Army, with the usual result. The whole military system broke down as soon as it was put to the test. The scandals of the Crimean campaign led to the establishment of a 'Topographical and Statistical' department in 1855, and its principal activities seem to have been devoted to studying the topography of foreign countries. The nature and strength of their armies were treated as minor matters, relegated to the background, and the department enjoyed a long slumber from the time when the memory of the Crimean scandals faded into the past

B

until a certain amount of public interest was awakened by the conspicuous successes of the German Army against Austria in 1866 and against France in 1870.

'Mobilization' then became a word to conjure with. To it was attributed the speed with which the French (supposed to be 'ready to the last gaiter-button') had been overcome by the Germans, who had thought over and had worked out their problem beforehand. Mobilization required preparation, and preparation was impossible without information. The principal interest of some of the highest authorities in the British Army in those days was devoted to the Dress Regulations. Everything depended on Discipline, and they held that Discipline depended chiefly upon Dress, upon Parades, and upon cleaning and pipe-claying equipment which was quite unsuitable for campaigning. The more uncomfortable the uniform and the more useless the equipment, the stronger the devotion to Discipline that was required for making the best of things. It was dangerous to allow soldiers to think. They must not 'wonder why'. Experiences gained in the American Civil War in 1861–4 were ignored.

After 1870 the whole of Europe sat at the feet of the Germans as the most efficient soldiers in the world. Their uniform was copied. Special tributes were paid to their helmets, the *'pickel-haubes'*. In Britain the old head-dresses of the artillery, engineers and infantry were abandoned, and a hideous form of brass-bound helmet, topped with a spike, was adopted in imitation of the *pickel-haube*. It has endured to this day.

While there is some element of truth in these views of Army Reforms, they do not cover the whole ground. As a result of the 1870 war the 'Topographical and Statistical' Department was awakened from its long period of repose—devoted to the production of artistic and ornamental topographical masterpieces—and additional officers were at last appointed to obtain and to classify information about foreign armies. The name of Lord

Cromer, of Egyptian fame, then Lieutenant E. Baring, R.A., appears amongst those pioneers of Army Intelligence.

Once started, the idea that the British Army was maintained, partly at all events, for waging war began to take root, with the obvious corollary that the more that it knew about foreign armies the better. The result was the establishment of an Intelligence Branch (under the Adjutant-General of the Forces) on a separate basis on the first of April, 1873.

Amongst the names of distinguished officers who were appointed to the new department we find that of the late Sir H. M. Hozier (then a Captain), a distinguished intellectual soldier who served as secretary to the important Carnarvon Royal Commission on British Empire Defence and, as an authority on shipping, was Secretary to Lloyd's. He was father-in-law to Mr. Winston Churchill.

In those early days Topographical and Intelligence officers were bandied about from pillar to post. A house in Adelphi Terrace, near the Savoy Theatre and Hotel, was at one time the scene of their activities. So was a coach-house and stable near the Government Offices in Whitehall. Then they were better sheltered in a house at the top of Whitehall in New Street, Spring Gardens, since pulled down; and at last, in 1874, they found a more permanent home in Adair House, near Nell Gwynn's old residence and the old War Office in Pall Mall, where they remained for ten years.

We now begin to find traces of a long rivalry between the Adjutant-General's and the Quartermaster-General's branches of the Staff of the Army, the relative importance of whose work used to depend for the time being upon the personality of their respective heads. In 1875 'Intelligence' rose steadily in importance. The idea began to be grasped that a War Office was intended to aid in the conduct of warfare and that the necessary preparations, as the Germans had shown in 1870, must perforce be carried out in time of peace. 'Intelligence' began to come into its own, and it was then transferred from the Adjutant-General's to the Quartermaster-General's sphere of influence.

The Military Authorities were still under the influence of the Palmerston Royal Commission of the early sixties, which was responsible for the idea that fortifications could do the work of warships, the theory being that the introduction of steam propulsion had rendered obsolete Raleigh's old principle that it was better to deal with foreign invading armies at sea, before they had 'our Kentish capons in their stomachs'. 'Intelligence', in those early years, was mainly devoted to studying how to deal with a foreign invading army after it had landed, leaving the British Navy out of account.

The Royal Engineers had a strong voice in military policy, and the name of the late Sir John Ardagh, a highly intellectual Sapper with wide views, began to appear in connection with the Intelligence Branch. I had made his acquaintance in the Sudan War of 1884, in connection with a beach-landing at Trinkitat before the battles of El Teb and Tamasi, and I found his friendship and guidance of great value in later years.

By 1884 'Intelligence' at the War Office was moved from Adair House in Pall Mall to a pleasant old house in Queen Anne's Gate, overlooking St. James's Park with a view of Buckingham Palace in the distance.

There, in 1886, I began to spend many profitable hours learning from Army Intelligence officers, with the gathering force of experience behind them, how to get great government departments to *do* things, instead of perpetually discussing them without doing anything. When the late Sir Henry Brackenbury, an artillery-man equipped with good brains and great administrative capacity, became the head of the department in Queen Anne's Gate, it began to be realized that gathering information about foreign armies was only a means to an end. The next step must be to make the best possible use of whatever Army Parliament consented to provide, and at last the lesson of speedy 'mobilization', which Prussia had taught to the world in 1870, was grasped. Mobilization was then brought within Brackenbury's scope at Queen Anne's Gate.

In 1887 Brackenbury's department was put under the late Lord Wolseley, whose prestige as the winner of wars had given him a dominating position in connection with Army policy and a voice in public affairs. The Adjutant-General's Department then absorbed Brackenbury's organization in 1888. The section dealing with mobilization and other matters not coming within the description of foreign intelligence was transferred to the War Office in Pall Mall, and three years later (1891) Brackenbury, the reformer, was sent to India on important Army work. He was followed by a series of distinguished successors, including, from 1896 onwards, Sir John Ardagh.

No tale of army reform during those years would be complete without referring to Lord Sydenham, then Captain G. S. Clarke of the Royal Engineers serving in the department of the Inspector-General of Fortifications and Works at the Horse Guards. He was the best friend that the British Navy ever had amongst soldiers. He held revolutionary ideas on defence, and to these his position as secretary to the Colonial Defence Committee enabled him to give full play. There was sore need for co-operation. One of the productions that emanated from the Army Intelligence Branch at Queen Anne's Gate showed how, on the outbreak of a great war, it was proposed to re-distribute the troops employed on garrison duties abroad. The navy was not consulted either about the safety or about the convenience of sea-transport. The table of movements included one of thirteen men from St. Helena to Aden, and a re-sorting all round which would cause a dislocation of naval arrangement at a critical period. I tell the tale as typical of the old days, and to mark the progress that was made during the years which intervened before the Great War.

My next experience of military intelligence and Secret Service was with the field-army, and we now come to the Anglo-Boer War of 1899–1902, when 'Deputy Assistant Adjutants-General for Intelligence' first began to appear on the staff of divisions in a British expeditionary force. There had been a field-intelligence department in Kitchener's campaign which resulted in the conquest of the Sudan in 1898, but I can vouch for the fact that their functions were ill-defined. The tradition had survived.

At Lord Roberts's head-quarters at Bloemfontein, where I spent some time with such colleagues as Field-Marshal Sir William Robertson (then a Captain), I was sent off to one of the divisions to relieve Field-Marshal Sir George Milne, now chief of the Imperial General Staff (then a Captain in the Artillery), who was wanted at Lord Roberts's headquarters for other duties. There I found that the new intelligence officer was looked upon as a sort of handy man, expected to undertake odd jobs of every description.

In Kitchener's small army which had conquered the Sudan, staff officers had exchanged duties constantly, and Kitchener did much of his own staff work. The precedent was followed, and intelligence officers did so much of other people's work that they had little time for their own, so I soon found myself employed as a sort of Landrost or Mayor of an occupied town (where I had to arrange for all police duties, for the baking of bread for the troops, and for pacifying Old Boer women who complained that they were running short of matches); as a requisitioner of sheep (the business of the Army Service Corps), and as responsible for the custody of hundreds of prisoners, their arms, horses and saddlery (the business of the Provost-Marshal's department). That was all in addition to the responsible work of locating the enemy, providing maps, guides and interpreters and all the usual matters which come within the scope of the present-day intelligence officer. I had no office equipment whatever, and no staff.

Experience in South Africa caused the British public to take an evanescent interest in army reform. The Intelligence Department in the War Office was strengthened, and its influence steadily increased. The department was moved in 1901 from Queen Anne's Gate to Winchester House, near the old War Office in Pall Mall, and when that was removed to the present imposing building in Whitehall army intelligence and the Secret Services connected therewith were brought for the first time under the same roof as the highest military authorities.

The credit for establishing a General Staff, of which 'Intelligence' is an important branch, is due to the late H. O. Arnold Forster, who took that step just before he gave up his office as Secretary of State for War when the Conservatives went out of power in 1905. The credit for developing the British General Staff on its present basis is due to the late Lord Haldane, the best of all our Secretaries of State for War, who created the little Expeditionary Force which earned the admiration of its enemies in the Mons Retreat. From 1906 onwards the serious nature of the German menace became more and more obvious to all thinking soldiers, to a very few responsible statesmen, and to an infinitesimal proportion of the nation at large. Public attention was devoted chiefly to domestic questions, including troubles in Ireland.

It was not so at the Army Staff College at Camberley. As one of the Directing Staff there between the years 1904 and 1908, I was in constant touch with an old friend and fellow-student at the Staff College who had become Director of Military Operations, with the Intelligence Branch under his control. I can vouch for the completeness of information about foreign armies which his branch furnished to those of us who wanted information for working out schemes for using the new Haldane

Expeditionary Force under all conditions that we could imagine against the armies of every conceivable country. The War Office Intelligence Department contained by that time a geographical branch and a strategical branch (charged with real plans on parallel lines with the imaginary ones which we were working out as an instruction), and soon there was a 'Special Branch' charged with the most secret work. We shall come across some of its activities connected with marking down foreign secret agents.

There we can again leave the War Office Intelligence for the time being. Early in 1908 I became head of the General Staff of the British Army under Lord Methuen in South Africa, with a Secret Service of my own. My main attention was then devoted to the chance of native troubles during the critical time when the Union of the old colonies in South Africa was being established, and to German South-West Africa. I will not enlarge upon the question of native troubles. The less said the better. Traders had been passing up-to-date rifles in large numbers to Basutoland at great profit to themselves. Certain organs of the Press and less reputable authorities, likely to profit by a war against the Basutos, were constantly starting scares with no reasonable foundation whatever. Through my intelligence organization I was able to tell the High Commissioner (Lord Selborne) that there was no basis for the rumours. Hoping to put an end to them, he had the blocked-up passes specially opened through the Drakensberg Range (between Basutoland and Natal). Accompanied by Lady Selborne he then trekked, without military escort of any kind, from the Orange Free State right across Basutoland from west to east into Natal. Even after that object-lesson the rumours persisted.

The main incident which affected our knowledge of German South-West Africa was a breakdown in the cable to Swakopmund at about the time of the Agadir crisis of 1911. That caused the Germans to put their defence-scheme into operation, believing that war had been declared. I thus knew every detail of their plans and that knowledge was of great value to me in August 1914, when I was called upon to advise the authorities in Whitehall on the subject.

The late Lord Haig was Chief of the General Staff in India while I was in South Africa, and there were new General Staff officers all over the Empire. We arranged, independently of the War Office, a system to keep each other posted up every month with news of what was going on in other parts of the world. Our information was thus passed more rapidly than if it had been sent *via* London. The system worked well.

I returned to England in 1913, when my allegiance was transferred from the War Office to the Admiralty, still watching the activities of my old colleagues in the army with interest. At the War Office, the little section of the 'Special Intelligence' group that was charged with detecting spies, which numbered fourteen souls in time of peace, had risen to about 800 by the end of 1918. From the outset there was also a cable censorship, established by the Committee of Imperial Defence, and a huge extra staff, of which the number rose to over 4,000 during the War, was maintained for postal censorship. That work involved the examination of millions of communications, and the aid of experts in every language in the world; of chemists able to lay bare the secrets of the many forms of invisible ink which German agents employed; and of skilful solvers of the most complicated of ciphers. Propaganda, counter-propaganda, and much other work were added.

In course of time (January, 1916) the General Staff was reorganized by Lord Kitchener, and the Special Section became a large Department of State with a Director of its own, charged with duties affecting not only the Army, but all the fighting services and their activities. For some extraordinary reason this great department, employing more than 6,000 people as early as February 1915, and serving several other Departments of State, remained subordinate to the Military Intelligence Department, of which the proper business was work connected only with purely military operations. That procedure was a mistake, but the branch of 'Special Intelligence' with which we shall be mostly concerned will be Counter-Espionage. That involved the control of aliens (there were 30,000 Germans resident in the United Kingdom) and of undesirables, in conjunction with the Home Office authorities; the discovery and punishment, working with Scotland Yard, of hostile secret agents; and watching all ports and frontiers which civilian traffic must cross in order to reach or to leave areas in which military operations were proceeding. Besides all these activities, it was necessary to examine carefully the status of every foreigner who tried to obtain employment in munition factories, in Red Cross organizations, and in any other form of work which afforded special facilities for sabotage or for spying. Touch had also to be kept with similar work all over the Empire, and with seditious movements in India and in the Far East.

I used sometimes to wonder whether those hosts who were employed on Military Intelligence and on 'Special Intelligence' in the Great War ever thought about the little party of soldiers who worked in a Whitehall coach-house and stable after the Crimean War, and were bandied about from pillar to post until they were housed in the new War Office in the early part of the century. They were probably far too busy over the problems of the moment. Nevertheless, one trembles to think what would have happened to the country if the great emergency of 1914 had found 'Intelligence' without the organization of which those early pioneers laid the original foundations in the old days when few of the higher authorities in the Army took the least interest in their labours.

In a subsequent chapter we shall come across some examples of the contributions that were made by the counter-espionage branch to the winning of the war. I had the good fortune at the time to enjoy the friendship of one of the mysterious members of that particular branch. He wears many well-earned decorations, few people know how well. His name is—shall we say 'X', the 'Unknown Quantity'?

CHAPTER II

PERSONAL MEMORIES OF THE NAVAL INTELLIGENCE DEPARTMENT
1886–1890

UNTIL the year 1887 there was not, to my knowledge, any permanent department of the British Admiralty that was specially charged with collecting and issuing information about foreign navies and coast defences, though a certain amount of detail, of value to shipbuilders, was noted by the Naval constructors. The Hydrographic Department was pre-eminent in producing charts, at the disposal of the seamen of the whole world for purposes of navigation, but the land topography depicted on most of the charts was too inaccurate to be of value for coastal attack or defence. Only the positions of points that were likely to be of use in navigation were fixed with any accuracy; intervening features of the ground were sketched in roughly by eye, without being surveyed. Additional information which might be useful in landing operations was to be found in Admiralty 'Sailing Directions' and 'Pilots', emanating from the same department. There was also a 'Dock-book' covering the whole world and a 'Coal and Telegraph Chart' showing the principal coaling-stations and cables.

When the late Sir George Tryon, an Admiral with views far in advance of those of his contemporaries, was Secretary to the Admiralty, he used his influence to appoint a 'Foreign Intelligence Committee', with a naval officer as chairman, to tabulate such information as might reach the office about matters of importance likely to be useful to the Admiralty. The general impression at the time was that, when once the information had been tabulated, a very small staff would suffice to keep it up to date. In the original plans for the new Admiralty building, now stretching all the way from the Mall and Horse Guards Parade to Whitehall, only two small rooms were allotted to the Naval Intelligence Department. It now occupies a large proportion of a whole block. Some personal experiences of the work in the old building may be of interest.

In the spring of the year 1886 I was crossing Hungerford Bridge over the Thames on my way from Waterloo Station to Whitehall with a fellow-traveller whose acquaintance I had made in the train. We discovered that we were both bound for the Admiralty. I was a young subaltern in the (late) Marine Artillery, fresh from three years' experience in a ward-room mess at sea. He belonged to the Higher Division of the Civil Service, and to the Department of the Secretary of the Admiralty, then Sir Evan MacGregor. Hearing what my destination was, he said: 'Then you must be the new "intelligent" officer,' and he initiated me into some of the secrets of my new life as a member of the 'Foreign Intelligence Committee of the Military, Secret and Political Branch of the Department of the Secretary'. All that I had hitherto been able to do, as a young officer of Marines, to promote British Sea Power was to spend three years on guard every alternate day in the Mediterranean flagship, presenting arms to Admirals and visiting my sentries at intervals. The saying used to be that the two idlest men in a British man-of-war were the Chaplain, who did nothing, and the Major of Marines, who did less, as he had two subalterns to help him, and three years doing one-third of nothing seemed a poor preparation for an 'intelligent' officer whose previous training had not been very helpful. In the gunnery schools at Eastney and on board the old *Excellent*, and in the Vernon torpedo school, I had learned how to handle every sort of gun by sea and land, and the torpedoes and mines used in the fleet, but my ignorance of foreign affairs and of geography and modern languages was abysmal. The chief asset that had gained me the appointment seemed to have been a report from the Captain of my first ship (the late Sir Henry Rawson) that I 'had tact with men', and that I had conducted myself for three years with sobriety (unless that clause was inserted the implication to the contrary held good in the Navy of those times) and entirely to his satisfaction.

The Foreign Intelligence Committee was presided over by the late Captain W. H. Hall, R.N. (father of Sir Reginald Hall, then a naval cadet, who became the celebrated Director of Naval Intelligence at the Admiralty in the Great War). In those old days the motto of the authorities charged with the responsibility for defending the British Empire seemed to irreverent youth to resemble that of the amateur actor in that old play, *The Pantomime Rehearsal*—'It will be all right on the night.' Preparations for war did not exist. When the relations with any foreign power (usually Russia) became strained, popular panics resulted. The House of Commons then hastily voted sums of money, which allayed public uneasiness. The Russian scare of 1878 (the 'Peace with Honour' period) had produced the 'jingoes', who did not want to fight but by jingo if they did, proclaiming that they had the ships, the men, and the money for the purpose, a view that was more prevalent with the public than it was amongst the experts behind the scenes in Whitehall, or, I believe, amongst members of the Russian Secret Service. British ships had prevented the occupation of Constantinople by Russian troops, but 'battleships cannot climb mountains', and India was proverbially apprehensive of any further approach by Russia to her north-west frontier. The Pendjeh scare of 1885 raised another acute panic, both in India and in London, where public opinion was permanently aroused, and questions were showered upon the Foreign Intelligence Committee of the Admiralty.

It was not generally known that, at the time of the Pendjeh scare, no preparations had been made for war.

The fleet could not have been mobilized. This was discovered by the late Lord Beresford (then Lord Charles) when he joined the Admiralty as Junior Sea Lord in 1886. He made up his mind that, in the event of a sudden war, naval affairs would become a pandemonium and that Britain might be beaten at sea. His colleagues would not pay any attention to his representations, and he obtained the permission of the First Lord, Lord George Hamilton, to put the situation before Lord Salisbury, the Prime Minister, who, after consulting three senior admirals outside the Admiralty, directed the First Lord to establish an Intelligence Department for the Navy as soon as possible.

The old Admiralty was an attractive place in which one worked with pleasant companions. They were cultured men, mostly from the Universities, who wrote good English and ran the business of the office itself and correspondence with other departments with great ability. The Secretary's department was a close community into which no naval officers had been permitted permanently to intrude. The few in the Foreign Intelligence Committee were there only on sufferance, to help in matters which required technical knowledge of a nature which will appear in due course. Subjects connected with the peace administration of the Navy were dealt with efficiently by the Board, and if the Foreign Office wanted what they usually called a 'gunboat' in a hurry, to enforce an argument in any part of the world, a ship was at once forthcoming. The work went smoothly, with occasional light interludes (as, for instance, when the bailiff of Their Lordships' farm on the Island of Ascension asked for collies to start a breed to look after his sheep, and was sent two, both dogs). While these interludes occasionally relieved the monotony of peace routine, my chief, Captain W. H. Hall, had to contend with a dead weight of indifference about the lesson which had been taught by the Germans to the Army in 1870, that, under modern conditions, wars can be won by careful preparation before they have begun. For such preparation to be possible it was first necessary to know as much as possible about all foreign navies, defences, communications, and cognate matters.

Very little was known about them at the Admiralty, since it had been nobody's business to find out. Lord Charles Beresford, as junior Sea Lord, insisted upon a 'plan of campaign' being drawn up, and he would not be quieted. A clever Admiralty caricaturist drew a picture, based upon a well-known advertisement of Pears' Soap, of Lord Charles in his 'birthday suit' as a fat baby climbing out of a bath to get at a cake of soap labelled 'Plan of Campaign' that was lying on the floor. The picture was entitled ' He won't be happy till he gets it '. He, and others like him, did get it in the end, but only just in time for the great ordeal of August, 1914. The ideas of junior officers in the Old Navy were looked upon by their seniors with grave suspicion. I remember an occasion when a Sea-Lord wrote, 'On what authority does this *lieutenant* put forward such a proposal?' across an important suggestion by the late Admiral of the Fleet, Sir Doveton Sturdee, then a lieutenant in the flagship in the North American Station, to enlist the sympathies of the coast population of Canada in joining a reserve for the Navy.

It was in such surroundings that I embarked over forty years ago upon my new career, an exciting one for the young as 'intelligence' seemed to imply spying, a subject in which I had taken an interest since, in early childhood, I had been shown a picture of two of them wending their way back from the Promised Land, staggering under the weight of a pole from which an enormous bunch of grapes was suspended. The spies had been aided by a woman who kept their secret and so obtained the salvation, when Jericho was burned, of her father, her mother, her brethren and all that she had. She subsequently dwelt in Israel, was held in great honour and 'lived happily ever after'. That story had left upon my youthful mind an impression that women can keep secrets, a lesson which I verified in later years at the centre of all secrets, the Office of the War Cabinet, at a time when the plans of commanders in the field were being freely discussed in London clubs.

There was no use in travelling about to unravel secrets before finding out first what was already known. Captain Hall had told me for what work of that sort I should be responsible, and I can still remember my instructions. I had to know all about British defended harbours at home and abroad, with their defences and their resources that might be of value to the Navy; about communications (submarine cables) British and foreign; about all foreign guns (at sea and in coast defences), gun-mountings, ammunition, armour, electric lights, torpedoes, submarine mines, 'and experiments connected therewith'. To which subjects there was soon to be added 'British and Foreign Commerce, Defence and Attack'. With the confidence of youth I cheerfully undertook the rôle of a grain of mustard-seed which grew into an enormous tree by the end of the Great War. Captain Hall added that he would like me to begin with Hong Kong, as our admirals at sea did not know how the harbours on their stations were defended, and that might lead to trouble.

Having discovered, with the aid of an atlas, where Hong Kong was, I sat down, before an unlimited supply of Government foolscap-paper, red-tape and stationery, to the work of an intelligence officer and to many years of labour in that interesting capacity by sea and by land. Another table in the room was occupied by a civilian member of the Secretary's Department, Graham Greene, who was afterwards Secretary to the Admiralty. He taught me what office industry means (he was usually the first to arrive and the last to leave, and he consumed his luncheon hastily amongst the papers on the table at which he worked), and also the secret of getting things done in Government offices in Whitehall—do not go straight to the heads through the official channel. First smooth the way with the brains behind them. You may find these in quite a junior official. Go and see him. Before writing an official letter to another Department the best plan was to go across to the office to which it was to be addressed and, if possible, to write the reply.

The other two tables were occupied by naval officers. All the countries in the world were divided into two groups. One of these officers had to find out about all the navies, dockyards and coast defences of the countries in each group. We had only one travelling Naval Attaché to obtain information from the whole of Europe. The British Navy was supreme. Britain was referred to by the whole world as the 'Mistress of the Seas', and other navies were deemed to be of so little account that representatives of Foreign Powers were allowed practically free access to all our dockyards and naval establishments. It was thought that the more they saw of our Navy the less would be the chance of complications with foreign Powers. I remember that in one matter the Intelligence Department of the Navy of the United States was very helpful. They sent us a 'card-index', the first that we had seen. We were too conservative to use one at once, and I used to write all the information that I collected in enormous ledgers, but the department is probably full of card-indexes by this time.

It was in February, in the year 1887, that the activities of Lord Charles Beresford and of others led to the establishment of the Naval Intelligence Department, embodying our Foreign Intelligence Committee, slightly strengthened, as the Intelligence Division. There was also a small Mobilization Division. The heads of the respective divisions were Captains Eardley Wilmot and Custance (now Admiral Sir Reginald). The work was strenuous, and for long periods it was very dull. We worked in the office for about nine hours a day for six days in the week, and we often took work home with us. Most of the time was spent in compiling and sifting the information which soon began to pour in, instead of embarking, as I had hoped, upon adventurous trips to 'spy out the land'. Captain Hall, our Chief, set a high standard. I only realized it when I came to know him and his family at their home in Redcliffe Square. He worked before breakfast from 5 to 8 a.m. He came to the Admiralty at 10 o'clock. He worked there until 7 p.m., and again for an hour and a half after dining at home. He died soon after he left the Admiralty, but not until the foundations of the later huge Naval Staff, with its plans, operations, intelligence, historical and mobilization divisions, had been well and truly laid. There ought to be a statue to him in the Admiralty.

There were some interesting incidents at times, and one of these gives me an opportunity of telling a few stories of how the information that we were constantly recording was sometimes obtained. Hong Kong has been mentioned. I remember receiving a valuable report from a young subaltern in the Army who was serving in the garrison there. We knew next to nothing about the guns in the defences of Vladivostock, so this enterprising young officer visited the place in snowy weather, crawled over the ramparts when the sentries were under cover, and obtained full information. With Siberia of dreadful association so handy, he must have had good nerves to undertake that enterprise entirely on his own initiative. Fired by his example, I took advantage of the next snowstorm to obtain a few days' leave to visit our friends across the Channel, not, of course, from any feeling of hostility to the French. Intelligence Departments collect information about all countries, however friendly; you never know what may happen in the course of years. The Germans in those days were urging us to strengthen our Navy to answer the French building programme. A predominant British Navy was relied upon as the best guarantee of peace in Europe.

It was bitterly cold, so all suspicious folk were under cover when I paid my visit to Dunkirk, Calais and Boulogne. Some imaginative panic-monger had conceived the notion that the new harbour-works, that were then being made at Dunkirk with railway lines along the quays, were intended for embarking troops in a hurry to invade England; and we knew nothing about the forts defending Calais and Boulogne, in spite of the stream of British visitors and travellers who had been living in or passing through those places for years. I was not quite sure what the ethics of such espionage were, as it was my first experience of the sort. On all occasions when I have visited foreign countries in time of peace, I have made no secret of being a British officer, and I was once approached by an obvious *agent provocateur*, who offered to sell me the plans of a fort. I replied that they did not interest me. The fort was a new one, not quite complete, and all that I had wanted to know was whether it yet held a garrison. That I knew already when the agent approached me, because the soldiers of that particular country wore boots with nails arranged in a particular pattern on the soles. The road to the fort was muddy. It showed the footprints of so many soldiers that the existence of a garrison could easily be deduced.

Any officer who knew his business could see what he wanted in foreign coast defences from afar off. 'Loading derricks' were used, for getting shell into heavy guns, and they were of a different size and shape for different sorts of ordnance. There were pictures of those derricks in the published drill manuals, and as they always showed up on the skyline, the rest was simple. If inspection of the interior of a fort was desirable, there was usually a high lighthouse in the neighbourhood which could be visited for a small fee. I went up one of them on that occasion, after asking a small girl whether it was permitted to *ascendre*, which was all the French that I knew at the time. She fled from me, and I hoped that her father was not a soldier or a gendarme. The incident did not land me in a French prison, but I was glad to arrive safely at Dover. I think that the folk whom I met at *tables d'hôte* in the little inns in which I stayed must have gathered somehow the impression that I had visited their seaside resorts in that snowy weather in order to find a cheap place to bring my (non-existent) wife in the summer. I certainly did not know enough French to have conveyed that impression purposely myself. I remember asking my way to the sea, and being understood to want my mother.

I carried my plans in an open suitcase, which reminds me that, when likely to meet suspicious folk, the best method of handling secret papers is to treat them as if they are of no importance. I confess to having hoped most devoutly that I was not mistaken in that view when I once carried about the plans of the minefields defending the naval ports of an important foreign Power, but they reached their destination. I can only remember two occasions on which I tried the theatrical sort of tricks attributed to people in spy-stories when they are carrying secret plans or papers. Once, when I was travelling by train, I crossed a frontier unexpectedly by night, having arrived there earlier than I had intended. I was ostensibly on a shooting tour, so I had with me a number of cartridges: at the frontier I was told that they were liable to a heavier duty than I could afford to pay. I had removed the shot from four of the cartridges and substituted some secret notes, ramming down the wads again over the charge, the idea being that, if I was arrested while I was out shooting, I could destroy the plans by firing them off. It was very difficult to slip those four cartridges into my pocket without exciting suspicion. It would have been better to have followed my usual practice and to have avoided 'play-acting'.

On another occasion I was told at Cook's tourist agency that the police were taking an interest in me, so I thought that it would be more convenient for both parties if I left by the next steamer. I went to my hotel to pack up, and I was sitting in my room there with a secret plan on very fine paper before me, touching it up, when there was a violent hammering at the door. I do not know whether psychologists have ever solved the mystery of the apparatus behind the brain which causes one to act in emergencies without conscious thought. A cricketer sometimes finds the ball in his hands when fielding at short slip without having an idea how it got there, so there must be some such apparatus. It made me ram my secret plan into an empty pipe, add a little tobacco and light it, before calling out the foreign equivalent of 'Come in'. The whole operation took about the same time as a catch in the slips. I should like to finish the story by describing how I was taken to durance vile by police-agents and searched while the object of their quest was vanishing in pipe-smoke before their eyes, but it was only the hotel 'boots' (coming to see about my luggage) who had knocked.

Only once did I have the misfortune to attract the attention of a gendarme. It was at the Paris Exhibition of 1889, which I visited to inspect the display of war material. He objected to my making a sketch of an apparatus for firing the guns of a ship when the deck was exactly horizontal, thus solving the problem of accurate fire from ships against forts on shore, which interested me intensely (the Gallipoli campaign might have ended otherwise if we had had a really reliable apparatus of that sort). The incident shook my nerve so much that I did not dare to prod with my umbrella some big guns which were shown at that Paris Exhibition, or to knock them with my knuckles. I sent in a report about the biggest of them all. That particular gun was shown by a new factory, and I impressed the lesson taught by the speed at which the factory had turned out so big a gun. I ascertained, after sending in my report, that the wretched gun was made of *papier-mâché*. Lord Sydenham (then Captain G. S. Clarke, R.E.) and Sir Desmond O'Callaghan (then a Captain R.A.) reported to the War Office on the same gun, but I persuaded them not to give me away, and to leave out the *papier-mâché* part.

At about that time a great fuss was being made about

the French explosive called *mélinite*, that was expected,
like most new inventions, to 'revolutionize warfare'. We
were allowed, within limits, to order any new foreign
books which we thought were likely to provide information of value to the Admiralty, so when I saw an advertisement of a book called *Mélinite*, I applied for a copy to
the Assistant Secretary (R. D. Awdry), who was not very
sympathetic with the activities of our new Naval Intelligence Department. Soon afterwards a risky French novel
with a picture outside of the heroine (*Mélinite* by name)
reached me with the Assistant Secretary's compliments,
and 'Does this sort of information come within the scope
of the new intelligence officers'?—'Above all, no zeal,'
was Talleyrand's advice to the budding diplomatist, and
I still had much to learn.

There were plenty of stories of other folk's mistakes
in those early days. A military attaché in Paris (now a
celebrated retired General) reported that the new French
rifle bullet was covered with leather (*cuir*), having been
told that it was covered with *cuivre* (copper); and other
similar stories tended to brighten our labours. A naval
attaché was invited to attend an important trial of some
foreign armour-piercing shell of secret composition. It
was a ceremonial occasion, so he attended in full-dress
uniform, with a tail coat, and there was a large attendance
of foreign senior officers. Our attaché picked up a piece
of one of the shells which had just been fired, intending
to forward it for analysis in England. The spectators
were soon afterwards entertained by the sight of a spiral
of smoke rising from his coat-tails. The metal was still
hot, and he was compelled to produce it for all to behold
after having tried for a time to copy the heroism of the
Spartan boy who concealed a live fox (on the other side
of his body).

Those years of hard work at the centre of a web which
was destined in course of time to stretch to all parts of the
world, afforded good training for the future, and I hope
that I have not been too prolix on the subject. The net

result of establishing a Naval Intelligence Department was to discover that, unless we increased our Fleet both in ships and men, certain foreign navies would easily be able to wrest from Britain the historic sea-supremacy which had not been challenged since Trafalgar. The Naval Defence Act of 1889 was then forced upon a reluctant Board of Admiralty by public opinion as the result of an agitation in which the London Chamber of Commerce, Lord Charles Beresford, the *Pall Mall Gazette* (and late W. T. Stead) and the Poet Laureate (Tennyson) bore prominent parts.

The intelligence work was done at a bare minimum of expense. Patriotism, rather than profit, was the incentive for those who provided the information about foreign fleets, coast-defences and armaments. The work required technical knowledge and a thorough mastery of what was known already before going in search of more. Otherwise, there would have been useless duplication. Obtainers of information had to be trusted with what had already been collected, and no foreigner, to my knowledge, was entrusted with such a mission and so tempted to betray his country. On the other hand, there were attempts by foreign agents, some of them harmless, some dangerous, to worm secrets out of our government employees. An Admiralty messenger got into serious trouble. One of their lordships went out to luncheon, leaving a drawer of his writing-table not quite closed. There was an attachment which rang a bell in the next room, which was occupied by a private secretary, if the drawer was opened. Directly after the Admiral left his room the bell rang, and the private secretary came in and found the messenger at the drawer.

We discovered the impossibility of keeping any printed matter secret unless it was sent to the Foreign Office Press, whence it emerged, printed on duck's egg green paper, in locked boxes. To number each copy and lock up those that were not officially distributed was useless, unless the type was broken up and all the proofs were burned. There was a lucrative foreign market for spare proofs, and even for torn waste-paper. I recalled that lesson during the Peace Conference at Versailles in 1919 when I received, two or three days after the discussions had taken place, my official printed copies of the secret proceedings of most of the Committees. I found that I knew most of their contents already, from what I had read in articles in the Paris Press.

When I left the Admiralty to join the Army Staff College at Camberley, my work was divided between two sections, each under an officer. These sections, in course of time, threw off more shoots to form the various branches and divisions of the Great War. I saw a good deal of the Naval Staff work in 1913 and 1914 when I was working at the Admiralty, and I dug out a good many papers reminiscent of the old days, including that plan of a foreign torpedo-boat station, stained with tobacco-juice. I do not think that it would be an exaggeration to add that, for the work which Captain Hall's little group of officers and others tried to do in time of peace in the eighties of last century, the Admiralty must have employed a thousand people in the Great War.

My other work in connection with Naval Intelligence was still more interesting, as I was my own master and I dealt direct with the Naval Commander-in-Chief in the Mediterranean, which was the first naval station to possess an intelligence department, established between the years 1892 and 1895. Unfortunately the system had not had time to spread all over the world by 1914, when there was still no intelligence officer in the flagship of the Australian squadron. A typical example of the result occurred when instructions were sent, to the Commander-in-Chief on the station soon after war broke out, to proceed to New Guinea and to destroy the high-power German wireless station at a place called Rabaul. He went there and he came away again, having been unable to find it. It was found and dealt with later. In August 1914 great difficulties were experienced in discovering the exact truth about the progress which the Germans had made with their new wireless stations in the Pacific. The information was urgently needed, and on all stations where intelligence officers had been established for some time everything of that sort was of course well known. Nevertheless it was something to have established in the Mediterranean in 1892 a system of Fleet intelligence which had spread nearly all over the world by 1914.

No funds had been available for the purpose when, in 1892, I was sent to Sir George Tryon's flagship ostensibly in place of a subaltern, who was removed in order to provide me with a cabin, but I had recently come into a small legacy which I expended upon the work. At the end of the third year the appointment was put on a permanent footing with extra pay, and one of the officers who had relieved me at the Admiralty came out to take my place. The system gradually spread to other naval stations, and it worked smoothly in the Great War.

CHAPTER III

RANDOM RECOLLECTIONS

BEFORE passing to the secret service which lay behind certain selected events in the Great War, it may be as well to recall a few impressions which were gathered during the early period that was covered by my connection with the Naval and Military Intelligence Departments, of which the history is given in the preceding chapters.

The incident which stands out most clearly, as having had a dominating influence upon my outlook towards public affairs, was a visit to Metz in the year 1891, while studying at the Staff College, after having discovered in the Naval Intelligence Department at the Admiralty the grave need for preparing the fighting forces for war. The visit to Metz was paid in company with a division of students at the Army Staff College who were in charge of a Professor (the late Sir Frederick Maurice). Our object was to study on the ground the various battles of the Franco-Prussian War of 1870. We certainly did learn something about the tactical use of ground, but the general impression that we gained was that the Germans overran the French before they were ready, and so won the war. We had been told constantly that the process by which this result was obtained was called 'mobilization', but very little about what mobilization actually meant. We had some idea of one feature of it, that the German army which was to be rushed into the field on the outbreak of war was distributed in time of peace so that the reservists who would fill the ranks should be living near the forces which they would join, while the French reservists were not so distributed; several days were lost in complicated railway movements and in sorting out the men. We did not realize the Prussian thoroughness and attention to detail which strove to save not only days but minutes. We were there to study history and to learn lessons in tactics, not in any way to spy out the land, and information which taught us by far the most important lesson came to us by hazard.

We were copiously entertained by a German cavalry regiment at Metz, the entertainment including a formal dinner at which we sat from 5.30 to 11.30 p.m. and for which the strongest of heads for liquor was needed. Next morning, with splitting headaches, we were shown round the Quartermaster's clothing-store in the barracks. There I saw at a glance that the clothing for each army reservist was in a pigeon-hole by itself with his blanket lying loose on the top. That attention to detail saved many hours on mobilization. All that was necessary was that the men should file through the store, pick up their blankets, shovel the rest of the things into them, and move on. That Quartermaster's store, which I compared with our own of the same date, impressed me more than anything else with the thoroughness of preparation for war in Germany. I believed then, as I still believe, that the most potent cause of the fear which Continental nations display towards their neighbours is not the potential strength of armies, but rather the state of immediate readiness in which the armies are maintained. When fear reaches a climax, war results. The lesson that was learned in France in 1870 has never been forgotten.

From the little incident at Metz in 1891 one learned thus about the speed of mobilizing the German field-army —far more valuable information than any about their forts could be. We took care to keep clear of those. If their army got off the mark first to invade a neighbour, that neighbour would never be likely to reach the forts. Our hosts were quite open about such matters, but in later years we at the Staff College looked with comparative equanimity upon their activities in Norfolk, where we heard that German officers were holding a sort of Staff Tour. We trusted the Navy. One recalls now the incidents, soon after the outbreak of the Great War, when orders were given to be ready to drive all the taxis and cabs inland from our seaside-resorts on the East Coast, lest they should be useful to an invader. The story of the invasion scares of the Great War will be worth telling some day. Sir William Robertson has told us in his *Soldiers and Statesmen* as much of the tale as it is possible to disclose at present.

Mention of what would, I suppose, be called 'spying' on foreign forts reminds me of an incident connected therewith which also bears indirectly upon developments in the Great War. Soon after the experience gained at Metz, of German thoroughness in war preparation, I was at Constantinople in 1892 on Sir George Tryon's staff, and we found there a German military mission which exercised considerable influence in Turkey. British influence, which had in former years been exerted through a Naval mission, was on the wane. We also found that, through some mysterious financial pressure, more attention was being paid to defending the Dardanelles than the Bosporus, and armaments ordered from firms in the Central Power group were being distributed accordingly, the inference being that it was considered more important to keep away the British Fleet than the Russian. Nevertheless, the Sultan (Abdul Hamid) appeared to be very friendly to us personally, as can be gathered from the incident which follows.

As an intelligence officer I was naturally interested in the Bosporus defences, and anxious to compare them with those of the Dardanelles, which I had seen during the voyage to Constantinople. The new Dardanelles forts had just been completed, and there was talk of new ones to defend the Bosporus. So my steps led me in that direction during an afternoon's walk with some of my shipmates. I had left them to visit some high ground on the European shore near Rumeli Kavak, where I sat for a time on a small eminence overlooking a new battery. The trace of the work could already be clearly distinguished, so I took

45

a photograph with a pocket camera. When I looked up after the click of the shutter, I discovered that, while I was looking into the finder, a Turkish sentry had spotted me on the skyline. He called out something, and a party of soldiers began to climb the hill.

Close to me was a shipmate, out for a walk. I concealed the camera in my pocket, hailed him, and asked him to sit down for a few minutes and look after my things while I went to meet Captains Noel and Wilson (the late Admirals of the Fleet, Sir Gerard Noel and Sir A. K. Wilson), whom I had just seen some way off in another direction. Being rather tired, my shipmate was quite pleased to oblige me. Then I joined the Captains as fast as I could and we returned slowly together to the hill. There we found my friend looking rather bewildered. He was surrounded by excited Turks, armed to the teeth, gesticulating and exclaiming in an unknown tongue. We joined the group. Then a Turkish officer who spoke a little French was fetched, and he explained to us that the soldiers had actually seen my shipmate in the very act of photographing their fort. We recommended our friend to submit, as an act of concession, to the indignity of being searched, in order to prove his innocence. They searched him and found nothing, not noticing the camera bulging in my pocket. We said that we hoped that they were quite satisfied, as we were all obliged to return to our ship, and we left them examining every crevice in the ground and crannies in the neighbourhood. The incident was doubtless reported to Constantinople, as I was sent for in the evening by the Admiral, who told me that the Sultan had asked whether we were interested in the defences of the Bosporus, if so, arrangements would be made for him to visit any forts which he desired. The result was that we were given every opportunity of verifying the rumours about more attention being paid to the defences facing the Mediterranean than to those which faced the Black Sea.

The reflection will doubtless occur to readers of this

old tale that the tragedy of the Dardanelles campaign of 1915, referred to in a subsequent chapter, might have had a different issue if the Russians, in whose interests that campaign was nominally conducted, had taken an active part in the operations by a simultaneous attack from the Black Sea, but political conditions are not always in accord with military effectiveness, as subsequent disclosures have proved in this instance.

As a further preliminary to the Great War chapters, it may be desirable to introduce here a few notes on appointments which I held, and on impressions of the German menace between the years of my direct connections with Naval and Military opinions in Whitehall and the outbreak of the Great War in August 1914.

There was no doubt in my mind when I left the Staff College in 1908 that military opinion, as embodied in the late Sir Henry Wilson, held that the immediate departure of the British Expeditionary Force to France in the event of war with Germany would be inevitable. Naval opinion, as far as I could judge, had not gone nearly as far. Further personal references will be made to these subjects under appropriate headings in subsequent chapters. By way of credentials, in order to enable a judgment to be formed of the amount of my authority about matters then, but no longer, secret, it may be as well to mention here the Defence Conference that was held in London in 1909, soon after it was discovered through confidential channels that the naval building programme in Germany had been accelerated. I attended that conference with the delegates from the old South African Colonies, who came to England in connection with the consolidation of Union, but were unable to speak of South Africa as a whole until that measure had been completed. The growing menace, from a naval point of view, of the German navy and the policy which lay behind it was realized by all. On the military side, the new General Staff of the Army performed yeoman service behind the scenes in furthering the policy of establishing uniformity in training, in organization and equipment of all the military forces in the Empire. Sir Spencer Ewart, then the Director of Military Operations, was the moving spirit. The late Sir Charles Callwell was an able assistant. At that time there was no realization of the demands for masses of troops that would arise in the event of war with Germany. Between that date and the outbreak of war it was believed that British sea-power, if adequately maintained, would be the dominating factor from the point of view of the British Empire, and the military view was that if a British Army of six divisions were to be sent to the aid of the French, that army would suffice to turn the balance. I was confirmed in that view by conversations with members of the General Staff at the War Office when I was serving at the Admiralty in 1913 and 1914.

While such were the soldiers' views, I find in my private diary for January 1909, evidence that the late Lord Haldane must have had a wider vision when he was Secretary of State for War, and a better realization of the great military effort that might be required of the British Empire if we should ever find ourselves 'with backs to the wall' as we were in the years 1914–1918. I had come from South Africa to England on a short visit to attend the first conference at Camberley of the projected 'Imperial' General Staff. An entry in my diary for Wednesday, January 27th, 1909, runs: 'Rather an important day. Lunched with Mr. Haldane, Sir Edward Grey and General Douglas Haig present. Mr. Haldane noted with pleasure that our local policy (in South Africa) had been to work on exactly the lines worked at home, and to fit in with the present and future policy which is contemplated. He hopes that the Imperial General Staff will be a success. He explained the proposals for forming a seventh division (from British troops in South Africa and elsewhere) and what an advance they are upon the Cardwell system in having a force available for service without taking the linked battalions. He hopes behind the seven divisions and those in India, to have fourteen of Territorials in the United Kingdom and more in the Oversea dominions.' I have a further note that Mr. Haldane, as he was then, was the first to realize the probability that, given a just cause, the whole Empire would rally to provide an army which would be numbered in army corps and in armies in the event of grave emergency. I remembered that note in an old diary when he was subjected to bitter attacks in certain sections of the Press in the darkest days of the Great War. As a result of these attacks, a rumour was current at one time that he (who had done more than any other statesman of our time to prepare the nation and Empire for the great ordeal) had been shut up in the Tower of London as a traitor!

In these days there should be little need for Secret Service about the fighting forces in foreign countries which are the members of the League of Nations, as they all are expected to provide full information about their armaments, which are published annually in an armament book, issued from Geneva. In the old days there was plenty of scope for officers on leave and other patriotic folk to report on such matters during visits to foreign countries. Here the question arose of sending information back. It was better to keep it in one's head if possible, even in peace when the penalty would probably only be unpopularity, though possibly incarceration in a fortress. In time of war it has been proved by experience that the danger of having to face a firing-party (sometimes the hangman's noose) is usually due to the methods used in sending the information to its destination. The hostile spies who were detected in the United Kingdom in the Great War were nearly all convicted on written evidence. I have added in an appendix, for those who are interested therein, a few notes on certain methods of communicating secret information by using ciphers, codes, and 'invisible inks'.

Great use was made of homing-pigeons by nearly all countries in the Great War, to transmit information, and it was sometimes as much as a man's life was worth to be seen in company with one of these interesting messengers, of which use has been made throughout the ages.

As soon as I was employed on naval intelligence work the use of homing-pigeons in connection therewith appealed to me strongly. In my early days in the Admiralty I used to study Nelson's methods of obtaining the sort of information which is most important to sea-commanders, which was news of the movements of hostile ships. Nelson kept frigates always watching harbours that were known to contain hostile fleets. Either the frigate brought the information direct, or (as happened before Trafalgar) signalled the news to vessels stationed to pass on the messages. When Whitehead torpedoes were invented and were constantly improved, it seemed to me that to station valuable cruisers off foreign defended harbours, swarming as some of them did with torpedo-boats, would be too expensive an undertaking. Numbers of small fast yachts or even fishing-boats could watch foreign harbours equally well. They could run away if they were chased, and send their messages by carrier-pigeons. I was too junior at the time to put forward the proposal myself, so I persuaded some friends in the Foreign Office and in the War Office to put the idea forward and to call the attention of the Admiralty officially to experiments abroad with carrier-pigeons, and the letters arrived at the Admiralty in due course. My proposal was killed, for the time being, by an official who wrote this 'minute' on the papers: 'No action. These birds might carry misleading intelligence.' I then decided to keep a pigeon-loft at Portsmouth at my own expense, and H.M.S. *Excellent* took up the question later. I am still puzzling over the idea that was in that official's mind. How can a pigeon flying across the sea be captured alive by an enemy, its message removed, and a false message substituted ?

When, later, I went to Malta, I took pigeons with me and started a flying club there. My object was to organize a daily pigeon-post from Sicily to Malta, in order to keep up rapid communication if the cables were cut in war. Then wireless telegraphy came in, and the project was allowed to drop. The German armoured cruiser *Goeben*, with the *Breslau* in company, put into Messina during the night of August 2nd/3rd, 1914. They coaled and they left at 5 p.m. on August 6th. The news reached the British Admiral later. The *Goeben* escaped from superior British forces and her success in reaching Constantinople uninjured on August 10th was the main factor that made Turkey join the Central Powers. That completely altered the aspect of the war, and probably prolonged it for two years. I still think that an intelligence agent at or near Messina could have sent the news of the *Goeben's* movements more rapidly to the British Navy if he had had homing-pigeons at his disposal.

CHAPTER IV

1914
WELL-KEPT SECRETS OF THE WAR

WE CAN select two well-kept secrets from the early days of the War, the secret despatch of French's little 'B.E.F.' of Old Contemptibles to France, and the surprise which the Germans sprang upon the French by putting in the field an army far stronger than the French General Staff expected. Luckily for the Allied cause, the first was a set-off against the second.

Only complete ignorance of the strength of the German army with which they would be immediately confronted could have induced the French military authorities to conceive their celebrated 'Plan 17', which landed them at once in grave disasters, in the 'blood-baths' at Morhange and elsewhere, and in the wedging of Lanrezac's Fifth Army into the sharp angle between the Meuse and the Sambre, attacked by German masses from the east and north, and open to attack from the west too, resulting in a colossal 'Sedan'—if the first secret had not been kept. He would have been struck on three sides by more than three-quarters of a million enemies.

It is interesting to study how the keeping of the British secret saved the situation, and how the secret was kept.

A difficult problem faced the British military authorities. In a land teeming with the enemy's spies in all walks of life they had to assemble secretly from many places thousands of men, horses, guns and vehicles innumerable to form a 'little' army which, if you strung it out along a road, would occupy about a hundred miles. The whole had to be put into trains and moved to British and Irish ports—to Southampton, to Avonmouth, to Newhaven, to Liverpool, to Glasgow, to Dublin, Cork, or Belfast, as might be needed. Rolling-stock had to be collected at various railway-stations before the troops could be moved (1,800 special trains were needed in five busy days). Eighty actually ran into Southampton Docks, easily watched by spies, and figures for other ports were in due proportion.

Then came the Navy's turn to keep the secret. The Admiralty moved troops by sea in those days (the Board of Trade does so now). The transports had hurriedly to be collected, a very suspicious proceeding. Ships for men. Ships for horses, needing special fittings, and for vehicles. Ships for motor-lorries (only a few in those days). Ships for stores and ships for supplies. Ships of all sizes and speeds. They had to be loaded, moved and unloaded both safely and secretly—and secrecy spells safety in war. They had to run the gauntlet of hostile eyes which might be distributed on the long coast-lines of Southampton Water, the Solent and the Isle of Wight.

Then came the Army's turn again—to take over these masses of men, horses, guns and vehicles and to move them to their destination just in time, as it turned out, to fill a yawning gap between Lanrezac's left flank of the whole French Army and the sea. Such was the problem: 'secrecy first' under conditions that seemed to be impossible; and personal memories of one who remembers those days well may be of interest. For the first time in history British soldiers had been given enough notice to prepare their plans, although they did not know whether the Cabinet would sanction them at the last moment. The Government had only promised definitely to confer, not to act. For that statement I can vouch. The General Staff did not and could not commit the Cabinet to further action.

The General Staff of the Army was of recent growth. It was established while I was teaching 'Imperial Strategy' at the Camberley Staff College under the late Lord Rawlinson and Sir Henry Wilson between the years 1904 and 1908, and all the 'teachers' became General Staff Officers. As soon as Lord Haldane, the best War Minister of modern times, established the Expeditionary Force, we worked out, as was our way, schemes for using it under every imaginable condition in every conceivable part of the world, including Belgium—especially in Belgium from 1906 onwards, and partly for the following reason.

Henry Wilson, who had been serving in the innermost sanctuary of War Office secrets, came to us as Commandant. He knew all about the 'military conversations' with the French General Staff that dated from about that time. Thenceforward the question of how to use the B.E.F., if Belgian neutrality was violated by Germany, came into special prominence. Henry Wilson spent much of his leave bicycling on the Belgian frontiers, and he encouraged the students to do the same. In due course new railway-sidings were discovered, and other indications of Germany's intention to mass troops some day in the Aix-la-Chapelle-Malmédy area. We thus found out, all those years ago, the general nature of the celebrated 'Schlieffen Plan', which had recently been adopted by the Great General Staff at Berlin. The full details of that plan have never yet been disclosed. They may still be amongst the records in that sinister building that was occupied by the Great General Staff in Berlin. They are not to be found amongst the wilderness of words uttered or written by statesmen and diplomatists. The military archives have been jealously guarded against unbiased researchers.

So now we have three plans. The German Schlieffen Plan, the direction of the great blow foreseen by us at the Staff College, its strength unknown; the French 'Plan 17', obviously based upon ignorance of the enemy's strength and intentions (the British Military authorities apparently knew little or nothing of 'Plan 17' until August 1914); and the British General Staff plan for using the British Army, which the Germans, to their cost, failed to discover.

At one time British military authorities had thought

that it would be most effective to send the Army by sea to Antwerp, ignoring the fact that both banks of the Scheldt belong to Holland. It is inconceivable that the support of any wise British Cabinet would have been obtained for such a plan. We, at the Staff College, thought that the best scheme would be to disembark in French ports and to get into touch at once with the left of the French Army, wherever that was to be found. Everybody knows now that it was the plan that was actually adopted in 1914, and it is amazing that, as will appear, the secret was not discovered by the Germans. I will first add some personal details, to bring the experiences of pre-war days up to date.

After serving as head of the General Staff under Lord Methuen until 1912, I stayed in South Africa until early in the spring of 1913, to help the new Government of the Union in which General Smuts was Minister of Defence, to start and to train the South African Defence Forces. We were then coming nearer and nearer to the brink of the precipice. I came to England several times, so I was constantly in touch with my colleagues on the General Staff of the Army, with the Committee of Imperial Defence and with the Admiralty. From Henry Wilson himself I knew of that personal friendship with his French colleague, General Foch, which led to an aftermath so momentous.

On returning to England I joined the new Admiralty 'War Staff' to work out certain problems of preparations for any war, especially guarding places of which the loss would sorely handicap the Navy.

I have no desire to save foreign secret agents the labour (it took me nearly a year, with the aid of everybody of any consequence in the Admiralty) of compiling a list of such places, and we all know that, Pacts or no Pacts to abolish war, the intelligence departments of the most pacific of nations are still busy prying into each other's secrets. It will be quite enough to mention that, from the naval point of view alone, I discovered numerous places where what

Whitehall calls 'evilly-disposed persons' might in those days have worried the Navy. That experience gave me some considerable acquaintanceship with the genus in question, and with the best ways to defeat their nefarious objects. I have presented my credentials, and we now come to the story of the great British secret, and of how it was kept.

The true tale has never, to my knowledge, been told of the two dinners that were attended by Cabinet Ministers in Queen Anne's Gate on the night of that fateful Sunday, August 2nd, 1914. Lord Haldane told me, not long before his death, the story of the one at his house, when news of the German ultimatum to Belgium at 7 p.m. on that evening was brought to the table.

The other dinner was held at a celebrity's house, a few doors to the eastward. The two parties looked, I believe, at the news from different angles, but when the significance was fully grasped at the meeting of the Cabinet on the Monday morning all opinions were reconciled, with the loss of two Ministers to the Government, Lord Morley and Mr. John Burns. Then, at 3 p.m. Sir Edward Grey made the great speech which pulled the whole nation and Empire together. It was on August Bank Holiday. This sorely handicapped the War Office. The German ultimatum had come, to all intents and purposes, as a bolt from the blue, so the assembly of the Territorials for their training had not been cancelled. To stop the training would have doubled the activity of German espionage, and on the Friday there had still been hope of peace. We need not delve any further into unknown history. We had to do so to get our dates right, and every hour counted. The Germans invaded Belgium early on the Tuesday. The order to mobilize the British Army went out at 4 p.m. The Fleet had already been mobilized. By midnight Britain was at War with Germany.

On the Wednesday I met Henry Wilson (then Director of Military Operations) in a corridor of the Admiralty, in great distress. The arrangement for possible British support for the French, arrived at during the military conversations with which he had so much to do, was that the British Army should be mobilized on the same day as the French, and that the six Divisions of the Army should be sent over. The detailed calculations had been made on that assumption.

It was not until Thursday, August 6th, that the Cabinet finally decided to send four divisions at once and that the French should choose their destination. Now let us go to the Admiralty 'War Room', with its map of the world covering a whole wall. By day and by night the door was guarded by a messenger to bar the entry of the unauthorized, whether evilly or well-disposed. There, in the early days of the war, we watched the movements of the *Goeben* and *Breslau*, slipping through the Straits of Messina (neutral waters) and so escaping from their British pursuers a few hours before war was declared, never again to come within range of British ships capable of tackling the *Goeben*. There were many distinguished visitors to that secret room, including at least one 'Personage'.

Then, in another room, we could watch the movements of the armies facing each other on that long line with its southern flank on the Swiss frontier. The Cabinet had ordained that the British Army should begin to move on the 9th, a Sunday. The ships were ready before the troops. On the 14th Sir John French crossed. By the 20th his army was assembled between Maubeuge and Le Cateau. By the 22nd it was about Mons, well beyond the left flank of the French, preparing to advance into the jaws of the German Army, not knowing, as we read in '1914', anything about the strength of the huge German force that was north of the Meuse.

Did the enemy know? Those were tense moments for the watchers of the movements of the little flags, knowing what they represented, and all that they stood for—nothing less than the saving of the situation when 'Plan 17' was heading towards its inevitable conclusion. I had discovered its nature from a French officer, I forget the exact date in August. Mystified by the movements of the flags on the war-map, I had turned to him and asked, 'What is Joffre's plan?' He answered with a gesture. Placing a fist near Nancy, he struck a blow north-easterly, which, even if it succeeded for a time, could not affect the far-away left flank in time to avert impending disaster.

The Belgian General Staff by the 22nd had plenty of chances of identifying the great German masses wheeling through their country north of the Meuse, and I have never been able to understand why Sir John French knew so little. Bülow's Second Army was attacking the French. Namur was on the point of falling. Kluck's First Army, the furthest north of all, was on the rim of the great wheel, and beyond him was Marwitz with his whole corps of cavalry. The Belgians, in face of such overwhelming force, had fallen back to Antwerp. From the 18th onwards, the map was emptied of flags between Kluck's long columns and the 'Old Contemptibles'. Kluck *must* know, we thought, that he had only that little 'B.E.F.' in front of him, and where it was, though perhaps he did not know its strength, or rather its weakness. He himself had no less than six *Army Corps*, of which two were 'reserve corps' (the surprise which the Germans sprang upon the French). He had, or rather there was, a whole corps of German cavalry besides. This was not under his command at the time, though it was on the spot and only needing knowledge of the position of the British to burst its way round their outer flank, while they were attacked in front by Kluck's masses.

Did Kluck know? That was the point. We can, I suppose, wave aside the fact that the German High-Power Wireless Station at Nauen broadcasted to the world that the British had deserted the French by not sending their army across at all. That was probably 'propaganda'. We know that the Germans had gathered from their spies before the war that the British, if they came, would land at Zeebrugge, near the Dutch frontier of Belgium (I once reported on Zeebrugge myself as being excellent, but in the wrong position). That spoke well for the British counter-espionage. To the end Kluck believed that the British Army had intended to land in Belgian ports, and that they afterwards chose French harbours of Dunkirk, Calais and Boulogne instead. We did not intend to land troops in Belgian ports, we landed no troops at Dunkirk or Calais, and only a few at Boulogne. It was not until August 20th that Kluck 'believed' that the B.E.F. had landed in some 'French harbours' by the 18th. He did not know which harbours, or anything about the direction of their advance.

Late on the 22nd (9.30 p.m.) he had found only one squadron of British cavalry. He then issued ordinary march orders, believing that the country for 50 miles ahead of him was clear. On that fateful Sunday, August 23rd, his advanced guards, unwarned, came suddenly upon the British Army stretching across their path. The German Cavalry Corps, which might then have been sent round its flank to cut off its retreat, was nearly 40 miles away, searching for the British near Courtrai. Secrecy had brought salvation; and this brings us to the question how Kluck was mystified and misled in that well-kept secret of the war.

We have heard much about the 'Mobilization' in those early days of August, and very little about the 'Precautionary Stage' which came first. There was no need to advertise it by proclamations calling up reservists. The 'precaution' that saved Sir John French's handful of 'Old Contemptibles' by blinding their enemies is the one with which we are concerned. (One's thoughts naturally go to the precedent in the Old Testament when Elisha dealt single-handed with the 'great host' of Syrians, equipped with horses and chariots, who surrounded him in the night. Having blinded them he offered to guide them on their way, led them into Samaria when they were bound for Dothan. Kluck was blind for as long a period.) To understand what follows we must know something

about the German spy system. We can easily compare it
with the British by quoting the two mottoes which sum
up the teaching of German and British Army officers in
the pages of their pre-war text-books. The 'Mystify and
Mislead' of the British, the 'Violence and Cunning' of the
German War-book. There is something more subtle
about the former, more aggressive about the other. On
the German side a massed attack by a host of spies trained
—almost drilled—to work in the same way and to look
to higher authority for instructions about how to deal
with a 'stupid' inferior foe. On the British side a few,
carefully selected, proved by trial in small missions before
entrusted with great, and then perhaps advanced to the
higher grade of British 'counter-espionage' which earned
high post-war tributes from such men as Colonel Nikolai,
the Chief of the German Secret Service during the Great
War, and from one Winfried Lüdecke in articles in the
Press of Switzerland and Germany two years ago.

At an early hour on Tuesday, August 4th, 1914, the
German hosts began to cross the Belgian frontier. There
were three great armies of about 320,000, 260,000 and
180,000 men—Kluck's, Bülow's and Hausen's. Bülow
and Hausen were to overwhelm Lanrezac's French Army;
Kluck's great mass was to swing round its flank. Britain
was not then at war, but technically at peace. Nevertheless, every minute being priceless, British counter-espionage acted before the order to mobilize the Army was
issued, and only a small handful of German spies, working
as they thought in complete security, were arrested. Why
take only the few, leaving the many? Counter-espionage,
like every other sort of competition, depends for success
upon being able to look at things from the other man's
point of view. Either learn, or better still know instinc-
tively, how other people are likely to think and to act.
Politicians have to guess at the next vagary of the 'popular
whirligig', Public Opinion. So do Pressmen. The soldier, as Foch taught, must know his enemy's character
and how it will react to different conditions.

For at least four years before the war (the Agadir crisis, when we were on the brink of it, came in 1911) many German spies were marked down. They were not arrested. They could do little harm in ordinary times, and if they were taken there would be new ones at the critical time. Colonel Nikolai said, as far as my memory serves me, that we arrested five. We may have done so, but I do not recall the incidents; I can only remember the trial of one beguiled and unfortunate British officer. The idea was that the supreme need for secrecy would come at the last moment if we should ever be faced with a war with Germany. The big secret would then be the day and the time when our Army began to move and where it went to. They could not help knowing its strength because that had been freely advertised. They could know something of its fighting value by watching its manœuvres and by studying the published records of its performances on the rifle-ranges. (That they had not studied those records is beside the point; if they had done so, they would not have mistaken British rifle-fire for machine-gun fire at Mons.) The great secret to be kept was about the despatch and the destination of the British Expeditionary Force, so it was from 'Der Tag' onwards that the great General Staff of Germany must be blinded.

Here I must interpose a note about secrecy, with which all who have had anything at all to do with Secret Service, and sympathizers outside that inner circle, will be in hearty accord. Those of the elect do not tell their secrets, even to each other; they know their own constant strain of anxiety lest they themselves may, in some unguarded moment, give away a secret. The fewer secrets they know, the better for their own comfort, so they resent being told secrets unnecessarily, and they do not burden their friends with them. I did not know any details of the despatch of the Expeditionary Force at the time. Only the localities from whence it would be desirable to exclude the 'evilly-disposed' came into my province, and I rejoiced when results showed that they had been excluded, though there were more than 30,000 Germans in the country when war broke out. There was not a single case of sabotage in the United Kingdom, and obviously I cannot give the names of those to whom the credit is due. I knew most of them in pre-war days, some of them well, and I had seen them at work in their rooms, without being told what they were doing, there or elsewhere.

Their idea was that Germans, spies and others, needed leaders, and that they were helpless without them. That they liked working 'according to plan', according to the *letter* of a plan; if left alone to interpret its *spirit*, they were likely to fail, they would probably await instructions. No matter how big a swarm of German spies there might be in England, Scotland, Wales, or Ireland in pre-war days, they would look for guidance to certain leaders and organizers, and if the leaders were taken away the followers would be helpless. Those leaders must be removed at exactly the right moment, when it would be impossible to replace them, and there, as the head of the German Spy Service has since pointed out, Britain had the great advantage of being surrounded by sea, instead of by land frontiers across which secret agents can trickle. It is easier to watch a few harbours where a stream of travellers passes through barriers, and a coastline approachable only in vessels visible from afar off, than it is to watch hundreds of miles of country with the frontier line marked only by posts, with long gaps between them. We learned that lesson ourselves with the long line of block-houses, even when they were joined by wire fences, in the last of all Boer wars.

News of our naval mobilization reached me at Portsmouth between 3 and 4 a.m. on the 2nd August, a Sunday morning, when German espionage was still working at full pressure in England. Early on July 29th the First Fleet, which had full crews, slipped away from Portland for an unknown destination. That fact, and the naval mobilization, were known in Germany, as Bülow the Imperial Chancellor and others have disclosed. For the influence of counter-espionage, in blinding the enemy before the Army was mobilized or moved, we will take our accounts from the German side.

In Berlin, nothing was known of the fact that the British counter-espionage officers had for some years read every letter that passed through the hands of twenty-two German secret agents in Great Britain and their employers in Germany, or that that correspondence had laid bare the whole network of which Berlin was the centre. Those far-reaching results had been achieved by shadowing a certain German officer of high rank, who, when he was in attendance upon the Kaiser on one of his visits to England, wandered away from his official duties to visit an out-of-the way district (Caledonian Road) in the north of London. There he went to visit the hairdressing saloon of one E——, a German born in England, who had a German wife. It turned out that the hairdresser was a mere 'letter-box', working on a salary of only five-shillings a week, which had recently been increased to about twelve-and-sixpence. Ostensibly he was working for a business agency, really for the German Secret Service from which many letters emanated. Thenceforward E——'s correspondence was examined, and the discovery was made that he received numerous letters from Germany to which he affixed English stamps and then forwarded them to various addresses. That gave away the identity of a large group of German secret agents distributed all over the country. It was a tremendous *coup*. Luck, some would say, but partly due to the German passion for organization and for centralization. If all those letters had been sent, with German stamps, direct to the secret agents themselves, it is probable that nothing would have happened to them, and so we come to our climax, the quiet and inconspicuous arrest by the police—no display of armed soldiers—of twenty-one out of the twenty-two German secret agents located in peace, trained as spies for war, all of them known for years to British counter-espionage, if not 'known to the police'. The name of the

63

agent at Southampton was Thomas Kegnamer. There were five in London, three in Newcastle, one in Warwick, one in Brighton, one in Winchester, one in Barrow-in-Furness, one in Sittingbourne, one in Padstow, two in Portsmouth, one in Weymouth, one near Plymouth, and one at Falmouth. They were simply interned. There were no conspicuous trials to advertise their capture. Their employers were left with a puzzle to solve. E—— being a British subject, was awarded seven years' penal servitude for working for the Secret Service in Berlin. One agent escaped to board a ship, lying at Hull. That his information, if such he had, of the secret about the British Army was harmless was proved by the deception of Kluck and the salvation of Lanrezac's force, the left flank of the whole French Army.

Besides the twenty-one agents who were arrested, about 200 more were strictly watched. Thousands of aliens were interned and, early on the morning of the next day, every German submarine telegraph-cable was cut. And so we can leave Kluck's army and the Cavalry Corps of Marwitz (as an old eighteenth-century writer described soldiers on land awaiting the arrival of an enemy about to descend upon them from some unknown spot on the sea-coast) 'in the dark, moving to and fro, distracted and at a loss which way to go to guard against the stroke of an Invisible Hand'. The stroke was to be struck, through Galliéni's influence, on his right flank by the French Sixth Army, while the British pressed through the gap on his left.

Meanwhile sections of the British public in the early days were seething with indignation. Locally, it may have been noticed that some little newspaper and tobacco shop kept by a foreigner had mysteriously put up its shutters. A foreign waiter at a big hotel who knew one's taste in luncheons had disappeared—his day off, perhaps. A learned foreign scientist, interested in the geology of the east coast of Scotland, was not seen about as usual. 'Society' ladies missed a pet French (?) 'beauty-doctor'.

Superstitious folk could not make out what had happened to their favourite palmist or fortune-teller, and we heard much of those arts in the early days of the war. Little account was taken of these incidents, but many rumours were current and the military authorities were severely criticized by those who believed them.

A lady looking into a shop window in Bond Street was said to have stepped back and trodden inadvertently upon the toe of a fair-haired, well-groomed man who had let slip the German equivalent of 'Damn!'—obviously a German officer. Hard lawn-tennis courts, recently made in alien gardens in the suburbs, had concrete foundations which were suspiciously thick. These were clearly designed as platforms for hostile howitzers (which could shoot far better from any modern road-surface). Dwellers in upper flats were signalling up their chimneys to Zeppelins in the sky, and suspicious lights were showing in the back premises of basements. And so on—— Criticisms were officially encouraged, as a reputation for stupidity is an asset in counter-espionage.

The moral of the whole story is that in the Secret Service it is unsafe to assume that any people are stupid. Try, for instance, to get the better in a bargain of the British 'bucolic' mind, as displayed by the old English stock in villages. I learned my own lesson in South Africa, from an apparently stupid old Boer.

CHAPTER V

THE RAID TO OSTEND IN 1914

MAKING feints with small bodies of troops and spreading disquieting rumours are recognized forms of Secret Service in war, and we now come to a piece of bluff, which was initiated by Mr. Winston Churchill as First Lord of the Admiralty and member of the War Council of the Cabinet when things were looking black for the British Army on August 25th, 1914. Though a small affair, the story may be worth telling as an example indicating what might have been done with more mobile 'amphibious' forces, properly equipped. It is not a story of keeping a secret, but of making sure that the 'secret' reached and misled the enemy in order to affect the military situation. The British Expeditionary Force was in full retreat after the incident at Mons. It was the day before Smith-Dorrien's fine stand at Le Cateau which held up the advance of Kluck's First German Army and the Cavalry Corps of Marwitz, and so enabled the bulk of Sir John French's army to continue its retreat unmolested.

Late in the evening of Tuesday, August 25th, 1914, I was hard at work with the late Admiral of the Fleet Sir Henry Jackson in a luxurious room in the Admiralty overlooking St. James's Park. It was a hot day, and having worked practically continuously without a complete night's rest since the 3rd of August, I was half asleep on a sofa waiting for the next batch of telegrams to come in when the late Sir Doveton Sturdee, Chief of the Staff, came hurriedly into the room and asked me whether I had any uniform. I was a Colonel at the time, having recently given up the rank of Brigadier-General on the General Staff of the Army on my return from

South Africa. I told the Admiral that I thought that there was some rather tight blue uniform at my tailor's, but it was the uniform of a Brigadier-General. 'That's all right,' he said, 'then you will have to be promoted to Brigadier-General. There is no time to change it. The First Lord has a job for you. He will tell you all about it in his room.'

I found Mr. Churchill with the Adjutant-General of Marines (the head of my Corps), and a map of the military situation in Flanders covered with little flags showing masses of German troops in Belgium. He explained his plan which, roughly speaking, was to land a brigade of Marines, hastily assembled, at Ostend. The force was to be under my command, and he asked me what I wanted in order to carry out the instructions which he outlined to put up a good bluff in order to draw as many German troops as possible in my direction and so to ease the situation for Sir John French.

He told me to study the map and to let him have my answer as quickly as possible. Judging by what I saw on the map, a commodious coffin seemed to be the most likely requirement, but that was obviously not the reply that was expected. In about three minutes I replied: 'A good staff officer; 500 rounds of ammunition per man; 500 bicycles; maps of Belgium; and my orders in writing.' 'That will be all right,' he said. 'You must catch the late train from Victoria to Chatham, where the Commander-in-Chief (Sir Richard Poore) will rush you down to Sheerness to embark in the *Euryalus*.' While I was securing uniform, a packet of Maggi's soups, and a supply of money in English sovereigns, my old friend and colleague in the old days in the Intelligence Department, Sir Graham Greene, Secretary of the Admiralty, rushed the orders through. They read thus:

'1. At daylight to-morrow, 26th August, *if circumstances allow* [My italics. I remembered those words afterwards when I heard of Sir Douglas Haig's message from the

Cabinet about sending British troops to Marshal Foch, and his reply], you will disembark such portions of your Brigade as have arrived at Ostend, and occupy the town. You will push out a reconnaissance of cyclists to Bruges, Thourout, and Dixmude. You will establish yourself at Ostend, forming an entrenched picket-line round the town in such a way as to enable you to cover the debarkation of a Division of the Army. A squadron of aeroplanes will reach you before noon, having previously made an aerial reconnaissance of the country within 30 miles of Ostend. These aeroplanes will be placed under your orders.

'2. The object of this movement is to make a diversion favourable to the Belgians who are advancing from Antwerp, and to threaten the western flank of the German southward advance. It should therefore be ostentatious. You should not advance inland from Ostend without further orders, but some enterprise may be permitted to the patrols. Information about the enemy will be supplied to you personally at the Admiralty. [No more reached me.]

'3. The object in view would be fully attained if a considerable force of the enemy were attracted to the coast. You will be re-embarked as soon as this is accomplished.

'You are accorded temporary rank of Brigadier-General.'

These orders were issued with the authority of 'Their Lordships' and signed and dated August 25th, 1914. To them Mr. Churchill added verbally (to be kept secret) that he thought that I should be back in a week.

Sir Doveton Sturdee appended a note that the Brigade would operate in close proximity to the coast and would be 'so equipped as to be capable of swift debarkation and embarkation.' They would be based on and supplied from the ships.

As I was leaving the Admiralty courtyard in a taxi for

Victoria, this paper was thrust hastily into my hand by a messenger:

'*For Information.*

'Telephone from *Daily Mail* (Mr. H. W. Wilson).

'*Daily Mail* correspondents just arrived from Ostend and telephoned following to the Admiralty (8.30 p.m.). They left to-day as German troops were approaching.

'The entire Ostend garrison of 4,000 was removed to Antwerp on Friday, leaving Ostend undefended except for about 200 gendarmes.

'The gendarmes engaged about 300 German Uhlans, who came from Thielt. The gendarmes suffered about 45 casualties, and having defended the honour of the town, now intend to surrender when larger forces of Germans arrive.'

This message was endorsed 'First Lord informed, who decided to make no change in the orders. Lord Kitchener is being informed. First Sea Lord informed' and initialed by the chief of Staff.

I arrived at Chatham in the course of the night, and after a few minutes' talk Sir Richard Poore, the Commander-in-Chief, sent me down the Medway in his own barge to join the *Euryalus*, flagship of the late Rear-Admiral Arthur Christian, who made me comfortable in a spare cabin for the remaining hours of the early morning. Then the Chatham Battalion of Royal Marine Light Infantry arrived with an immense amount of baggage and stores. There was no question of arriving off Ostend 'at daylight'. The *Euryalus* did not leave the Nore till later in the day. In the evening an interesting message came by wireless in secret code from the Admiralty. It contained a suggestion, which we attributed to the First Lord, that if we found the German Army in occupation of Ostend we might land somewhere else and turn it out. It was from the Admiralty to the *Euryalus*, dated August 26th (the day of Le Cateau and of the sack of Louvain) at

6 p.m. and it was received in the *Euryalus* at 7.5 p.m. It read:

'For senior Officer present and General Aston. If on arrival you find Ostend occupied by the enemy you must act according to circumstances and their strength. Endeavour to avoid bringing calamity upon the town for the sake of minor operations and if convenient (land?) some other point near by and so turn them out. This is left entirely to your judgment. Acknowledge by telegram.'

The Admiral and I talked things over. It was blowing freshly with a choppy sea, and a beach landing was out of the question on that shoaling coast where ships could only anchor miles away from land. We decided that the best course would be to wait until we reached Ostend before we made up our minds. The Admiral, it appeared, had a pressing engagement elsewhere, in the Heligoland Bight (action off Heligoland, August 28th, in the histories of the War). It was almost dark when we arrived and anchored about 6 or 8 miles off Ostend. The Admiral decided that it was out of the question to land the men and their heavy equipment in ships' boats in the dark in the choppy sea. An officer who went in in a picket-boat reported that there were no German troops in Ostend, so I decided to sleep on board a smaller vessel anchored nearer to the town and to land by 3.30 in the morning, ahead of the troops.

I landed accordingly in the dark of rather a chilly morning, with little but what I stood up in, the Maggi soup tablets and English gold in my haversack. I had no staff, and none of the personnel and paraphernalia for communication with the troops that go to make up 'Headquarters' of a brigade as understood in the Army. There was not even a map of an unfamiliar country. The lack of staff was made up for by a naval officer, Lieutenant-Commander Clarke-Hall, R.N. (now an Air Marshal in the R.A.F.), who made an excellent Brigade-Major; and, at the last moment, I remembered the need of a Union

Jack, which he borrowed from the ship and carried ashore under his arm. In the huge echoing railway-station by the quay at Ostend we found the Mayor and many Belgian dignitaries who, as I found out, had been waiting for me there for some hours in the cold station.

I felt rather like the frog in the fable who tried to blow himself up to the size of an ox, when explaining that my force would soon land, to save them from the expected German Army. To cut a long story short, the Chatham Marines landed. The *Euryalus* then went off to the Heligoland Bight. Another ship arrived with another senior naval officer during the day. He signalled to me, giving his requirements in fishing-boats for landing troops from afar off, and then he faded away. The Portsmouth Marines then landed, and also the Marine Artillery from Eastney. By nightfall a third senior naval officer (Admiral the Hon. Sir A. E. Bethell) arrived.

At 1 p.m. on the 27th I reported to the Admiralty in cipher:

'Firmly established by noon to-day. Bruges and Dixmude reported clear of the enemy whose main columns are using the Brussels-Renaix-Tournai road [the right of Kluck's Army]. Cavalry at Menin and Ypres yesterday.'

By nightfall I surrounded the town with a line of pickets about 7 miles long with the aid of a town-map which I managed to purloin from one of the magnates who accompanied the Mayor. There was no time for me to see the ground myself, but the battalion commanders played up well.

Then there came a panic in the town. A report arrived of the approach of a German aeroplane. Thinking that it might possibly be one of the machines which I had been promised, I went off at once in a commandeered motor-car to warn the outposts. I was too late. They had greeted the leading machine (Commander Samson's) with a fusillade, luckily harmless, and he landed on the racecourse, followed by other machines, and, on the next day by some more. (There were nine in all, and a small airship.) The Plymouth Marines arrived too, and we settled down to spread ourselves out and to dig. My main object being to bluff the Germans and to draw some of their heavy columns on the Brussels-Tournai road in my direction, events then began to play into my hands.

There were some minor drawbacks. Instead of the 500 bicycles for which I had stipulated, only a dozen or so had been despatched. The 500 rounds of ammunition per man had been sent (judging by the heavy job of landing it), but it was not 'charger-loaded', which meant that we would have to use all our magazine rifles as single-loaders. Of my other requests, no Brigade Staff had arrived, and no maps of Belgium. In view of my special orders 'to be equipped so as to be capable of swift embarkation', it was embarrassing to find that nearly 300 tons of various stores had been sent ashore—almost everything conceivable except what I wanted most, which was plenty of signalling equipment and machine-guns, and, above all, those missing bicycles. I gathered that there was a German Division quite near, at Audenarde, and bicyclists might have teased it in our direction.

I had left instructions on board the *Euryalus* about the men landing as light as possible, with a list of what they must have, but as there were three senior naval officers in twenty-four hours my orders must have gone astray. Some field-guns and ammunition were sent, with no transport. These I refused to receive. I did not want to leave guns behind me for the enemy to crow over when the time came for the hasty withdrawal which seemed probable. Meanwhile the men dug in for all they were worth, in positions covering all the approaches to the town. The favourable events overshadowed the trifling difficulties. Commander Samson's airmen, when they arrived, were an enterprising lot and they made a good show in the air. He went out himself in an armed car via Bruges to Thourout, and one of my own officers (Lieut.-

Colonel Osmaston), in a motor-car with some Belgian
officers and a small armed party, went nearly as far as
Menin, of historic memory in the light of later events.
We succeeded in hiring about fifty bicycles and I pushed
patrols of cyclists out into the country, to make as much
show as possible.

The outstanding occurrences which were most helpful
were the 'Russian troops rumour' (about mysterious Russians arriving in Scottish ports and travelling southward
by night) and the news that the Belgian division, driven
out of Namur, was embarking at Havre and coming
round to Ostend. The Russian troops rumour, told me
by the correspondent of *The Times*, was very useful. My
marines were dressed in blue, with round caps with no
peaks. They might easily be taken for Russians by German spies. Crowds of civilians were travelling through
Ostend for the south, and spying was very easy. I hoisted
my huge Union Jack in the railway-station for them to
report, and I took care that the Russian troops rumour
was told as a *strict secret* to as many people as possible.
That is the best way to make sure of wide publicity; but
although I heard afterwards that the rumour was believed
by vast numbers of people in England, I thought at the
time that it was almost too much to hope for its belief by
experts in the German General Staff.

Here are the actual messages about the Belgian troops;
the first is from the Admiralty to Admiral Bethell commanding the 7th Battle Squadron off Ostend. It was sent
at 1.45 a.m. on August 29th:

'4,000 Belgian troops are being embarked (at) Havre
to-day for Ostend. On Sunday and Monday (August
30th and 31st) another 12,000 Belgian troops will be sent
from Havre. French authorities suggest Zeebrugge for
landing troops due to the draught of water of transport(s).
Inform General Aston.'

The message concluded with the news of the Battle of
Heligoland Bight, to which the *Euryalus* had gone.

I told the Admiral that I agreed with French opinion that Zeebrugge was better, as it did away with my difficulties about guarding the huge civil population of Ostend, but it was a question for the Belgian military authorities whether suitable camp and water-supply were available at Zeebrugge. (My own idea was that it would be a good thing to move my force to Zeebrugge, to reinforce it with plenty of guns and engineers, and to let me form an entrenched camp there and hold on to the place. At all events, the more harbours that were used for landing troops the better, if a good bluff was the object in view.)

Then the Chief of the Staff of the French Governor of Dunkirk came to see me, and urged upon me the greater suitability of Dunkirk with its defence inundations, garrison of about 20,000 and far better harbour than Ostend. By 6.15 I had sent a secret signal to Admiral Bethell for the Admiralty, giving my views, which (as I heard at 10.30 a.m.) the Admiral sent on to the Admiralty with his own backing. Meanwhile the Admiralty seemed to be getting a little nervous about my little force, as they sent me a message, received at 10.30 a.m., to entrench strongly and to hold the perimeter of Ostend (about 8 miles, with about 3,000 men) 'against *all* attacks', to cover the disembarkation of 1,600 troops arriving at Ostend on their return through Holland [*sic*] from Namur.

I gave the decipherers credit for having in their haste dropped an o from the number and for having made a mistake about the violation of Dutch neutrality which would be involved in a retreat through Holland. I sent the Admiral at 9.10 p.m. a reassuring signal about my defences, adding that I hoped to receive notice about when the Belgians were expected. From two Admiralty signals and a message that 3,000 Belgian recruits were due to arrive by train, I made the total 20,600. (The message was sent secretly, but I hoped that the 'secret' would leak out.) I added that I was trying to find out whether the Belgians had any ammunition. It seemed to me that Winston Churchill's bluff was succeeding well.

I must not omit to mention a tribute by a French naval officer to marines at Ostend, which appeared in the Press:

'I saw them land at Ostend. No one ever would imagine that they were at war. They seem to see only the humorous side. They laugh, they crack jokes, they engage in rough play with each other, and their laughter is Homeric, it is infectious. No wonder the crowds laughed with them. Nevertheless there is a grim doggedness about the firm-set lips. At the least obstacle there comes into their eyes a serious purpose.'

Before we close this story we will take account of the effect of Mr. Churchill's Ostend enterprise upon the minds of the German General Staff. We can now read all about it in Sir J. Edmonds's excellent official history. This is what Lieutenant-General Tappen has written on the subject:

'At this time (August 30th) there was no lack of alarming reports at General Headquarters. Ostend and Antwerp took a prominent part in them. One day countless British troops were said to have landed at Ostend and to be marching on Antwerp; on another that there were to be great sorties from Antwerp. Even landings of Russian troops, 80,000 men, at Ostend were mentioned. At Ostend a great entrenched Camp for the English was in preparation. The security of the rear and right flank of the army requires constant attention.'

Liddell Hart has recently reminded us in his book, *The Real War*,[1] that Colonel Hentsch, when he visited Kluck's head-quarters during the crisis of the Battle of the Marne, said that 'the English are disembarking fresh troops continuously on the Belgian coast. There are reports of a Russian Expeditionary Force in the same parts. A withdrawal is becoming inevitable.' Liddell

[1] Published by Faber & Faber, 1930.

Hart adds: 'We know from other sources that the 3,000 Marines had grown in the German Command's imagination to 40,000 and that the Russians were said to be 80,000,' He attaches much value to the amazing Russian myth which spread 'so mysteriously'.

Thinking over these events fifteen years later, I wonder whether more could have been done, and what the German Staff would have thought if I had been given the 500 bicycles for which I had asked, and had made intelligent use of them. In the actual event, 6,000 Belgian troops from Namur via Havre were disembarked at Ostend, covered by my defence-line, on the 30th of August. I made friends with a Belgian General who was with them. We had luncheon together at the station restaurant, and I took him into my confidence. He only asked me one question: 'Have you plenty of bicycles?' I told him that I had found only a few in Ostend, the remainder had apparently been commandeered for the army. His comment was *'Bonne chance!'*

My friends at the Admiralty seemed to be getting more nervous about my safety, and the Admiral told me that he was receiving messages about supporting me by gun-fire from his ships, which was the one thing that I did not want. My secret plan for getting away with as little loss of life as possible was to concentrate my small force to attack the heads of the German columns (if they came) in the defiles formed by the road-causeways across the water-logged country; then to leave weak rearguards behind, avoid giving trouble to the civil population by retreating through the town, and march to Dunkirk, if necessary along the beach under cover of the sand-dunes. Admiral Bethell's ships were far away on the horizon, a line of high sand-dunes hid the flat land from the sea gunners. I had been one myself in the Fleet for twelve years, and I knew their limitations against targets which they could not see. I had no idea where my own men would be; that would depend upon where the enemy was. To have the Germans in force on my front would be enough, without having to dodge heavy shells from friendly ships behind me. Finally the Admiral told me that when, after many long signals, he had been asked by the Admiralty why he would not support my men with his gun-fire, he had answered: 'Because the General does not want me to.'

A few days later there came, at 4.30 a.m., a signal from the Admiralty to embark my force. Then a message from the Admiral that German wireless signals were coming closer to his ships, and that he wanted us all on board by nightfall. The ships were out of sight from the shore. Then I was handed a message that they had put to sea, which proved to be false. The men worked splendidly, though depressed at the order to withdraw. They and all the stores (between 200 and 300 tons) had been embarked from that inferior harbour, with its one little crane, by 5 p.m., when I followed them with the Union Jack, which did not return to Ostend for over four years.

In the next chapter we will develop further the subject of rumours, and mention the first of the German spies to be executed in England.

CHAPTER VI

SPY-RUMOURS AND A REAL SPY

R UMOURS and their secret origin in times of war form an important branch of the subject of Secret Service because they exert an important influence both upon armies and upon the peoples behind them who react, in their turn, upon the morale of their armies. It is seldom possible to trace such rumours to their original source because the most deadly ones are passed by word of mouth and, like ordinary scandal, much exaggerated in the process.

Admiral Mahan, in his account of the Spanish American War of 1898, mentions the harmful influence upon American naval dispositions of an absurd rumour that the unfortunate Admiral Cervera's handful of small ill-equipped cruisers was on its way across the wide Atlantic to attack the strongly defended east coast of the United States. He drew a picture of panics in the hotels and bathing-beaches on that coast, and the influence that was brought to bear upon the authorities to provide local protection by warships. This caused delay in the rounding-up of Cervera's vessels which succeeded in reaching the defended harbour at Santiago in Cuba, and their destruction involved the despatch of an expeditionary force, under General Shafter, which suffered severely from sickness in an unhealthy climate.

There were serious scares amongst the civil population of Germany when war broke out in August 1914. Counter-espionage was looked upon as a purely military affair, and it was left in the hands of the various Army commanders, who were too much occupied with other concerns. The Government, it is alleged, had not established any responsible authority to control counter-espionage in the homeland. The results were serious. A wild epidemic of spy-fevers began to rage all over the country, largely, according to German authority, on account of the 'stupidity and incompetence' of ignorant local officials who assumed the responsibility for counter-espionage, and took no steps to deal with false rumours.

The rumour which led to the most unfortunate results was a tale (apparently the product of imagination) that thousands of motor-cars, filled with gold, were crossing the Fatherland. The gold was to be expended by Germany's enemies upon Secret Service, and Germany was thus to be disintegrated (as Russia, Germany's enemy, was later in the War by Germany herself) by agents spreading disturbing doctrines and spying out military secrets. I have good authority for a story of a highly-placed German diplomatist who, when he was asked how long it would take the German Government to create a complete change of opinion amongst the German people, replied, to the astonishment of his interrogator, 'About a fortnight.' It is easy to imagine the effect of a rumour, believed to have official backing, upon such a docile people. The result of this extraordinary tale spreading all over Germany was that in some districts every motor-car was held up. Their occupants were fired upon, and considerable loss of life was caused. Government officials travelling on duty were killed.

Public disorders and panics became so serious that they interfered with the important process of mobilization, and finally the General Staff of the Army were hampered by being obliged to take charge of the situation. Then there came a general reaction, and the local authorities, who had done much to foster an agitation which had speedily grown into a Frankenstein monster, stopped their activities altogether. The pendulum swung too far the other way. In connection with those fears of the effect of foreign gold upon possible traitors to the Fatherland, it is interesting to study the secret figures, since published by Colonel

Nikolai, which show the nationality of the people who were found guilty of offences against the treason laws in Germany during the War. 235 of them were Germans, and 176 were foreigners, including 4 Austrians, Germany's allies. Of the 172 remaining foreigners, 94 belonged to enemy races, including 46 Frenchmen and 3 English; 78 were of neutral nationality, including 31 Dutchmen.

Passing now to Britain. Although I spent most of the month of August 1914 in London, I can supply little information of much value about spy-mania or about absurd rumours at that particular period. I was staying in the Grand Hotel (now no more) which stood at the corner of Northumberland Avenue facing towards Trafalgar Square, and I spent all my days and much of my nights at the Admiralty. There were crowds in the streets by day and for most of the night. Sporting instinct seemed to move them, rather than panic. By day they stood watching some men mounting an anti-aircraft gun (a six-pounder!!) on the top of the Admiralty Arch, and I noticed many of them searching the sky to the eastward, as if they expected hostile aircraft to appear at once. They probably looked forward to the excitement of seeing them shot down by that inadequate little pop-gun, not realizing the foolishness of collecting in large crowds if air-raiders did arrive. That was before the days of the 300 lb. air bombs, which taught their lesson. By night constant streams of people processed past my hotel, singing and shouting, but things soon quieted down.

A report which reached me in private correspondence was typical of the attitude in the country. It came from a hunting district: 'The people here are willingly sending their sons. They are grumbling at having to send their horses!' I heard of no public disturbances or panic anywhere, but spy-stories and rumours were rife in the towns. There was a heavy strain upon the 'Special Branch' at Scotland Yard, and upon police authorities all over the country. The 'Special Branch' was really established for political reasons in time of peace, England being a notorious refuge for aliens of all nationalities. It did invaluable work in war. Francis Bacon wrote in the sixteenth century that 'all states that are liberal of naturalization towards strangers are fit for empire', but the England of his day was not faced with the modern problem of harbouring anarchists and others of a type likely to prove a nuisance to other nations, or of calming the dense population of aliens in the East End of London who panicked or fled to sleep under hedgerows in the country when the air-raiders did arrive. During the war the Special Branch at Scotland Yard and the 'Special Intelligence' counter-espionage officers at the War Office vied with each other in the control of dangerous aliens: each department was the complement of the other. In the actual event, I have been told on high authority, that not a single man or woman of British descent was convicted of espionage in the United Kingdom in the Great War.

Spreaders of rumours were another affair. There were plenty of those in the War, as there always are in the West End of London in peace. In the days when ladies first took to bicycling a 'cautionary tale' went the round of the tea-tables about a foolish lady who *would* ride with her hands off the handle-bars of her bicycle, even when she was in traffic. . . . When she was crossing Knightsbridge from Hyde Park she fell under an omnibus. The horses trampled on her. The wheel ran over her neck and cut off her head. The tale was widely believed, though it never appeared in the Press, where a report of an inquest upon the poor lady's remains would have been published if the story had been true. Some people were quite upset if their versions were not believed. The origin was probably a remark by someone of the old school, shocked by the idea of lady bicyclists, that, 'Mrs. X is *so* rash. She *will* ride her bicycle without holding the handle-bar. Supposing she lost her head in the traffic!' In the most embroidered versions the omnibus-horses were splashed with the blood, and other gruesome details were added.

In the war atmosphere rumours were similarly 'improved' in passing from mouth to mouth, and amateur spy-hunting developed on quite a large scale. Certain types of gossip made it their business, like the fat boy in *Pickwick*, to make each other's flesh creep. 'Foreign waiter' stories were the most common. Many of them left the country hastily to fulfil their military obligations in their own armies, and it is possible not a few of them may have been spying, though I do not believe that a case was detected. Some perfectly harmless ones above the age for military service who remained at their work had a very bad time. I can give the example of one 'Fritz', whom I knew from the days of his and of my own youth. I first knew him in 1887 as a waiter in the luncheon-bar of the old Grand Hotel in the Strand, and he rose steadily to manager in the grill-room when it was established underground round the corner. I can vouch for his harmlessness. He was, I believe, an Austrian by birth. Much to the regret of his British colleagues with whom he was popular, he was forced to leave his work in response to public opinion. It was a sad business. I was told by an English waiter who liked him that he was nearly starving. Then I lost trace of him.

The rumours covered every conceivable subject. Signalling to hostile aircraft. Feeding pigeons that might be carriers (homers) in the public street. Blowing up munition works. Destroying railway bridges. Mystery motor-cars with forbidden headlights (I was nearly arrested myself once by a zealous spy-hunter, because the dimmed lights of my Ford car glowed a little more brightly when I took the clutch out on being held up). There were suspicious Swiss governesses in distinguished families. Great men in public life were being detained in the Tower. I have given other examples elsewhere, and I have read in some reliable source that at one time about 400 people were reported daily as spies to the London police.

On the whole not much harm was done, though some of the suspects suffered some inconveniences. There was a certain amount of value in having plenty of amateur detectives to reinforce the police, and the spreading of false rumours of a type likely to mislead the enemy was not a disadvantage. Take, for example, that rumour about swarms of Russian troops landing in Scotland and travelling southward secretly in sealed vans. I referred to it in connection with Winston Churchill's raid to Ostend at the end of August 1914, where, on account of an experience in the South African War, I attributed the starting of the rumour to Lord Kitchener. (We had reached a place called Kenhardt to put down a rebellion in the north-west of Cape Colony when we received a telegram, partly in clear and partly in cipher, from 'K'. The clear portion told us that he was marching himself to Kenhardt. The cipher portion read, 'This will be of great interest to the enemy', so it seemed probable to me that as Secretary of State of War he was using similar methods of deceiving the enemy.) Many other stories are told of the origin of the Russian troops rumour. I quoted it exactly as it reached me at Ostend. A reliable friend—an eminent historian versed in methods of research—told me afterwards how it reached him in England. He had enough knowledge of military matters to treat what he called the 'monstrous legend passed from mouth to mouth in August and September' as a mere *canard*, though nine out of ten people who heard it believed the story in this exaggerated form: That four Russian Army Corps, or even that 250,000 Russian troops, were being conveyed through Scotland and England via Archangel (with its single line of railway!). Exaggeration, my friend thought, was caused by the hope in those critical days that this immense surprise army from Russia would roll back the German invaders of Belgium and France. Apart from the vast amount of rolling-stock which such an army would have required on both sides of the sea, their sea-transport would have kept hundreds of large vessels constantly plying from Archangel to Scottish ports, and from where could the ships have come?

Mention of that rumour now affords an opportunity to pay a tribute to a real German spy of the highest type, who had the misfortune to be taken in by it and to pass it on to his employers with picturesque detail of huge bearded men, with snow still clinging to their boots, being seen in transit. I refer to Karl Lody. The mention of his name takes us from fiction to grim reality.[1]

Karl Hans Lody, specially selected (it is said) by his Kaiser, risked his life when he came to England to fill the gap created by the arrest of the twenty-one German spies at the instigation of the Special Intelligence Department on August 4th, 1914. The tale of his proceedings from the day when he landed upon his dangerous mission, to the day on which he faced a firing-party in the Tower of London, has often been told, but it is still worth the telling. Originally in the German Navy, Lody retired because he could not afford the necessary expenses of an officer serving therein, and thenceforward he belonged to the Reserve of Naval Officers. He tried to obtain employment under Thomas Cook & Son's travel agency, but he was not successful. Then, as a guide to tourists, he served the Hamburg-Amerika Line. He was so serving in Norway in those days of strain that preceded the Great War. He reached Berlin on the day when Britain came into the War (and those twenty-one spies were interned, escaping the death penalty because their offences against the law had been committed in time of peace). Then, inspired by patriotism, he came to England. As a tourist's guide he had travelled much, and he knew England well. He spoke English fluently, with an American accent acquired in the United States, and also through his association with American tourists and passengers travelling by the Hamburg-Amerika Line. He carried a passport. It was made out in the name of an American, Charles A. Inglis. What happened to the original owner of the passport I

[1] In accounts of this, and of other secret agents who are mentioned, the author's personal knowledge has been supplemented by Felstead's *German Spies at Bay*, for which official authority is claimed.

do not know. The real Inglis asked his Embassy in Berlin to obtain a *visa* which would cover travel in Europe. The Embassy sent it to the Berlin Foreign Office for the purpose. The Foreign Office 'lost' it, removed the photograph of Charles A. Inglis, and substituted a portrait of Karl Lody.

Where Lody landed I do not know. Crowds of Belgian and other foreign refugees were pouring into the country just at that time. Proper examination of papers and of all the host of immigrants was impossible, since the staff was too small to cope with the work, and it may be that Lody joined one of those crowds. He first committed himself at the North British Hotel, Edinburgh. Thence he sent a telegram to Stockholm, addressed to one Adolf Burchard. This telegram caused suspicion, as the address was known, and thenceforward all his letters were opened and read by the postal censors, who were then beginning their activities. He used no cipher or shorthand. His letters to Sweden were in plain English or in German. They described coast-defences, ships' armaments and other confidential matters, and his four communications in his writings to Burchard would alone have sufficed to condemn him. The whole business was a tragedy.

Lody soon moved from his hotel to private rooms in Edinburgh, where his landlady, judging by his American accent, imagined that 'Charles A. Inglis' was simply an American tourist, interested in local sightseeing. While he was in the neighbourhood of the Forth, Lody spent a couple of weeks bicycling about and making his observations of the defences and of Rosyth, the naval base above the Forth Bridge. Then he went to London to an hotel in Bloomsbury, a district which seems to have been a favourite resort for foreign spies. In London he reported by the same channel upon anti-aircraft armaments and upon protective arrangements.

Then he went back to Edinburgh, and he was under observation all the time. On September 26th he went to Liverpool. As an expert in merchant-shipping he addressed useful reports to Berlin about the fitting of ocean liners with armaments. Then he went to the Grand Hotel, Dublin, via Holyhead. From Dublin he reported to his correspondent in Stockholm that he had chosen the Holyhead-Dublin route as being favourable for obtaining information, but that he was afraid that he was now being watched. From Dublin he travelled to Killarney, and he was arrested there on October 2nd by the Royal Irish Constabulary and detained to await the arrival of Scotland Yard representatives who took him to London.

There had been no subtlety at all in his methods, and no concealment of damning evidence. His bag contained nearly £180 in English money, besides Norwegian notes and German gold coin. Also a note-book, containing information about the latest naval action in the North Sea, and copies of his communications to Burchard. He was taken to the Tower of London, tried by Court Martial on October 30th and 31st and found guilty. He was shot five days later, facing his fate bravely and thinking of others to the last.

He told the members of the Court who tried him that he would accept their decision, whatever it might be, as coming from just and righteous men. To his relatives in Stuttgart he wrote, during his last hours in the Tower:

'A hero's death on the battlefield is certainly finer, but such is not to be my lot, and I die here in the enemy's country, silent and unknown. But the consciousness that I die in the service of the Fatherland makes death easy. . . . I have had just judges, and I shall die as an officer, not as a spy. Farewell. God bless you.'

To the officer commanding the battalion in the Tower he wrote:

'I feel it my duty as a German officer to express my sincere thanks and appreciation towards the staff of officers and men who were in charge of my person during my confinement. Their kind and considerate treatment has called up my highest esteem and admiration regarding good-fellowship even towards an enemy, and if I may be permitted I would thank you to make this known to them.'

Felstead tells us further that Lody said wistfully to the Assistant Provost-Marshal who fetched him from his cell, 'I suppose that you will not care to shake hands with a German spy?' 'No,' was the reply, 'but I will shake hands with a brave man.'

When his fate became known in Germany he was, for the time being, a national hero, and in his native village there thrives an oak, planted in his memory and called by his name, so that the tale of Lody will be told to future generations. There we take leave of the first spy who was shot in England in the Great War, and the first man who was executed within those grim grey battlements of the Tower of London for a hundred and fifty years. Nothing seemed to bring home to Londoners the reversion to stern conditions, which war must bring in its train, more than the executions in the Tower.

Over thirty spies in the pay of Germany were brought to justice by the British counter-espionage. Of these twelve were shot, one was hanged, and one committed suicide. . . . We shall make the acquaintance of others, of a type different from Lody, in due course. No woman spy suffered the death-penalty at the hands of British authorities. Lody, of the finest type of war-spy, came over solely from patriotic motives. He was a fine character, and the stern necessity to revert to execution for the safety of the realm was looked upon, in his case, as a tragedy.

Few of the others who spied for Germany in the United Kingdom were of German nationality. Most of them were from neutral countries, working for money. Some were of low type, steeped in vice, and accounts of how such folk face death in agonies of fear and cowardice need find no place in this record of Secret Service. I do

87

not believe that any men or women of that stamp obtained or reported information of naval or military importance, and it seems a pity that any country should employ them. According to some authorities, they were under suspicion and sent over as 'fool-spies' in the hope that they would be executed.

CHAPTER VII

THE WORST-KEPT SECRET OF THE WAR: THE DARDANELLES, 1915

THE STORY of the worst-kept secret of the War can appropriately be begun with a parallel in history, described in the diary of a midshipman who took part in the famous Walcheren Expedition early in the nineteenth century:

'The fact was that, no sooner was the idea suggested by Ministers than the secret was across the water—like most of our secret affairs at that time; certain it is that, in almost every instance in which the success of an expedition depended upon secrecy, the only persons mystified were the officers who were appointed to the command of it.'

My personal acquaintanceship with the Dardanelles and with the defences of the Straits leading to the Sea of Marmora dates from the years 1883–6, when I was serving in H.M.S. *Alexandra*, flagship of the late Admiral of the Fleet Lord John Hay in the Mediterranean Squadron. The late Captain the Hon. Maurice Bourke was her Gunnery Lieutenant. He went up the Straits to Constantinople with the Admiral in the old *Helicon*, then the Admiral's yacht, and he made some useful notes while he was passing the batteries. Taking pity upon my idleness as a young marine officer, and knowing that I had lately passed through a stiff course on coast fortification as an artilleryman, Bourke enlisted my aid in putting his report into shape.

We produced between us a voluminous document, profusely illustrated by plans and charts, in which we arrived at the conclusion that to run the gauntlet of the forts guarding the Narrows opposite to Chanak, delayed by the strong current which sets always from the Sea of Marmora into the Mediterranean, would be a very hazardous operation; it might just be possible perhaps, if effective machine-gun fire could be directed from the ships' tops against the detachments working the heavy guns in the lower batteries, for whom no effective overhead cover had been provided. We received the cordial thanks of the Lords Commissioners of the Admiralty for our report, and it may have been partly through that incident that, in 1886, I was given my start on Intelligence work at the Admiralty at so early an age.

I have mentioned my next visit to Constantinople in 1892 in H.M.S. *Surprise*, Admiral's yacht, on the staff of the late Vice-Admiral Sir George Tryon, Commander-in-Chief, when I was then engaged in starting under his direction the first branch of the Naval Intelligence Department which was established in the British Fleet, and I mentioned the greater activities in the Dardanelles defences than in those covering the Bosporus. Large parties of Turks were working hard upon improvements to the forts, which were much more formidable and more heavily armed than when I had first seen them. The Admiral saw me using my field-glasses to look at the forts, and he called me up to the bridge and said, 'Did you notice anything special about those forts?' I told him what I had noted, and he added: 'You missed one point. Only a few of the picks and shovels that the men were using were bright. The remainder were rusty. They had started digging to impress us.'

That visit, owing to the slow progress of the *Surprise* against the strong current, gave me an opportunity to make a thorough investigation of the defences of the Narrows, and I was specially interested in certain shielded slits in the hillside, near the water, which I decided were intended to protect look-out men in charge of minefields. The existence of mines completely changed the problem of running the gauntlet past the Narrows to clear water beyond.

When H.M.S. *Victoria*, with Sir George Tryon on board, went down after collision with the *Camperdown* in 1893, the late Admiral Sir Michael Culme-Seymour became Commander-in-Chief, and I joined his staff to re-establish the new Intelligence Department because the whole of the records and notes of the system which I had established had been lost in the ship. My work was completed in the years 1893–5. In 1894 the Admiral visited the Sultan at Constantinople in the *Surprise*, and some months later he sent for me and told me that he had been asked to give an opinion whether, if such a course should ever be deemed necessary, the Mediterranean Fleet could run the gauntlet past the Dardanelles and reach Constantinople. As I had worked at the problem for many years, I could answer off-hand. 'As far as the forts go; Yes, with heavy loss, say one third of the Fleet. If the mines are in position; No. They will be in the narrow channel, which the sunken ships will block. An army is needed to capture the forts and the observation-stations of the minefields before the Fleet can pass. It must be strong enough to defeat the Turkish troops on the spot.'

Years afterwards his son, the late Admiral of the same name, told me that his father had reported in accordance with my opinion, and that he had expressed his views with his usual vigour and candour when the proposal to rush the Dardanelles was on foot in the early days of the Great War. Sir Michael was noted for his straightness and candour, and for the vigour with which he expressed his opinion. There is a story of an interview with a First Lord of the Admiralty, after which the First Lord said to a friend: 'I like Sir Michael Seymour. He is so delightfully indiscreet.'

Between the years 1904 and 1907 it again fell to my lot to come across the Dardanelles problem when teaching 'Imperial Strategy' at the Army Staff College at Camberley, with special reference to combined operations of fleets and armies. Hoping to induce the public to take some interest in the subject, I chose the title 'Amphibious Warfare' (now in current use) for a lecture at the Royal United Service Institution in Whitehall in July 1907. The late Admiral of the Fleet Sir Arthur Wilson was in the chair, and Lord Roberts opened the discussion. The Press gave plenty of publicity, and it was hoped that, through public opinion, the interest of the authorities in power might be attracted.

In our teachings at the Staff College, which were afterwards embodied in *Amphibious Wars* and other books, two conditions were laid down for success—secrecy first, then speed. Secrecy would depend upon discretion, speed upon careful preparation. The transports must be packed so that what was first required when the troops were landed was on the top of the baggage in the holds, and so on to the bottom layer. The authorities who were responsible for the Dardanelles campaign did not secure secrecy, and they made speed impossible. The impending attack on the Narrows was almost advertised. The stores, munitions, and supplies were so loaded that the holds had to be emptied in Egyptian ports and repacked, a process which occupied many precious weeks, of which good use was made by the German General (Liman von Sanders). He prepared a warm reception for Sir Ian Hamilton's force, which did not arrive off the Gallipoli Peninsula until the end of April. To the lack of secrecy, and to the delay which was caused by packing the holds of the transports badly, the holocaust of slaughter on the beaches can directly be attributed. It was the worst-kept secret of the War, though it was approached in that aspect by the Nivelle attack in France in 1917.

Sir Douglas Brownrigg, the Chief Naval Censor, has told us that during the Dardanelles days in 1915 his office was very busy indeed. Mr. Churchill, the First Lord, took a keen interest in the proceedings of the Censor's office. He said to Brownrigg, 'For this business

I am Chief Censor, not you.'[1] Brownrigg adds that he used at that time to see the last of the First Lord at 1.30 a.m. He took copies of the radios that had come in during the night, had them properly typed out, and was at Mr. Churchill's bedside with them at 9.30 a.m. He used to find him

'in a huge bed, with the whole of the counterpane littered with despatch-boxes, red and all colours, and a stenographer sitting at the foot—Mr. Churchill himself with an enormous Corona in his mouth, a glass of warm water on the table by his side and a writing-pad on his knee.'

It is inconceivable that Mr. Churchill could, as Chief Naval Censor, have allowed secrets to leak out, when their disclosure would wreck an operation upon which he had set his heart. The leakage must have been elsewhere. It was a matter of common knowledge at Portsmouth, where I was stationed, and, not being behind the scenes in Whitehall at that time, I wrote to a friend who was, and I asked him to try to get the authorities to study the problem properly before committing themselves; above all, not to ignore the Turkish Army. I had urged,[2] as a condition of success in amphibious warfare, that there must be no superior hostile army within striking distance of the landing. Hence my anxiety. Judging by the report which was written after the event by the Dardanelles Commissioners, the Turkish Army had almost escaped attention. Even if a fleet did succeed in running the gauntlet past the batteries and the mines, the helpless transports full of troops and the store-ships and fuel-ships that must follow could not expect to pass the Narrows. The mobile guns and howitzers of the Turkish Field Army would easily have stopped them.

An attempt by the Fleet alone to get through the Dardanelles was definitely repulsed with considerable loss by the 18th of March, several battleships having

[1] *Indiscretions of a Naval Censor*, p. 12.
[2] *Sea, Land and Air Strategy*, published in August, 1914.

been sunk by mines and others seriously damaged. The intention to force the passage was then widely advertised. By that time it had become obvious that an army would be needed, and Sir Ian Hamilton was selected for the command. In a letter which lies before me, he tells me that, on the 13th of March when he went into Lord Kitchener's room to say good-bye, he found the War Secretary in the act of deciding between three sets of instructions which had been drawn up for Sir Ian's guidance. All three bore this heading:

CONSTANTINOPLE EXPEDITIONARY FORCE

After reading that, Sir Ian at once realized that secrecy— the main factor in success—was likely to be sacrificed. Had he known that the mischief was already done, he would doubtless have asked that he might be given a free hand to form some entirely different plan which, if kept secret, might have had a good chance of succeeding. (That was the way in which the younger Pitt, as Prime Minister, treated General Craig when he sent him to the Mediterranean in the spring of 1805, the year of Trafalgar.)

Sir Ian tells me that, without reading beyond the headings of those War Office papers, he 'implored' Lord Kitchener to change those headings, chiefly because it was such a disclosure of the destination of the force. Kitchener then changed 'Constantinople' to 'Mediterranean'. The original document is in the custody of the Imperial War Museum.

During the long delay that followed for re-packing the holds of the transports, Sir Ian was waiting in Egypt. *Before the end of March* the Egyptian newspapers were publishing the details of every ship-load of troops or stores as it arrived, stating 'without any reticence whatever' that they were all bound for the Gallipoli Peninsula. Sir Ian wrote to Sir Henry MacMahon to complain about this, but no redress was obtained. Looking back at those eventful days, he tells me that the only way out of it for him would have been to let all the publicity run its course and then, without telling anyone (even Lord Kitchener or the Cabinet), to have landed at Andramita or at Smyrna. It was in that way (by landing at Ismailia in the Suez Canal and not at Alexandria as everyone, including the Government, expected) that Lord Wolseley had won the Egyptian campaign of 1882 so easily. I hoped, at the time when I was anxiously following the fortunes of my old Marine Brigade which was in the Gallipoli Force, that some similar change would be made in a plan which had been so widely advertised. The General also points out to me that he was not the senior General concerned, as Wolseley was in 1882, and that the French Government also 'came in'. This is his final summary:

'With as much cleverness as might have come to any schoolboy, they [the authorities concerned] could have made it so that half the Turks I encountered at the landing would have been waiting for me some hundred miles distant.'

Sir Ian's troops forced their way ashore with great heroism in spite of heavy losses. They failed in their object. Publicity was too heavy a handicap. The total loss by battle casualties reached nearly 113,000, of whom 30,500 were killed in action or died of wounds. The Gallipoli Peninsula was not taken from the Turks. The wastage from sickness and other causes may be judged from the total number of all ranks, combatant and non-combatant, who were employed. This number reached nearly 470,000, though the maximum number that were serving in the theatre of war at any one time did not reach 128,000.

The worst-kept of all war secrets at the beginning was succeeded at the end by a miracle of success through secrecy. The withdrawal of the Army to cut further losses in December 1915 and early in January 1916 was achieved without loss of life. To this day it is believed in some remote quarters that the secret withdrawal, when in close touch with the Turkish lines, was so astounding as to be impossible, so that the safety of the troops, then commanded by the late Sir Charles Monro, must have been secured by bribery. There is not a particle of evidence in support of that view.

The circumstances which caused the campaign to be undertaken have never been fully disclosed, and I am not in a position to supply the gaps in the evidence. The Dardanelles Commissioners (before whom I was examined as an expert on the difference between gun-fire from decks of moving ships and howitzer-fire from steady platforms on land) stated that the decision to undertake a big offensive campaign against the Turks, when we had not enough men and munitions for the offensive in Flanders which was sanctioned at the same time, could be traced back to an appeal by the Grand Duke Nicholas. It seems to have been mistakenly suggested that the Russians could not hold their own against the Turks in the Caucasus, but long before any decision was arrived at by the War Council about taking action, naval or military, in the Dardanelles, the situation in that area had been completely stabilized by Russian victories over the Turks.

Opinion has since been sharply divided on the subject of the advantages which might have accrued to the cause of the Entente Alliance if Sir Ian Hamilton had succeeded in driving the Turks out of the Gallipoli Peninsula, leaving them in possession of the Asiatic shore there and also of the environs of Constantinople on both sides of the Bosporus. It was believed at the time that the appearance of the Fleet off the Golden Horn would have caused a revolution in Turkey against the pro-German rulers, and that Turkey would have then forsaken her allies of the Central Powers. I have not been able to trace the origin or the authority for that important rumour. Had Turkey taken that course, a route into the Black Sea would have been opened up for the Allies to have supplied the Russian armies with sorely-needed munitions. The Russian armies which were fighting the Turks could perhaps have then been turned against the German and the Austro-Hungarian armies. Ferdinand of Bulgaria would have come down on the allied side of the fence upon which he was sitting, instead of on the German side. Serbia would have been saved. With Russia, Roumania, Bulgaria, Serbia, Greece and Italy in arms on the Eastern and on the Southern fronts, supported it might be by British and by French troops, the Central Powers would be hard pressed. The long-brewing revolution in Russia would have been averted. British Empire troops in Mesopotamia, those in Egypt, and those subsequently used in Persia and for the conquest of Palestine and of Syria, would all have been set free for more effective employment. The tremendous strain upon the Merchant Navy, and upon the Royal Navy for its protection, would have been eased.

That vision splendid of the results which might have followed the success of Sir Ian Hamilton's Gallipoli campaign goes far beyond our scope. It was written [1] of Craig's force, sent to the Mediterranean in 1805 (which caused the Battle of Trafalgar), that Pitt's little expedition, after painfully gathering at Portsmouth, was destined to prove the insidious drop of poison—the little sting—that was to infect Napoleon's Empire with decay. Over a hundred years later some modern Pitt—who conceived the vision splendid of the Gallipoli venture, will go down to history with failure (through lack of secrecy and speed) to his credit. In 1915 it was the expedition, and not a hostile Empire, that was infected with decay. The 'little sting' was not the expedition itself. It was the publicity that was given to the 'worst-kept secret of the War' which caused its failure.

[1] Corbett, *The Campaign of Trafalgar*.

G

CHAPTER VIII

A DANGEROUS SPY

1915

WE RETURN now to the United Kingdom, and to the hostile secret agents who were trying to pick up secrets, such as those affecting the Naval dispositions, the Dardanelles venture, and the transport of troops to the Western Front and elsewhere.

I have mentioned the round-up of German secret agents by the counter-espionage department on the 4th of August 1914, the endeavours that were made by the German Secret Service to fill their places, and the tragic end of Karl Lody, officer of the Reserve of the German Navy, a patriot lacking in the subtlety that is needed for successful war-time espionage. Nothing was known at that time about the presence in England of a far more dangerous agent, Karl Friedrich Muller, posing as a Russian, who escaped the notice of the authorities until February 1915. His whereabouts were only discovered through an apparently small mischance which he had not foreseen. His secret headquarters were located at No. 2,000 [1] High Street, and High Street is the only street in Deptford that contains a house so highly numbered. Truth is stranger than fiction. Legends have grown up around the memory of this spy, and the legendary story bears less resemblance to the thriller of present-day fiction than does the true tale of his patient trackers in following up their only clue to his whereabouts and to his personality.

The story has been told in several books, and in most

[1] A fictitious number, to avoid causing inconvenience to the present occupant of the real number.

of those with which I am acquainted it is recounted that he sent his messages to the German spy-agency in Holland by inserting them in newspapers and posting them openly to their destination. Some accounts say that he marked the relevant matter in pencil, others that he did so in secret invisible ink, or that he used that medium to write his messages in the margins. These stories may rest on a basis of truth.[1] Of that I know nothing: if he did use such methods, they did not lead to his discovery or to his sharing the fate of Lody in the Tower of London.

Though I was not serving in Whitehall in 1915, my work in London in connection with the defence of 'vulnerable points' against the 'evilly-disposed person' was constantly continued, and I can vouch for the fact that, though spy-rumours and spy-scares were at their height during the first half of the year, the mysterious Muller (of whose existence as a spy traces were first discovered in February) was one of the very few that caused any anxiety to the authorities.

In January the first of the Zeppelins arrived off the east coast of England. The same month was marked by the loss of the battleship *Formidable* from a submarine in the Channel and by the raid of German cruisers which resulted in the action of Dogger Bank and in the sinking of the German battle-cruiser *Blücher*. In France the Battle of Champagne was proceeding. On the Eastern Front the Germans won the winter battle of the Masurian Lakes against the Russian Army. In Egypt there had been anxiety about the security of the Suez Canal until the attack by the Turks across the Sinai Desert was repulsed in February. The first German submarine blockade of Britain began in that month. What brought the war home to the people of England most acutely in those days was the Battle of Neuve-Chapelle in March, followed by the Battles of Ypres in April and May. The drumming of distant gunfire could then be heard in Kent. That was the general setting for the spy-drama of

[1] For the authorities used in this chapter, see footnote on p. 84.

the tracking of Muller, the most dangerous German secret agent who was captured in England.

The man's life and motives have always been a mystery to me. The last picture that was taken of him shows a deeply-lined face with haunted-looking eyes, tragic in their sorrow. It is a puzzling face, leaving a strong impression of tragedy in one's memory. My own deduction from his story as I knew it, was that he had adopted his dangerous and difficult course from financial straits and the need to support others—'*Père de famille est capable de tout.*' His record shows the tendencies of a gambler, not more scrupulous than others of the kind in his methods. He had been many things, hotel-keeper, sales-agent for motor-cars, a promiser of easy wealth to men of high estate with the plausibility of the shady company-promoter, and so forth. Many years' residence in England had made him fluent in the language, and he passed easily as a Russian from the Baltic Provinces, a member of the allied nation which—in those early days of the War—suffered so much, and achieved so much, for the cause of the Entente. He was therefore a welcome visitor to British shores. So much for the hunted, and now for the hunters.

British postal censorship was in full swing by February 1915, and certain addresses in neutral countries were suspected as being those of recipients of reports from secret agents in the United Kingdom. Holland was a hot-bed of such agencies, and some were located in Rotterdam. Letters which contained only unimportant matter, not calling for the trouble of correspondence in war-time, were always suspected by the censors. One 'L. Cohen' wrote on such lines to a suspected address in Rotterdam, giving his address as No. 2,000 High Street, Deptford. No such man lived at that address.

In the Appendix I mention certain simple agents, milk and lemon-juice, which make forms of invisible ink, easily made visible (dark brown) when the paper is toasted before a hot fire. I thought of these experiments of my childhood when I heard of the methods that were employed by postal censors. They kept a hot flat-iron in readiness to test suspected letters and so to find out whether grown men and women, whose lives depended upon covering their tracks, were foolish enough to resort to infantile methods of concealing secret messages. 'L. Cohen's' letters disclosed, under the influences of the hot flat-iron, surprisingly accurate reports upon the state of readiness of the units of the New Army which the Germans were expecting in France, and equally important matters about the British Navy and about anti-submarine procedure. Here was the greatest discovery of leakage from the United Kingdom of really important information to the enemy since the outbreak of war. Who was 'L. Cohen', and where was he? All that could be done, for the time being, was to verify the suspicion about his correspondent in Rotterdam, and this was done. A whole month passed by, while 'L. Cohen', in letters to his correspondent, clamoured for payment for his undoubtedly valuable services to the German Reich.

Then the postal censors picked up in transmission a certain letter, with the postmark DEPTFORD, bearing the incriminating address in Rotterdam. The letter itself contained little of importance. There was a short postscript, in invisible ink, and this was all that it said: '*C. has gone to Newcastle, so I am writing this from 2,000 instead.*'

That was all, but it was enough to put the hunters on the line. The scene now changes to the Special Branch at Scotland Yard, to the 'sleuths' of the spy-story fiction. What did '2,000' mean? It was probably the number of a house in a street. Where? The postmark on the envelope was Deptford, and the police in Deptford reported by telephone, in reply to an inquiry, that High Street was the only street there with houses so highly numbered. 'Who lives at 2,000?'—'It is a baker's shop.' 'What is the name of the baker?'—'*Peter Hahn.*'

Thus we get another actor in our spy-drama. It

transpired in due course that Peter Hahn, born in England and the son of a naturalized German no longer in England, had established his business as a baker and confectioner in High Street, Deptford, in 1910; that within three years he had become a bankrupt with liabilities amounting to about £1,800, and only about three pounds with which to satisfy his creditors. Then Hahn had mysteriously been re-established, and it might be that, from 1913 onwards, Secret Service funds supplied by Muller or by some other German agent had set him on his legs again. With that we are not concerned, excepting in so far as it promised a motive for his becoming Muller's tool, destined unwillingly to betray his chief to death.

Scotland Yard acted promptly. The name of the occupant of 'No. 2,000' was enough to confirm suspicion. Hahn was immediately arrested by special police from London. 'Who is C.?' he was asked. He knew no such man. 'You have told somebody that C. has gone to Newcastle.' Hahn would give no information, so he was at once removed and detained in custody, care being taken not to give him an opportunity of communicating with the mysterious C. There we will leave him for the present, while we follow the hunt.

Deptford is densely populated. It is rather a grimy and shabby-looking district in parts, better in others. Hahn had many neighbours and customers. His business had been established for five years, and his bankruptcy and his subsequent prosperity had attracted attention. The Police searched his premises, and in a back room behind the shop they discovered what was 'C.'s' headquarters, at all events at times. A cardboard box which they found there contained equipment for writing in invisible ink; pens, wool, ammonia, special paper and other apparatus. Then the people about were diligently questioned by experts in such inquiries, and soon a woman mentioned a constant visitor to Hahn—'a tall man, a Russian, who lived in Bloomsbury, in Russell

Square or thereabouts.' His name, she thought, was Muller.

Then the hunt passed to Bloomsbury, where all the lodging-house registers in the vicinity of Russell Square were laboriously examined until in one of them the name 'Muller' was discovered. 'Who is Muller? Is he a Russian?' the investigators asked of the landlady of that boarding-house. 'Yes, he is,' was the reply, 'but he is away from London, *at Newcastle*, where he is visiting some friends.' 'Could you let us have his address?' After some hesitation the landlady gave it, and after that the hunt for the mysterious 'L. Cohen', who had despatched so much valuable information to the incriminating address in Rotterdam, was over. His identity had been traced to Karl Friedrich Muller, who was arrested at Newcastle on the next day and brought to London to stand his trial.

When he was arrested he was at first pugnacious, protesting that a grave mistake had been made in so treating a subject of an Allied Power, a Russian who detested the Germans and all their ways. At subsequent interrogations he denied all knowledge of Hahn, he knew no such man, nor could he speak the German language. Then, when he had been confronted with one of his own incriminating letters, he relapsed into silence. He was an expert linguist. He spoke German, English and Russian fluently, and also Dutch and Flemish. He could claim to be a Russian if his birthplace, apart from his parentage, could make him one. He was born at Libau, and his age was 58. Both Muller and Hahn (as a naturalized British subject) were tried at the Old Bailey in May 1915, at the time when, after the first gas-attack on the Ypres Salient in April, the newly-raised units and recruits, stiffened by Canadians and by the few surviving Old Contemptibles, were undergoing their terrible ordeal of 'Second Ypres', wedged into a narrow pocket after their left flank had been left exposed, heavily bombarded by day and by night.

The evidence at Muller's trial was definite, documentary and clear. The investigation was careful and deliberate. He was found guilty, and he was sentenced to death by shooting, as a spy. Hahn, whose defence was that he was only a subordinate, obeying orders, was sentenced to seven years' penal servitude. Muller appealed, without avail, and he was taken to Brixton Prison; thence he was taken on June 22nd across the City to the Tower. He met his fate the next morning, leaving a wife and children for whom he was known to grieve sorely. The authorities are naturally reticent about such subjects, but according to the sources which I have quoted, there was a touch of nobility about his end. There is no more trying work for soldiers than the shooting in cold blood of a convicted spy, so Muller, when he was brought to the place of execution, asked and was allowed to walk down the ranks of the firing-party, shaking hands with every man and telling them that he bore no ill-feeling against men doing what was their duty.

The tragedy of that morning in the Tower of London was followed by an incident to which grim humour has been attached in several of the (sometimes embroidered) accounts which have been published. No news of Muller's arrest and execution reached his employers either in Holland or in Germany. While he was in prison and for some considerable time after his death, answers to his communications, payments for them, and requests for further reports were intercepted by the censors, and full use was made of the opportunity. By a permissible *ruse de guerre* the Germans were thus provided with much war news—sent ostensibly by Muller—which it was fervently hoped that they would believe. I believe that, for this misleading information, the enemy was good enough to pay the senders four hundred pounds. The sum did not appear under 'Appropriations in Aid' in the Estimates to my knowledge.

Lody, the ingenuous and patriotic sea-officer, and the mysterious Muller stood far above the cosmopolitan agents, some of them steeped in fraud or in vice, referred to at the end of a previous chapter. There is little to be learned from the methods or motives of those others besides the lesson that Secret Service needs not only subtlety but steady nerves, to which a vicious life and low standards of conduct seldom contribute.

We shall make the acquaintance of typical women spies on a later occasion.

CHAPTER IX

JUTLAND, 1916—I

For an example of the information at the disposal of the commander of a fleet in a modern naval battle, we cannot do better than take the Battle of Jutland in 1916. Official histories have cleared up all doubtful points about what actually happened at the battle, so there is no need to drag up old controversies of which the public has had enough and the Navy too much, but there seem still to be some gaps in the public knowledge.

Preceded by Hipper's battle cruisers and light craft, Admiral Scheer put to sea early on May 31st, 1916, and he moved northward towards the Skagerrak after distributing his submarines off the Scottish and other ports, from the Humber northwards, which he thought contained parts of Jellicoe's Grand Fleet and Beatty's Battle-Cruiser Fleet. He hoped thus to get early news of the approach of superior British forces which he naturally had no intention of meeting. He was far too wise to seek an encounter, whatever his propaganda compatriots may have announced after the battle. He has since made this point quite clear in his own writings.

Scheer's first idea had been a raid upon Sunderland, using Zeppelins to give him warning if Jellicoe came out, and submarines to take their toll of British battleships on their way to cut him off. Lack of visibility for air-observation had ruled out that plan. The German submarines had left harbour on May 15th and they could not stay out much longer than May 30th, so early on the 31st Scheer put to sea to carry out an alternative plan, a raid in the Skagerrak, with the High Seas Fleet in support. It is not universally known that Jellicoe,

106

curiously enough, had formed his own almost simultaneous plan to get the High Seas Fleet out towards the Skagerrak, well beyond the shelter of German forts and minefields and far enough to ensure that it would be obliged to fight a battle.

The idea was that two British light-cruiser squadrons would be off the Skaw at daybreak on June 2nd, and that they would then sweep down the Kattegat and push on into the jaws of the Great Belt and the Sound entrances to the Baltic. One squadron of British battleships would go as far as the Skagerrak in support. Three submarines would take up a position near Horn Reef on the west coast of Denmark to seek an opportunity to observe and to attack whatever came their way between June 1st and 3rd. (They actually started, lay on the bottom not knowing what was going on during the Battle of Jutland, and returned to their base on expiration of the allotted time. The officers heard about the battle for the first time on board their depot-ship.) The *Abdiel* (mine-layer) would add some more mines to those that she had laid in that neighbourhood about a month before, while Jellicoe and Beatty, in full strength, would lie in wait for the High Seas Fleet somewhere north of the mined area.

That was the original idea on the British side. Mr. Balfour, then First Lord of the Admiralty, had proclaimed after the German raids on Lowestoft and on Scarborough in the spring (in which 3 civilians, including a woman and a child, and 1 soldier had been killed, and 17 civilians and 2 soldiers had been injured) that part of the Grand Fleet had been moved to the southward. A squadron of old battleships had actually been sent to the Humber, and by May 31st it had been moved to the mouth of the Thames. It was thought that Scheer, having read the First Lord's announcement, might believe that Jellicoe's force had been dangerously divided. That would give an opportunity for dealing with it piecemeal. Thus we get an idea of what was in the minds of the two combatants on May 29th.

It is curious that, after nearly two years of waiting, the dates of the two ventures should so nearly have coincided. Scheer's date was about a day ahead of Jellicoe's and it might have actually coincided with his if Scheer's U-boats could have stayed out for a day or two longer. As it was, Scheer was the first to put his plan into operation. He left the Jade roadstead between 2 and 3 a.m. on the 31st of May, and, in spite of all precautions that had been taken on the British side to obtain early news of his movements through Secret Service, it was not known until 4.38 p.m. that he had even left Wilhelmshaven, further to the southward than the Jade roadstead. He was met unexpectedly at sea by Beatty and his cruisers scouting for Jellicoe. We shall find out in due course how secrecy was achieved by Scheer. We must first recall something about broadcasting and 'directional' wireless—more or less of a mystery in those days, now matters of common knowledge.

The tradition in the British Navy is that wireless telegraphy was first discovered as a practical proposition on board H.M.S. *Vernon*, the Naval Torpedo-School, at the same time that Signor Marconi, who was investigating independently, produced his first inventions. The first and greatest naval expert in the science was the late Admiral of the Fleet Sir Henry Jackson, who has just passed away. He was a personal friend of the writer and old shipmate in H.M.S. *Alexandra*, flagship of the Mediterranean Fleet forty years ago. I saw him for the last time in his dressing-room in his London house, playing with new inventions connected with directional wireless. The room was full of mysterious apparatus, and he showed me how some of it worked, especially the 'directional'. With that I was able to get a line, within a fraction of a degree, on the sending station to which we were listening. I suppose that most 'listeners-in' are familiar with a certain portable apparatus for which no aerial is required, which you turn round until it points to '5XX' or to whatever station it may be. You can tell by the volume of sound whether the box is exactly on the line or not. The sound fades gradually away as you turn the box in either direction, away from that line. Subject to correction by experts, I suppose that that is the same idea, but in these days one sits at the feet of one's school-boy sons on subjects which, in the days of which I write, were jealously-guarded mysteries in their application to warfare.

Now that Britannia no longer holds Neptune's trident by the handle, it is, I suppose, possible that there will be a great sea-fight some day between nations which hold it by the prongs. Our descendants may then be able to sit in their studies listening to announcers proclaiming the progress of the fight, with assistants murmuring 'Square Six'—'Square Three'—at intervals. The combatants themselves may then be more visible to arm-chair critics, watching pictures of them on screens, than they are to each other. Meanwhile we now know all about the influence of directional wireless upon peace navigation. After the War I had an experience of that myself. When taking a trip down Channel with an old friend holding a flag command, we were approaching the Lizard with some heavy battleships, in a dense fog, on the way to an anchorage off Penzance. There had been no chance of fixing our position by sights, and the venture of rounding the Lizard seemed to me—ignorant of such matters—to be rather a hazardous undertaking. The ship's position was found quickly and accurately by directional wireless and we soon found ourselves at anchor, exactly where we wanted to be in Penzance Bay, when the fog lifted.

Experts tell me that in these days a good listener can tell not only the line of bearing of a sending-station, but whether it is in front of or behind the listener, and can also form a good idea of its distance away. The influence of the progress of this science upon future sea-warfare is obvious. Let us see how what was known in 1916 affected the Battle of Jutland.

I have mentioned that secrets about the 'vulnerable points' which needed protection against folk with a penchant for sabotage came within my province in the years 1913 onwards. Sir William Robertson, then a Director in the General Staff at the War Office, has published his opinions on the subject in so far as it caused the detention in Britain of troops for which the General Staff could have found better employment elsewhere (about 80,000 of them, at one time). Some of these points needed protection for reasons so secret that they were not disclosed even to me, and being in full sympathy with my old colleagues on the General Staff of the Army I hesitated before including them in my lists. I did so in the end, for two good reasons. Sir Henry Jackson, the wireless expert, was Chief of Staff at the Admiralty at the time, and someone referred in my hearing to 'Dionysius'. That gave me the clue.

Once, when on a trip from Malta to Syracuse in connection with the pigeon-post which I had hoped to establish between Sicily and Malta in time of peace for special use in war, I visited a cliff-bound spot with a cleft in the hill-side ending in a sort of cave. There was a hole at the top that went by the name of the 'Ear of Dionysius'. The floor of the cavity was used as a prison, and if anyone up above put his ear to the hole he could hear plainly what the prisoners were saying to each other. It was something on the lines of the 'whispering-gallery' under the dome of St. Paul's. (The more up-to-date method in the Great War was to conceal a microphone amongst prisoners.)

With that experience behind me, I drew my own conclusions that the mysterious 'vulnerable points' were 'Ears of Dionysius', with a very long radius of hearing. These could not fail to be useful to an Admiralty anxious, if war should ever arise, to hear what an enemy afar off had to say about his own plans. Spies, if obtainable, might somehow send the news of a hostile fleet leaving harbour. Only an Ear of Dionysius could tell what it was doing when out of sight of land; and even then, only if it used wireless telegraphy. The mere sending of a message would give the direction if his call-sign was known. A knowledge of what it contained would depend upon getting hold somehow or other (by 'fair means or foul' is the usual formula) of his secret ciphers or codes. I therefore starred every place that I believed to be an Ear of Dionysius as IMPORTANT, and now we have the setting for our sea-drama in the waves of the ether, or in whatever the last theory of the broadcasting marvel places them.

I know, from the evidence of German charts, that Scheer derived a certain amount of information from a somewhat similar Ear of Dionysius at Neumünster, but not enough to be of much value to him. The listener seems to have mistaken some mine-sweepers which put to sea for battleships or cruisers. Scheer also received some messages from the U-boats which he had placed outside Scapa Flow and the Firth of Forth to warn him of Jellicoe's or of Beatty's approach. From such messages as he received, he drew the wrong deductions. They were very scrappy and incomplete, and they gave a wrong impression of the direction in which ships that were actually seen at sea were steering. We can now put the characters on the stage, before ringing up the curtain.

On the morning of May 30th Jellicoe's Grand Fleet was at Scapa Flow in the Orkneys, with one of his squadrons of battleships farther to the southward, at Cromarty. Beatty's battle-cruisers and Evan Thomas's fast Queen Elizabeth class battleships ('Queen Lizzie' herself was not available) were in the Forth. The Admiralty listening-stations knew much about the activities of Scheer's U-boats since they left their bases on May 15th, especially when they came nearer to the Scottish and English east coasts.

(While on the subject, by the way, I note that the fact that our Naval Intelligence Departments on shore could follow the movements of German U-boats by listening to their signals, has recently been used as evidence to support the old 'Kitchener Betrayal' story, which I have done my best to scotch. I can say definitely that the Intelligence Department did not know that 'U75' had been off the west coast of the Orkney Islands and had laid her mines there early on May 29th. Why, when one comes to think of it, should she be so foolish as to advertise her presence there by using her wireless apparatus? Rumour-mongers are incorrigible.)

Something was expected by the Admiralty. Probably another 'tip-and-run' raid, like those on Lowestoft and on Scarborough. There was no object, so far, in sending the Grand Fleet to sea to use up fuel until something more was known. Then, during the morning of May 30th 'there were indications', as the official British historian puts it, that the High Seas Fleet was assembling in the Jade Roads, a protected anchorage some miles outside Wilhelmshaven.

Knowing that his U-boats could not remain at sea much longer, Scheer ordered Hipper's cruisers to the Skagerrak, to show themselves off the Norwegian coast, while he, with the utmost secrecy, followed with the battle fleet. The Ear of Dionysius in England was so sensitive that the movement of German call-stations from Wilhelmshaven to the Jade Roads was known at once at the Admiralty. At noon on the 30th it was decided that the time had come for Jellicoe and Beatty to move. They were then told that the German Fleet might go to sea early the next morning. It was not until after 5 p.m. on the 30th that conjecture changed to practical certainty that something was going to happen, though the idea of Scheer himself coming out seemed too good to be true. Hipper, yes, with cruisers and lighter craft for another raid, but not Scheer! After 5 p.m. a long operation order was sent out by Scheer. The news was passed at once to that centre of 'pink' secrets, the operation-rooms of the Naval Staff. (Pink was the colour of the most secret papers.) Every minute counted and, without waiting for deciphering, orders were sent to Jellicoe and to Beatty to put to sea. They left as soon as it was dark. Then Scheer transferred his call-sign from his flagship in the Jade Roads to the naval sending-stations at Wilhelmshaven to deceive the Ear of Diony-sius. The ruse succeeded. Neither the Admiralty nor Jellicoe knew that he put to sea, following Hipper before sunrise on May 31st.

How, it will be asked, were German messages under-stood? Did they not take the obvious precaution of using cipher? The whole secret cannot be disclosed during the lifetime of some who were concerned. There were, of course, the usual regulations in force in all navies to prevent secret documents from falling into the hands of an enemy. This is easy when a surface-ship surrenders as in days of old by striking her colours. A leaded box ought to sink. So should books with heavily-leaded backs. There is plenty of time to drop them overboard and, unless the water is very shallow and the spot is marked exactly, there is little chance of their recovery.

It is not possible for captains of war-vessels to keep the contents of all secret orders, charts of minefields and ciphers in their heads. There must be something in writing or in print. In a modern sea-fight surface-craft may burn fiercely and be abandoned; or they may be wrecked, as the *Magdeburg* was in her action with Russian forces in the Baltic in August 1914. In submarine warfare it is not easy for the Captain of a submerged and sinking vessel to eject his secret documents beneath the surface. There lie the clues to one method in which the cipher used in the German Fleet, and also the key to its changes, were obtained, some by the British, and some by the Russians from the German cruiser *Magdeburg* when she went ashore off the Aaland Islands on August 26th, 1914. The results will appear in the next chapter.

CHAPTER X

T HESE are some of the messages that were sent on both sides (in cipher) by wireless telegraphy during the period which covered the Battle of Jutland.

At 9.48 p.m. on May 30th Beatty issued (by wireless):

'Cease communication by W T except on sighting the enemy or replying to the Admiral after passing May Island.' (In the Firth of Forth.)

At 10 p.m. Jellicoe made a similar signal.

At 1.22 a.m. on May 31st Jellicoe told the Admiralty by wireless to what rendezvous he was proceeding, and the time when he would arrive there in the afternoon. If Scheer had read and been able to decipher that and certain other messages, the Battle of Jutland would not have followed. Scheer, by transforming his call-sign to the shore, scored a success in maintaining secrecy about his putting to sea, but the British Admiralty took the lead in reading and in deciphering the messages that passed from the High Seas Fleet. There is no need to repeat the often-told tale of the Battle of Jutland. It is enough for our purpose to recall a few points.

At 2.20 p.m. the *Galatea* reported by wireless to Beatty the presence of 'two cruisers, probably hostile'. A listener in the *Iron Duke* told Jellicoe the news.

At 2.52 p.m. one of Jellicoe's battleships, the *St. Vincent*, took in a German signal on a 2,300 feet wavelength 'Strength 10 Telefunken used' and reported to Jellicoe. Apparently it was not deciphered. The *St. Vincent* was evidently in the rôle of Dionysius, as she reported five more messages at 3.10 p.m. At the same time the

Admiralty told Jellicoe that at 2.31 p.m. an enemy's light cruiser and a destroyer were at sea, giving their respective positions, obtained by directional wireless.

At 3.31 p.m. a seaplane from the *Engadine* reported to Beatty the position of those enemy cruisers and five destroyers, steering north-west. This was the first example of that kind of air report to a fleet in the history of sea-warfare.

By 3.35 p.m. Beatty was able to report to Jellicoe that Hipper's battle-cruisers had been definitely located. Soon afterwards the wireless installation of the *Lion* was shot away.

Indomitable at 4.13 reported having heard Telefunken signals increasing in strength from '4' to '10', but it was not until 4.38 p.m. that the *Southampton*, a light cruiser with Beatty, sighted Scheer's High Seas Fleet. That was the first news that reached Jellicoe of Scheer's having put to sea.

Scheer, as we know, escaped, with the help of bad visibility, smoke-screens and torpedo attacks, from being forced to fight a decisive battle of which the issue was never in doubt. He was last seen steering to the westward. Jellicoe steered south to cut him off from the mine-swept channels leading to safety behind minefields and the forts of Heligoland. Scheer, as soon as he was out of sight of British vessels, steered (across Jellicoe's course and behind him) towards Horn Reef. He passed unharmed the three British submarines there, lost one old ship from one of the mines which Jellicoe had, at 9.32 p.m., ordered the *Abdiel* to lay out, and he escaped between Jellicoe's Grand Fleet and the land. Beatty was further still to the westward in the morning. What were the British and German listeners and decipherers on shore doing during that momentous night, when the fate of the High Seas Fleet was in the balance? Here are the recorded signals that were sent by and to their commanders:

At 9.27 p.m. Jellicoe signalled to his destroyers to 'take station astern of the battle fleet five miles'. This signal was taken in by the listener at Neumünster and passed on to Scheer, but it did not help him much. How it was deciphered, if in cipher, I do not know. My authority is the late Sir Julian Corbett.

At 9.6 p.m. Scheer had made an urgent signal asking for a look-out by airships off Horn Reef early in the morn-

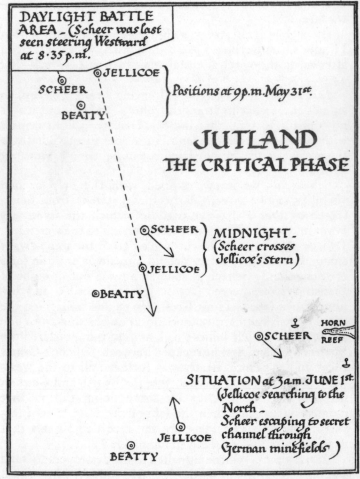

DAYLIGHT BATTLE AREA — (Scheer was last seen steering Westward at 8·35 p.m.

JELLICOE
SCHEER
BEATTY

} Positions at 9 p.m. May 31st.

JUTLAND
THE CRITICAL PHASE

SCHEER
JELLICOE

} MIDNIGHT —
(Scheer crosses Jellicoe's stern)

BEATTY

SCHEER HORN REEF

SITUATION at 3 a.m. JUNE 1st.
(Jellicoe searching to the North —
Scheer escaping to secret channel through German minefields)

JELLICOE
BEATTY

ing. The Admiralty read this, but I can find no record of its having been reported to Jellicoe at the time. Its importance cannot be exaggerated.

At 9.14 p.m. Scheer ordered retirement, and he gave the course to be steered by his ships. At 9.46 he altered that course, and gave the speed (16 knots).

At 9.55 the Admiralty warned Jellicoe that three destroyer flotillas had been ordered to attack him in the night; at 9.58 they gave him the estimated position of the rear ship of Scheer's battle-fleet, its course being 'Southerly' (the same as Jellicoe's); the message reached the *Iron Duke* at 10.23 p.m.

The Admiralty deciphered and made a summary of these messages. The summary, in cipher, was sent to Jellicoe at 10.41. It was received in the *Iron Duke* at 11.5 p.m. and it was in Jellicoe's hands, deciphered, by 11.30 p.m. My information does not support the view that Jellicoe was told anything about Scheer's signal of 9.6 p.m. asking for a look-out of airships off Horn Reef. There is no mention of its transmission in my set of secret Jutland messages, but that is not exhaustive. All that I know for certain is that the Admiralty, at 10.41. p.m., sent him the message in cipher stating that 'the enemy was believed to be returning to its [sic] base as its course was SSE¾E and speed 16 knots', and that, at 1.48 a.m. on the 1st of June, a further message was sent to him that 'enemy submarines were apparently coming out from German ports, and that a damaged German ship, probably *Lutzow*' (one of Hipper's battle-cruisers), was at a position of which the latitude and longitude were reported.

At 3.12 a.m. the Admiralty sent to Jellicoe a further report that a German 'light-cruiser', damaged, had been in a certain position, with destroyers standing by her, at 3 a.m. At 3.29 a.m. the Admiralty sent him a further message, *received at* 3.55, that the German main fleet was at 2.30 a.m. at a certain spot (latitude and longitude given) steering SE. by S. at 16 knots. It was then too late to cut off the enemy, starting from the position of the Grand Fleet at the time stated (3.55).

By 4.40 a.m. Jellicoe knew definitely that Scheer's fleet had returned to harbour. He informed Beatty, and sent him to locate the *Lutzow*.

At 5.30 the Admiralty told Jellicoe that the *Elbing* (light cruiser) had still been afloat, deserted by her crew, at 3.47, and they gave her position at that time. If other messages heard through the Ear of Dionysius were passed to Jellicoe, I can find no trace of them in official records of secret messages until 9.17 a.m. when the Admiralty told him that, at 6.20, enemy submarines had been sent to the *Elbing*. Her new position at that time was given. At 11.8 a.m. Jellicoe reported to the Admiralty that the whole area had been swept for disabled enemy cruisers, without result. (Both *Lutzow* and *Elbing* had sunk in the night.)

Scheer, on his part, relied a good deal upon his airships for information, and he was under the false impression that Jellicoe's fleet had been divided, a large portion being in the Skagerrak in the morning.

So ended the Battle of Jutland, as heard on both sides from the shore through headphones. A battle of words was substituted immediately afterwards for the battle of the ships, and that word-battle has lasted until this day. A similar one over the Battle of Trafalgar lasted for more than a hundred years. With the propaganda bearing upon Jutland I do not propose to deal in detail. The subject would fill a large book. With propaganda generally, as a supplement to the deeds of fighting forces in the Great War, I hope to deal in due course. (As a member of the War Cabinet Secretariat, specially charged with the subject, I was in a position to know much during the later stages when propaganda attained its maximum influence at the time when the issue was trembling in the balance, and much depended upon the spirit of the civil populations of the belligerent countries.)

The Germans reached their defended anchorage more

than two days before Jellicoe could cover the distance (400 miles) back to Scapa Flow, and they naturally made the most of the opportunity to claim a victory. The same thing occurred after Howe's 'Glorious First of June' in 1794, and after Trafalgar. I received private letters myself from various quarters, far apart, asking what had really happened; one was from the Governor of Malta (Lord Methuen), and one was from the Chief of the General Staff in France (Sir Lancelot Kiggell).

Nelson's definition of a naval victory ran thus: '[By] completely victorious, I mean able to remain at sea whilst the enemy must return to port.' That definition escaped for some time the attention of propagandists on both sides of the North Sea. The first news of the battle, from the German side, reported that the High Seas Fleet had met and had defeated a considerably superior main portion of the Grand Fleet. An excessive estimate of British losses was given, and a victory was claimed.

For what follows it will be best to enter another depository at the Admiralty of 'pink' secrets—'Room 37'. It was next to the inner sanctuary of 'Operations' from which orders to the Fleet were issued. The censor and his assistants worked there, and passed news to the Press Bureau. The inmates naturally worried about what to do in the absence of reports which were being collected and checked by Jellicoe before sending in his account. Wild rumours, based upon the German *communiqué*, were current. Ships returning from the battle were arriving at British ports nearest to the scene of action. Members of the ships' companies were telegraphing to their friends and relations to tell them that they were all right. Six thousand such telegrams were being held up, although there was no censorship under ordinary conditions of inland messages.

Reuter's report from Amsterdam of the German *communiqué* of May 31st, which had been held up, was released between 10 and 11 a.m. on June 2nd. Finally, at 7 p.m. on June 2nd, an announcement (which was afterwards severely criticized) was issued by the Admiralty.

The official history attributes its authorship to the First Lord (the late Lord Balfour). Sir Douglas Brownrigg, the Chief Naval Censor, has written that it was framed by the First Lord, the First Sea Lord (Admiral Sir Henry Jackson) and the Chief of Staff (Vice-Admiral Sir Henry Oliver). The material that was available was a wireless message from Jellicoe. The time of origin is given as 9 a.m., the time of despatch as 10.35 a.m. (the delay doubtless being due to enciphering), and the time of receipt (presumably after deciphering) at the Admiralty Censor's office was 3.30 p.m. The information in that message chiefly referred to British losses, the delay in ascertaining and in verifying them having been due to the British Fleet having remained at sea, in command of the area outside the German minefields, for so long a period after Scheer (in harbour) had been able to collect his reports. Jellicoe had not heard of the principal losses in battle-cruisers until the day after the battle. The Admiralty announcement confessed these losses freely, whereas the German Admiralty, in their first *communiqué*, suppressed the most important of their own (the battle-cruisers *Lutzow* sank, and *Seydlitz* beached just in time— she would have been lost if the battle had not been so close to the German base—and three of the light cruisers, *Elbing*, *Rostock* and *Frauenlob*). The British Admiralty account did, however, mention the crucial point, that the 'enemy returned to port, though not before receiving severe damage'.

Casualties appeal more strongly than strategic results to the average mind. Of that I had experience myself. My first news of the battle came from a messenger who rushed into my room to tell me of the loss of so many of my own men in the sunken battle-cruisers. It was at Portsmouth, where extravagant stories had been afoot, earlier in the War, of the likelihood of a German invasion. 'What has the enemy lost and where is his fleet?' was the obvious question to be asked. 'Losses are not known. The High Seas Fleet has gone back into harbour,' was the reply. But it took some time for many to realize its significance.

I have given the day and time when the German account was published in England through Reuter's agency. It was between 10 and 11 a.m. on June 2nd. What was happening in places, all over the world, which accounts from the German side had reached on May 31st and the German *communiqué* on June 1st? A whole day's start in 'news value' means much to modern journalism. There was triumph amongst pro-Germans, and sympathy, tinged with pity, for the British amongst neutrals favouring the cause of the Allies. At 7.5 p.m. on the 2nd of June, and again at 7.10 p.m., Jellicoe sent further information about British losses, and all that he considered definitely proved about the losses of the enemy. At 11.30 p.m. he sent a long and comprehensive despatch. All these came by land telegraph-line. A long report was sent by Beatty sixteen minutes after midnight.

At 2.40 p.m. on the 3rd of June, Jellicoe telegraphed about the Admiralty statement of the previous evening in these terms: 'Last night's [Admiralty] *communiqué* magnifies our losses and minimizes the enemy's casualties, and gives somewhat false impression of action generally.'

At 1.5 a.m. on June 3rd the Admiralty issued a little more information in order to relieve anxiety, but it was not until the Monday, June 5th, that the Press Bureau was supplied with a comprehensive statement which touched, for the first time, the crux of the situation in these words: 'When the main body of the British Fleet came into contact with the German High Seas Fleet, a very brief period sufficed to compel the latter, who had been severely punished, to seek refuge in their protected waters. Sir John Jellicoe, having driven the enemy into port, returned to the main scene of action, and scoured the sea in search of disabled vessels.'

Had there been a competent 'publicity agent', with a free hand to write what he liked, on board the *Iron Duke* at noon on the 1st of June an identical statement might have reached all other Ears of Dionysius tuned to the British wave-length at that time. There would have been no need for delay to encipher or decipher such an announcement. It could well have been sent 'in clear'.

There is mere wisdom after the event. Judging by the aftermath, it was better in the end to underestimate than to run the risk of overestimating results. That leads to retribution, and 'purple prose' has no lasting effect. 'To lie like a bulletin' was proverbial in the Napoleonic wars, and the bulletin describing a victory of Villeneuve over Nelson after Trafalgar in 1805 is a document still worthy of the attention of propagandists. Its effects lasted in out-of-the-way country districts in Europe for many more years than the early Jutland *communiqués* have endured. The wording of that Trafalgar bulletin carries more than transient interest. It was dated from Cadiz, October 25th, 1805, four days after the battle, and the parallel with the Battles of Jutland and Verdun in 1916 is striking. This is how it is said to have read.

'The operations of the grand naval army [have] secured in the Atlantic those of the imperial army. . . . The English fleet is annihilated! Nelson is no more!

'Indignant at being inactive in port whilst our brave brethren in arms were gaining laurels in Germany, Admirals Villeneuve and Gravina resolved to put to sea and to give the English battle.

'They [the English] were superior in number, forty-five [true number twenty-four] to our thirty-three; but what is superiority in numbers to men determined to conquer?

'Admiral Nelson did everything to avoid a battle. He attempted to get into the Mediterranean, but we pursued, and came up with him off Trafalgar. . . .

'After having acquired so decisive a victory, we wait with impatience the Emperor's order to sail to the enemy's shore, annihilate the rest of his navy, and thus complete the triumphant work we have so brilliantly begun!'

In Denmark, after Jutland, the lack of news from England was taken as confirmation of the German report. In Holland the Press took the British silence as no very favourable sign, and there, as in Sweden, the first Admiralty statement was held to confirm the reports of a stupendous German victory. As late as June 5th, the Dutch *Standard* proclaimed a complete transformation of the position at sea. In Zurich, the British losses were held to give the Germans a right to claim the victory. Then, when the loss of the *Lutzow* and *Rostock* had perforce to be confessed, there was a violent revulsion, accompanied by lasting distrust all over neutral Europe—in Denmark, Norway and Sweden, in Holland and in Spain—in German 'victories'. The balance of belief by neutrals in achievements and in prospects of victory in the sea-war hit the beam at the German end.

So much can be written, I hope without indiscretion or offence, about inspired publicity on the Battle of Jutland. Behind the scenes on the British side there was one real and jealously-guarded secret, of national importance —the truth about one of the causes of the heavy loss in British ships. After receiving a report by Sir Eustace d'Eyncourt, the expert in naval construction, the Admiralty wrote after mature consideration that they had been forced to the conclusion that 'in some of the ships engaged in the action of May 31st, the precautions necessary to the safety of the cordite cartridges were, to a certain extent, subordinated to the great desire, necessarily felt, to achieve a rapid rate of fire', and they issued stringent instructions that measures must be taken to safeguard the charges and to diminish the risk of their explosion, which might reach the magazines. The danger of such explosions on gun-decks passing by ammunition passages to magazines was well known by our ancestors who fought at sea. I have lately glanced through a sea-dialogue, printed in 1685 and written, I believe, at least fifty years earlier. There I found cautions to Master-Gunners to beware of such risks. That is the earliest warning of the kind with which I am acquainted. There have been many later, including one from Rodney in a private letter to a nephew, and perhaps some earlier.

I was told the secret myself privately, immediately after the Battle of Jutland. I was Commandant, at the time, at Eastney Barracks, Portsmouth, where hundreds of gunners were being trained for service in the Fleet. A few days after the battle I went to London upon some Admiralty business, and I attended a luncheon-party in Belgravia between my visits to Whitehall. To my amazement my hostess announced to her guests (we were about ten at luncheon) the secret of the cause to which some of the most serious of the Jutland losses were being attributed in official circles. I was appealed to for confirmation, and I could only think of interjecting, 'What an extraordinary story!' or some equally inadequate remark. I took care to be the last to leave the house, in order to ask my hostess where she had heard the story. 'It *must* be true,' she said. 'I was at a working-party this morning, and all the ladies there were talking about it, including X and Y!' (mentioning the wives of two eminent officials of my acquaintance in Whitehall).

So the most jealously-guarded secret about the Battle of Jutland became a *secret de Polichinelle* in London 'society' within a few days. It says much for the discretion of the many to whom it was repeated that it never to my knowledge reached the ears of the enemy. Even if it had, perhaps no harm would have been done. Whatever the relative total losses in ships may have been, the general result was that the Grand Fleet had fuelled and was ready for sea again on the night of June 2nd after having travelled 400 miles from the scene of the action. Heavy repairs delayed, until well into August, the date when the High Seas Fleet was ready.

The sources of information about the extent to which Secret Services were an aid to Jellicoe are more complete than those pertaining to Admiral Scheer, who seems to have been badly served during the approach, in the battle, and in his subsequent retreat. According to his own showing, he was misled by his submarines, which were stationed off the Scottish coast early on May 31st, and again by the Zeppelins which were scouting for him early on the 1st of June. From them he gained an impression that Jellicoe's fleet had been divided, a portion of it being in the Skagerrak, far away to the northward.

CHAPTER XI

1916

MEMORIES OF LORD KITCHENER AND HIS END

FOUR days after the conclusion of the Battle of Jutland (the 5th of June 1916), Field-Marshal Earl Kitchener of Khartoum passed from the scene of his earthly activities, and immediately afterwards there arose legends about the manner of his death, and even rumours of his survival. These continue to this day, and it seems impossible to follow them all up and to kill them once for all. One point has never to my knowledge been made quite clear, the connection between the sinking of H.M.S. *Hampshire* off that cruel cliff-bound and rocky coast of the Orkney Islands and the Battle of Jutland.

It is too soon for us to attempt a measure of Kitchener's greatness. Events in the Great War are too recent. Dwellers in the plain must travel far from the mountain-ranges before they can even see, much less judge the relative heights of the lonely peaks; and Kitchener when nearing his end, was a lonely man, with few intimate friendships. My own personal knowledge of him dated from the South African War (*the* war, as we all called it in England until August 1914), and I recall a vivid picture of the surroundings and circumstances in which we first met. It was at De Aar, an important railway junction 500 miles from Cape Town, on the lines of communication leading from the sea (where the British Navy was supreme) to the front-line troops; to Lord Methuen's force to the northward, facing the formidable heights of Magersfontein beyond which Cronje's Boer

Army was surrounding the garrison of Kimberley; to Sir John French's to the north-east beyond Naaupoort, at Colesberg near the frontier of the Orange Free State; and to General Gatacre's, farther to the eastward, facing Stormberg. Sir Redvers Buller, in supreme command until the arrival of Lord Roberts in January, was away with the main force on the Tugela in Natal, facing Spion Kop and the heights about Colenso, which screened the main Boer Army besieging Sir George White's force, shut up in Ladysmith.

'Black week' in December, which marked the 'disasters' of Colenso, of Stormberg, and of Magersfontein, had been followed by a period of confusion and bewilderment on the 'Western Front' in Cape Colony. Cape Town was a centre of depression and of gloomy prediction, of rumours which spread like a miasma up that long railway crossing the wilderness of the High Veld, the vulnerable line of communication upon which the fighting forces depended for their sustenance, even as a diver depends upon a long air-pipe for his breath. (Lord Methuen's troops at the front were quite cheery and confident. I had found them playing football.) There was incipient rebellion, fostered by enemy agents in the districts along the line. Every one of the hundreds of miles of railway-line had to be guarded against sabotage.

De Aar, the important junction, had its own garrison and commandant. It was my headquarters as staff officer to the Inspector-General of the whole Western Line, and soon I became the sole depository there of the jealously-guarded secret of Lord Roberts's plan to concentrate on the left at Enslin and Graspan, behind Lord Methuen, bringing French round through De Aar for the purpose, and then to strike north-east to cut off Cronje. Everything depended upon secrecy. Secrecy depended upon good organization, upon quietly concentrating transport for the move, and then upon decisive movement. All depended upon finding a man with broad views from whom to seek guidance. For instance, a hundred and eighty ox-wagons, with their masses of oxen, had to cross a long bridge over the Orange River and there was only room for the single line itself between high iron girders. One team of oxen met a train, and the poor brutes were squeezed through the girders into the river below. 'Have you held a court of inquiry upon the oxen?' was the message that came to me from the pundits at the base.

It was then that Kitchener came up the line. The battalion which was guarding us at De Aar had a great surplus of mule-transport for its needs. For instance, a mule-wagon, with its team of six fine mules, was sent out to look for a pipe which had been left behind on a kopje by a picket on night outpost duty. 'All regimental transport is to be pooled at once for army use,' was Kitchener's immediate order.

Then a staff officer (R.E.) arrived at De Aar from Kitchener with a table of railway movements. Trains would be at certain places at certain hours on certain days and the troops must be ready to get into them. I was to be responsible for that part, and the troops were to be told their starting-points, but not their destination. We did not know then where all the troops were, so I had to find out and do my best, which I did, but I could not find one of the field companies of Royal Engineers. The work of enciphering and despatching the orders occupied twenty-three continuous hours, strong soup and strong coffee being my chief sustenance. I fell into a dead sleep at the end, and was soon roughly aroused by an orderly. 'Pressing, *in red ink*, sir, from the base to you.' I opened the envelope and I read this: 'Two bags of lime were sent to De Aar station on the 3rd inst. The Contractor will charge as per margin for the empty bags if not returned forthwith.' Fourpence was the sum mentioned in the margin. Of such small matters some of the staffs were thinking, and then Kitchener turned up in the night. His advent was not advertised. My chief, who had just returned from speeding up the ox-wagons, told me privately, 'By the way, K. will be on No. 52 up train during the night. You will have to meet him. He will arrive at about 3 a.m.'

Washed, shaved and carefully brushed, I was on the platform in good time, and I found Kitchener sitting at a table in his saloon. He made a large soldierly figure, carefully 'groomed'. His belts and boots were highly polished, and his buckles and buttons gleamed. I had an impression of keen eyes, with a cold light in them, and of heavy brows. There was an air of mystery about him, and above all, of dominance. He asked me only one question. 'Where is the nth Field Company R.E.?' (The one that I had lost.) Every detail of the complicated move must have been in his head, and he had only one staff officer with him, Hubert Hamilton (killed when in command of the 3rd Division in the Mons Retreat). Hamilton, who was an old friend of mine—we had been at the same private school—called me aside afterwards and told me that 'K' was really quite pleased, though he had not said so. He added that, from a staff officer's point of view, K. abhorred the cumbrous system of army correspondence, with its recording and pigeon-holing then in vogue. Hundreds of telegrams reached him. He read them, memorized them and crammed them, crumpled up, into his pocket, concentrating upon the action most important at the moment. Hamilton had great difficulty in retrieving them, to keep some sort of record. At that and subsequent meetings 'K' always radiated confidence with me, as a man unperturbed in the gravest emergency, patient and inscrutable as the Sphinx.

Not long afterwards the rebellion in Cape Colony came to a head. The safety of the railway-line depended upon its immediate suppression. K. sent me off to Victoria West, far away to the southward, to pull indignant troops (bound for the front) out of their trains and to go with them hundreds of miles to Kenhardt, a centre of disaffection. He came back himself from the front to De Aar, to deal with a worse situation at Prieska. His name there was enough, his presence was advertised, and the rebellion fizzled out. Then Cronje was cut off at Paarde-berg, and Bloemfontein, the capital of the Free State, was taken. Such was my first knowledge of 'K's' personality.

In order to understand his influence at the time of his death, we must recall the atmosphere that prevailed amongst those in high places when war came suddenly upon them and the magnitude of the task had not been realized by our statesmen or by our soldiers of the General Staff. Sir William Robertson, one of its Directors when war broke out, has made that quite clear. The veteran Lord Roberts had warned the Government and the nation, but his warnings had fallen upon deaf ears. Kitchener's prestige stood high. The nation knew him as the victorious hero of wars in Africa; as the saviour of the Sudan, and perhaps of Egypt itself, from the incursions of fanatical desert hordes; as a military reformer in India, a man strong enough to stand up to a powerful Viceroy, at whatever cost to his own future career; as a soldier towering by achievement above his colleagues of the day, and as a man to lean upon in a grave crisis, better perhaps as an autocrat than as a colleague or as a subordinate.

The Prime Minister (Mr. Asquith) judged public opinion aright when he recalled Kitchener, just in time, as he was leaving England to return to his work in Egypt. Thirty-six hours after the declaration of war, 'K' was installed as Secretary of State for War and a member of the War Council, charged with the execution of plans in the making of which he had no hand. Most of the leading members of the General Staff were then busy packing up to go with the Army to France. Kitchener, and he alone amongst responsible statesmen and soldiers in Britain and in other countries, foresaw the magnitude and prolongation of the sacrifices that would be needed before victory would be within reach of the Allied armies, still less within their grasp. Walter Page, the American Ambassador to Britain, paid in the fewest words the best tribute to Kitchener's work for the Allied cause. 'His name has raised a great army.'

We pass over, as still well remembered, his personal visit to Sir John French in France, five days before the 'B.E.F.' arrested its retreat and turned northward to bear its part in the victory of the Marne; his meeting with French statesmen and soldiers at Dunkirk in November 1914, when he explained that the newly-raised British armies could not be thrown into the maelstrom of the conflict until they were fully trained and equipped, which would not be before 1916; his change of attitude in the autumn of 1915, when he ordered French and Haig, against their better judgment, to meet the appeals of Joffre and Foch and to undertake the costly autumn offensives in that year; his trip to the Mediterranean in December of the same year to lend his great prestige to the policy, already recommended by Sir Charles Monro on the spot, to cut our losses in the Dardanelles—a confession of failure in that ill-starred venture which could not (and did not) fail to shake public confidence in the conduct of the War. Then, in 1916, there came the sore plight of the French Army in stemming the massed German attacks from February onwards at Verdun, and the fear that those would succeed if the attackers were not drawn away to other parts; the decision to launch 'Kitchener's new armies' (before they were ready) in the costly Battle of the Somme, which was destined to relieve the situation; and, last but not least, the Russian battles on the Eastern Front. The Battle of Lake Naroch, which opened in March, was successful till near the end of April when the ground gained was lost, and preparations were made for Brusiloff's victorious advance which was to open on June 4th, the day on which Kitchener was starting on what was to be his last journey. Why was he sent?

In the welter of corruption in Russian high places and inefficiency and sedition amongst those of low position, which left their armies in the front line to fight without arms or munitions adequate for their needs, Kitchener, whose fame carried weight over the whole Eastern Hemisphere, was called upon to go to Russia himself as the one strong, disinterested personality whose presence might avail to initiate wiser councils. The secret of his journey and of his destination was jealously and safely guarded. In the Grand Fleet at Scapa Flow, in the Orkneys, no one besides the Commander-in-Chief and, in due course, the Captain of the *Hampshire*, a cruiser just back from the Battle of Jutland—which was to convey him to Archangel in the White Sea—knew anything about the journey. The *Hampshire* had returned to Scapa Flow at 5.30 a.m. on Friday, the 3rd of June.

We have had glimpses behind the scenes of counter-espionage in Britain, up to the day when the *Hampshire* was lost. We know how the whole system of German spying at various places, mostly on the coast-line, was paralysed on the day when war was declared. We have noted the endeavours that were made to get efficient spies into the country in their place—men of fine character like Lody in 1914, a hero far too guileless to be a spy, and the more dangerous Karl Friedrich Muller in 1915. After the great run of captures in that year, and after the occasion, in April 1916, when the last spy was executed (a Peruvian—no German spies having been sent for some time), the spy-offensive had definitely failed. It was impossible, even for a British observer dwelling in the Orkneys, to know that the *Hampshire* would steer as she did on leaving Scapa Flow until she actually shaped her course.

The scene of his last days now changes from Whitehall, where he had been in the inner conclaves of the War Committees of the Cabinet, to the north of Caithness, the Pentland Firth and the Orkneys. I have records of German spies having reached various parts of Scotland, but I do not believe that any such agents wandered as far north as the north of Sutherland, Caithness, and the Orkneys. Those who know the country there will not be surprised. After following the east coast of Sutherland, the railway-line which Lord Kitchener's train followed turns sharp inland, following the course of the Helmsdale with its salmon pools and touching that of the Halladaile at Forsinard, then to Georgemas, the junction for Wick and Thurso, and then one gets glimpses of the river of that name till arriving at the terminus at Thurso itself. Kitchener embarked there in the destroyer *Oak*, attached to the flagship of the Commander-in-Chief of the Grand Fleet. Caithness is a country of grouse-moors, deer-forests, salmon-rivers and trout-lochs. It is sparsely populated by people all well known and mostly related to each other. I remember an incident there some years ago when a visitor asked the driver of a post-cart: 'Is *everyone* in Caithness either a Sinclair or a Sutherland?' The driver's reply was, 'I'd no say that—the Gunns are coming on well!'

I can vouch myself for the fact that before the War, when various rumours of German aggression and of possible invasion were afoot, the keepers and stalkers, the gillies and the river-watchers kept, on their own initiative, a keen watch for any suspicious aliens, and, under the war-restrictions for travellers bound to the north, it would, by 1916, have been certain death for any foreigner spy to reach a destination so vital to the Navy as its base in the Orkneys. Every mile of the coast-line, too, was constantly patrolled by experts in matters affecting the sea. In clear weather even the periscope of a submarine would have stood little chance of escaping attention. At night, or in thick weather, nothing could be seen from hostile U-boats, though it is true that they were fitted (long before the British were) with wireless apparatus of long enough range to report to German naval bases in the North Sea. Two of those U-boats, Nos. 43 and 44, had been stationed off the exit from Scapa Flow that was used by the Grand Fleet late on the 30th of May and again on the 2nd of June. They failed to send Admiral Scheer the information of its movements which he hoped to obtain in order to enable him to avoid a meeting with Jellicoe. And that takes us back to Jutland and to the way in which the plan of Scheer—who can by no possibility have known anything of Kitchener's prospective movements—caused the loss of the *Hampshire* and her passengers.

Admiral Scheer became Commander-in-Chief of the High Seas Fleet in January 1916, after the death of Admiral von Pohl. The pressure of Allied sea-power was then being felt in Germany. 'Why a High Seas Fleet that never leaves harbour?' was asked. After some raids upon Lowestoft and upon Yarmouth in April, Scheer, as we have already noted, formed a plan for a raid, with the High Seas Fleet in support, upon Sunderland. A ring of airships (Zeppelins) was stationed to give him early notice if the Grand Fleet approached and, from May 17th to May 22nd, a line of nine U-boats was stretched, well to the northward of the Dogger Bank, to take their toll of Jellicoe's force if it should get the news early enough to sally out and enforce a fleet action. The raid was to take place on the 18th.

From that date onwards visibility was not sufficiently good for observers in the Zeppelins to make sure of giving Scheer enough notice. He then made the new plan, to sally forth in the direction of the Skagerrak on May 31st —the plan that led to the battle. Air observers having failed him, Scheer decided to move his submarines to positions near the ports containing Jellicoe's and Beatty's ships, as far as he knew where they were. Two were to watch for Jellicoe's departure from Scapa Flow in the Orkneys; seven to watch the exits from the Firth of Forth, and another precaution was taken, the one which caused Kitchener's death.

The secret of how all these things were discovered belongs to another tale. We are now concerned only with U-boat 75, which was fitted for laying mines. Scheer sent her to lay them west of the Orkneys, to catch vessels of Jellicoe's fleet which might use that route. My authority for the statement that the mines were laid to catch a portion of the Grand Fleet, and for no other object, is that of the captain of U-75—Kurt Beitzen himself. I give her track between the 27th and the 31st of May, the drawing being based upon a confidential German chart. It settles all doubts that have arisen about the cause of the loss of the *Hampshire*. The mines (22 in number)

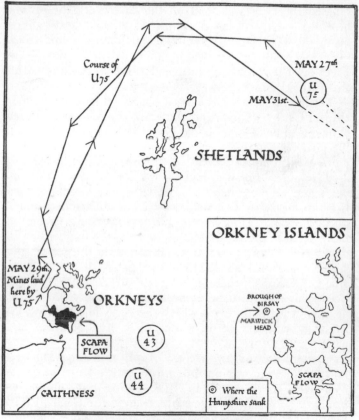

WHY THE HAMPSHIRE SANK

were laid, between 6 and 8.35 a.m. on May 29th, about 4 fathoms below the surface at high tide.

The story of the last hours is better known than the real cause of the catastrophe. Lord Kitchener, with Brigadier-General Ellershaw, Sir F. Donaldson, Colonel Fitzgerald,

Mr. O'Beirne, from the Foreign Office, Mr. Robertson (Ministry of Munitions) and Second-Lieutenant McPherson of the Cameron Highlanders, arrived at Thurso by train on the morning of Monday, June 5th, 1916, and crossed the Pentland Firth in the destroyer *Oak*. It was blowing freshly at the time, but in Scapa Flow—almost an inland sea, the only sheltered anchorage suited to the Grand Fleet—the sea was calmer. Most of the Grand Fleet lay there, having returned three days before from the Jutland Battle.

Kitchener went to the *Iron Duke*, Jellicoe's fleet flagship. First he went round the ship, the officers and crew showing many tokens of respect for his personality. He lunched in the Admiral's cabin. His talk was a little pathetic. He looked forward to his expedition to Russia as a holiday. He was feeling the strain of the last two years and he mentioned his difficulties in handling questions discussed in the Cabinet. (Lord Fisher had undergone the same experience.) He was working to a time-table because the Battle of the Somme, the baptism of fire of his new Armies, was to be launched on the 1st of July, so he could only spare three weeks. With not a day to spare, he hoped that the voyage to Archangel would occupy as short a time as possible.

Such was the problem which the Navy had to face. We know now where those mines of U-75 had been laid, early on the 29th of May. Jellicoe did not. Up to that time there was no knowledge of any mines having been laid by German submarines north of the Firth of Forth. With the short nights in June giving only about two hours of darkness, hostile surface-ships could hardly have ventured to lay mines so near to the Grand Fleet's anchorage. Their approach would have been observed. Nevertheless, it had been the practice to sweep for mines on both sides of the Orkney Islands. Owing to heavy weather there had been no sweeping for the past few days.

German U-boats, using torpedoes, would be the real

danger, and to counter that an escort of destroyers would be needed for the *Hampshire*. Those destroyers were ready, and the intention was that she should use the eastern channel, and the Captain had sailing orders to that effect, dated the 4th of June. Then a heavy north-easterly gale raised a heavy sea on the Monday, on the *east* side of the islands. Destroyers could not possibly keep up with the *Hampshire's* speed in such a sea, with such a gale, and speed meant safety, so Jellicoe decided that the *Hampshire* should take the western route, which was used by his fleet auxiliary vessels and constantly watched.

Kitchener and his party boarded the *Hampshire* at 4 p.m. She left at 5.30, escorted by two destroyers, *Unity* and *Victor*, to be sent back if they could not keep up. The *Hampshire* was to steam at 19 knots, trusting to her speed in case of torpedo-attack by a submarine. Then the wind changed, and a gale blew from the north-west (50 miles an hour). The *Hampshire* and her attendant destroyers were not sheltered by the land, so the destroyers were sent back. Soon after 7.30 p.m. the *Hampshire* struck one of U-boat 75's mines, between Marwick Head and the Brough of Birsay, and she sank, bows first, in about a quarter of an hour. Kitchener came on deck. The Captain (H. J. Savill) had ordered a boat to be lowered for him, but it was not possible either to hoist out or to lower a boat in that tremendous sea. Only fourteen men, drifting on a Carley unsinkable raft into a cleft in the rocks, reached the shore, and two of them died of exposure. The remainder were rescued by some of my men of the old 'Blue Marines', one of whom told me the tale of the rescue.

Shortly afterwards, sixteen of the mines from U-75's minefield were swept up; one, which was recovered, was set to float 7 metres (about 24 feet) below the surface, and on account of the dip of the moorings in a tideway, mines set at such a depth would be innocuous even to a vessel of heavy draught excepting in slack water at low tide with considerable motion on the ship, due to heavy seas. These unfortunately were the conditions under which the *Hampshire* struck the mine on that Monday night.

Kitchener was never seen again. It has been said of him that he lived to see the whole of his life's mission fulfilled. Did he? His name, it is true, had raised on a voluntary basis a great army, but we know that the closing months of his life as a subordinate, without the final voice in the disposal of that army, were not happy ones. We know, too, how some others in high places sought shelter behind the authority of his name after his lamented death, and that, late in 1915, attempts had been made to prevent his return from the Mediterranean (as Sir William Robertson has told us) to the inner councils of the Cabinet. He had resigned on his return, but the Prime Minister (Mr. Asquith) had not accepted his resignation.

Whether his influence could be spared by the Allied cause after he died, we cannot tell, without knowing what course he would have followed. When the General Staff, early in 1918, was in direct conflict (as Sir William Robertson has also told us) with the War Cabinet, and Sir Douglas Haig was left too weak to stem the great German attack of March 1918, would Kitchener have backed the General Staff? We do not know.

I was at Portsmouth at the time of his death, and I can vouch for the sorrow and dismay with which the news was received by the garrison, as it was by all soldier friends whom I met a few days later in London. I was not then, as I was later, at the hub of secret affairs, so I cannot answer the question of the date when the news of Kitchener's projected visit was first known in Russia. It was, I know, the subject of conversation there for some days before he started, but I have never been able to establish the exact date. I do not believe that it was known there when Admiral Scheer decided to send U-boat 75 to lay mines west of the Orkneys, to catch vessels of the Grand Fleet. Kitchener consented about a week later (May 26th) to undertake his mission.

Was the manner of Kitchener's death a reflection upon the British Secret Service? I think that I have proved that it was not. Was it a reflection upon the British Navy? The answer to that is that it was due to Scheer's preparations for his sally into the North Sea, to a heavy gale from the north-east, and to a sudden change in the direction of the wind as the *Hampshire* started. The German War Book did advocate the exploitation of the crimes of third parties, *including assassination*, as justifiable methods if they led to the prejudice of the enemy, and it was claimed on behalf of a certain woman spy that she had brought about Lord Kitchener's death—that she had even led the submarine to the spot where the mine was laid to cause it, an utterly absurd claim. I do not believe that any German in a responsible position had anything to do with the boasting of having brought about Lord Kitchener's death. It was claimed in some quarters in Germany that Kitchener's loss was a depressing blow to the spirit and determination of the British public. It had no such effect. Walter Hines Page, the American Ambassador, was right in his statement that, 'You could almost see the grim determination rise in their minds, as you see the hot sun raise the mercury in a thermometer'; and the foolish rumours which followed the catastrophe—to whomsoever the responsibility for them can be attributed—came, like the use of poison gas, the ruthless torpedoings by U-boats, the killing of women and children by air-raids, and the shooting of Edith Cavell and of Captain Fryatt, as a stimulus to Britain to hold out at all costs for victory.

With the individual rumours—foolish ones if really started by hostile spies in Britain and elsewhere—we need not deal in detail. They were wild in their improbability, and in their divergence. 'Kitchener is still alive'; then 'Some of the crew of the *Hampshire* [really men of the Hampshire regiment] are in a prison camp in Germany.' 'Kitchener is conducting Secret Service in Germany.' 'He is hiding in Berlin.' 'He is in Russia.' 'He is raising troops in China and Japan.' And in a later year someone had the culminating effrontery to bring a coffin from Norway to England, claiming that it contained Lord Kitchener's body.

To one possible cause of the rumours it is necessary to refer. The news of Lord Kitchener's death was made public on the Continent, and probably all over the world, before it was generally known in England, and this was the reason. At about 10.12 a.m.[1] on the Tuesday (June 6th) the Prime Minister heard of the catastrophe from the Admiralty, and after telegraphing to Sir John Jellicoe for details, an announcement was prepared by 11.38 a.m. Two copies were sent to the Press Bureau and the British and foreign news agencies had the information at about noon. Then more details came in from Jellicoe, and an attempt was made by telephone to stop publication of the original message. It was too late. The foreign agencies had already spread the news which had doubtless reached Berlin by telephone from a neutral country, probably Holland. The amended message, to which it had only been necessary to add two lines, was rushed across to the Press Bureau, and the British public knew at about 1.30 p.m. My authority is Sir Douglas Brownrigg, Chief Naval Censor at the Admiralty in the Great War, an old station-mate when I was serving in the Fleet. He published a book after the War, and for the past nine years has tried to get the truth known. The loss of nine *minutes* in war may be felt for ninety *years* if historians are not careful about their 'sources'.

I have been asked on occasions whether I believed the story that Lord Kitchener had been warned by a teller of fortunes that he would lose his life at sea, and that he had some premonition of his approaching death. With that I cannot deal. We all have our own views on such subjects. My object has only been to show the part that German Secret Service took, or rather did *not* take, in the tragedy. Kitchener lies, with those who formed his mission to

[1] Sir George Arthur heard the news at the War Office from the Prime Minister at 10.30 a.m.

Russia and with all but twelve of the officers and ship's company of the *Hampshire*, at the bottom of the sea about a mile and a half from the inhospitable western coast of the Orkneys, between the Brough of Birsay and Marwick Head. The scene is overlooked by a great mound on the cliffs—the tomb of a prehistoric warrior. There let us 'leave him alone in his glory'.

CHAPTER XII

SOME WOMEN SPIES—1915-17[1]

ALTHOUGH the employment of women as spies or as secret agents is not favoured in Britain, no record of Secret Service in the Great War would be complete without some reference to their work in that connection. It is not easy to deal adequately with the activities of the sex to which 'infinite variety' has been so freely attributed, although there are many dramatic tales of their exploits in espionage, both in fiction and in real life.

I remember reading some years ago an interesting novel—the name, I think, was 'Cronstadt'—about a girl, a governess with a Russian family, who risked the probability of facing a firing-party in order to secure the plans of that fortress. The usual love interest was introduced, and such influences must obviously come into fiction, but their introduction into the realities of war espionage is unfortunate, as experience has often proved. There are many stories of women—and of men through love of women—who have been torn between the two great forces of patriotism and of human attraction. I know one of a woman who, as an intelligence agent, was set the task of worming secrets out of a foreign officer in a high place. The end of the story was that she fell in love with him, abandoning her mission, and 'they lived happily (?) ever after'.

Let us hope that with her allegiance she did not transfer any military secrets of the country whose cause she abandoned. Of that side of the story I know nothing, and there must always be that risk. On the other hand, I agree with those who maintain that women keep secrets

[1] For sources of information, see footnote on p. 84.

of national importance better than men do. There is a stamp of man who wants to earn a reputation for being 'in the know' about naval and military affairs, especially in time of war, while taking very little interest in the family lives of his colleagues. With the other sex it seems to be the other way round.

The main point is that, so far, women have not yet in any nation taken over from men the naval and military positions in which the most important war secrets are discussed, so the woman-spy must obtain her information from a man. This introduces uncertainty in the relationship between the spy and the victim of espionage, which is one reason why the use of women as spies is not favoured in Great Britain. Other nations do not all share these views. There is also with us a strong objection to subjecting women to the death-penalties which would be meted out to them if discovered.

The Germans did not send or use many female spies in Great Britain in the Great War, and only three were brought to trial for espionage. One was a Mrs. Smith, wife of a naturalized British subject, who reported so high a spirit amongst the British people to her employers that she probably did more good than harm to the cause of the Entente, so she got off lightly. Another was a certain Lizzie Wertheim, of German birth, whose husband was of British nationality, being the son of a naturalized German. There is not much of interest to tell about her. Her husband, for sufficient reasons, did not live with her, but apparently they were not actually divorced. She was addicted to luxurious living, a cocaine-taker, and lacking in moral standards.

It was thought by the German Secret Service folk that she would be useful to obtain naval information in Scotland and elsewhere for a spy called Breeckow, who was sent over with others in the spring of 1915 with a forged American passport, made out in the name of Reginald Rowland. (The American Eagle on the seal of his false passport had one claw missing. It is upon such

details that the lives of Secret Service agents depend.)
The pair were tried by Civil Power at the Old Bailey on
September 20th, 1915, before Judges of the High Court.
Abundant evidence of espionage was produced. Mrs.
Wertheim was awarded ten years' penal servitude and
sent to Aylesbury to serve her term, and her subsequent
fate took her to Broadmoor Criminal Lunatic Asylum,
where she expired on August 4th, 1920. Her companion
Breeckow died of heart failure at the moment when he
was facing a firing-party in the Tower. Mrs. Wertheim,
by the way, was living in Bloomsbury when 'Reginald
Rowland' came to England, and we constantly come
across references to that 'highbrow' district behind the
British Museum in notes of foreign espionage. I do not
know what its attractions can be for secret agents, but
there seem to be a good many hotels there that still cater
for alien travellers not of the rich classes.

The third woman spy to be tried and sentenced in
England was Eva de Bournonville, a Swede in German
pay, who drew attention to herself by foolish questions
and by constant assertions of her place of birth in
Denmark. She also was arrested in Bloomsbury (Upper
Bedford Place) after living at various other addresses.
She worked for a salary of only £30 a month, which she
drew from the German Military Attaché in Sweden. It
was not very high pay, for the most efficient woman spy
with whom we had to deal, to risk her life. She would probably have lost it in a country less lenient to woman spies.

There was practically no defence, and there were no
extenuating circumstances when she was tried at the Old
Bailey, found guilty, and sentenced to death by Mr.
Justice Darling on January 12th, 1916. Her punishment
was commuted to penal servitude for life. She joined
Mrs. Wertheim at Aylesbury, and in course of time the
two were allowed occasionally to converse with each
other. We must go to other countries for more interesting tales of female espionage. I have mentioned Eva
de Bournonville's case principally to show the strength

144

of the 'ruling passion' of her kind. She wrote a letter to ask if she might have in prison her manicure-set and part of her large wardrobe, adding rather pathetically: 'Please kindly hang up my evening dresses and cover them well.'

There seemed to be quite a spate of German spies sweeping into our country in May and June 1915. Several of them, like Mrs. Wertheim's accomplice or employer Breeckow ('Reginald Rowland'), and one Anton Küpferle (only at large for five days), relied upon an American accent and passport for safety. We can remind ourselves that 1915 was the year of the first ruthless U-boat campaign, of the Battle of Neuve-Chapelle (initiated by Sir John French), of the Second Battle of Ypres, of the Allied offensive which immediately followed, and of the costly autumn offensive initiated by Joffre and Foch in which the British Army took part at the bidding of Lord Kitchener. The centre of interest for German military espionage during the year was therefore the Western Front, rather than the United Kingdom.

The Dardanelles venture, as we have seen, was freely advertised in Egypt, so there was little to be learned about that, and the main object of the German Secret Service agents in England and especially in Scotland in 1915 was to obtain naval information.

By 1916 the training of Britain's large 'New Armies' was being completed, so the importance of military information from Britain constantly increased. Early in that year Joffre (Foch assisting) and Haig—who had then succeeded French in command of the British Army on the Western Front—completed their first plan for a great offensive on the Somme, which was countered by the Germans getting in the first blow, at Verdun. Great efforts were made by the German Secret Service to obtain information about the Somme offensive which, in order to relieve the situation of the French Army at Verdun, could not be postponed to a date later than the 1st of July, although Haig had hoped for more time in which to train his newly-raised divisions.

This affords us a favourable opportunity to introduce a description of the German organization for espionage connected with the Western Front in Europe, and the mysterious German woman who is credited with having taken a leading part in it from her headquarters at Antwerp after that fortress had been occupied by the German Army. Many accounts have appeared since the war about her personality, her methods, and the names by which she was known behind the scenes in Allied countries. *Mademoiselle le Docteur* was the principal pseudonym used for her in France, to which country her activities seem principally to have been directed, but she had other more lurid descriptions, 'Red Tiger' being one; 'Tiger Eyes', 'The Black Cat', 'Frau Doktor Elizabeth' and 'The Queen of Spies' are other samples. Her agents worked behind the fighting Front, and she was the head, using terrorism as her method, of the whole of the secret organization seeking to solve naval and military secrets in the United Kingdom and in the Departments of France lying, roughly speaking, westward of the line Boulogne-Paris-Epinal-Belfort to the Swiss Frontier. Richard Rowan has written much about her in his book *Spy and Counterspy*, and there are references, more or less (chiefly less) accurate, in nearly all books on Secret Service in the Great War.

Rowan describes her as dominating with a glance, adding that her characteristics of boldness and ferocity were easily to be read in the 'flashing frigid blue of her eyes'. That her agents worked in fear of her is undoubted. She is credited with being the inventor of the 'Fool-spy' method of getting rid of the inconvenient or incapable, a method which was ruthless, but quite simple. All that was necessary was to send the unfortunate man or woman on some mission involving the certainty of capture and execution.

Joseph Marks, a Dutchman, who came to England in July 1915, affords a possible example of the 'fool-spy'. He was detected at Tilbury. Sir Basil Thomson, head of the Special Branch at Scotland Yard, happened to be there at the time, and to him Marks confessed the nature of his mission. If his death had really been foreseen by an inhuman employer, then that employer must have been disappointed. Marks was sentenced by court-martial sitting at the Westminster Guildhall to five years' penal servitude on a charge of holding communication with an enemy Secret Service agent abroad and then trying to land in England. He has since been repatriated, expressing much gratitude for his treatment; an English prison was certainly the safest place for him if he was really the victim of a sentence pronounced by the malignant 'Tiger-eyes'. Incidentally his capture put our Counter-Espionage Department on to a new and ingenious method of sending naval information to Germany via Switzerland by means of foreign postage stamps of different nationalities, each representing some class of war-vessel; but the chief interest in the methods of *Mademoiselle le Docteur* in connection with the subject of this chapter was her appreciation of the dangers of introducing the 'love-interest', to which we have referred, into so serious a business as war-time espionage.

She had much to do with the training of spies in the German spy-schools, and I have seen a good account of the instructions which she gave to one trusted agent. She trusted him to do well, so she impressed upon him that he must above all things be temperate and sober. He must be an early riser. If his work compelled him to go to haunts of 'pleasure', he must be careful not to get involved in any love affair. His enemies employed female counter-spies. (There is on record a case of a Dutchman, sent by her to Paris, who disregarded similar advice, drank too much and was indiscreet when 'in his cups' in conversation with a French cabaret girl, an agent of the French Intelligence Department. He even told her his mission and tried to enlist her help. He was left free by the French police, in the hope that his indiscretions would involve others. Rowan tells us that he met his end by night in one of the back streets of Montmartre, stabbed in the back by a German knife which had been left in the wound as a warning to others.)

We cannot take leave of the ruthless and unattractive female patriot who is credited with such great efficiency combined with terrorism in her methods, without a few notes on the various legends about her origin and her social status. She was a 'buxom good-looking creature, who probably relied much upon her powers of fascination to induce unfortunate neutrals to turn spy'. She posed as the Baroness d'Aspremont, as the Countess of Louvain, and as a member of a German family entitled to the prefix 'von'. She is reputed to have been a *demi-mondaine*, enjoying the friendship of a Prussian General who had enough influence with the Intelligence Department to secure employment for her therein. 'Heinrichsen' is believed to have been her original surname, but her true origin was uncertain to the end. Her strength lay in her frenzied devotion to her mission, facing all risks in its advancement. From her headquarters in Antwerp she travelled constantly in Holland, where she was well known to secret agents of the Allies in Rotterdam. She moved much by motor, and she was always guarded by an escort of two men, whether she was driving or on foot.

The story goes that the Allies gained their principal success against her by introducing a young Belgian, posing as pro-German, into her central office in Antwerp as her trusted subordinate; and that, when in due course she detected the ruse, she shot him with her own hand. Tales of this sinister woman appear in the works of Felstead, Lüdecke, Rowan, and others. She disliked employing women as spies, for reasons already given— the instability which 'love-interest' may introduce into serious and momentous work.

There we can leave her, and return to the women spies who reached our shores in the Great War, whether with or without her connivance. The most notorious of them, Marguerita Gertruda Macleod (*née* Zelle) only enjoyed our hospitality for a few days. She was sent to Spain, and it was partly through her interest in the Somme offensive of 1916 that she was destined to meet her fate in France in 1917.

She was a dancer of European reputation and a fascinator of men. Her stage name of 'Eye of the Morning' (Mata Hari) has been surrounded by many tales. Here are some of them. The most prevalent story is that she was the daughter of a Dutchman by a Javanese (one account says Japanese) wife, and that she was born in the Dutch East Indies. That she inherited from her mother the subtlety, obsequious bearing and diplomacy of her Eastern origin. That after her father's death she was taken by her mother from the prospects of labour in the sugar-fields of Java to Burmah and placed in an equivocal position as a dancing-girl in a Buddhist temple. That a British officer, fascinated by her charms, aided her escape from the temple and married her. That she bore him two children, but soon became tired of the monotony of official life in 'India', so she escaped to Holland, and from there to Paris. Thenceforward she was in the limelight as a dancer, so we need not follow farther that picturesque and highly imaginative legend of her early years. Her appearance, dusky skin and luminous black eyes, naturally tended to give currency to the story, and so did what has been described as her 'insatiable thirst for luxury and money'.

Less glamour was attached to the written evidence of her identification papers, which described her as a divorcée, her married name being Macleod; born of Dutch parents at Leeuwarden in Holland in 1878, and christened Marguerita Gertruda, her parents' name being Zelle. At the age of 18 (March 1895—her nineteenth birthday was in August) she married an officer in the Dutch Colonial Army, who was apparently of Scottish descent, his name being Macleod. He took her to Java, where their union was anything but happy. The popular account is that he treated her with cruelty and brutality, that a native servant murdered their baby son in hatred for his master, and that the mother shot the murderer. They had another child, a daughter. During their six years in the tropical and enervating climate of Java—in a part of the world where, as Rudyard Kipling once put it, 'there ain't no ten Commandments and the best is like the worst'—Marguerita Macleod gained a mastery over the dancing and dancing-lore of the East, which was to be her stand-by in fulfilling her ambitions as a beguiler of mankind in later years.

The ill-assorted couple returned to Holland in 1901, bringing with them the small daughter (Marie-Louise), then aged about 5 years. We need not dwell upon the four years between 1901 and 1905 which were spent by the wife in Holland. For the first year the ill-assorted couple lived together, under the eyes of 'in-laws' who seem occasionally to have intervened in times of special crisis. These culminated in her abandonment by her husband, who took the daughter with him. She seems to have been left in penury, supported by relations, and in course of time to have become bored with life in a Dutch village. In her twenty-ninth year (1905) she went to Paris with that chequered experience behind her, surrounded herself with picturesque legends of her early years, and was successful as a lightly-clad performer of seductive Eastern dances, for which she became known all over Europe.

Her profession enabled her to make friends in high places in France, in Germany, and in other European countries, and it took her farther afield, always earning very high fees. The date when she first became a secret agent for Germany is not known. She is believed to have been so before the War, on the evidence that her number, as such, was 'H 21', and that the letter H was not attached to such agents after the outbreak of war. Her notoriety was against her, and in the end even the most highly-placed acquaintances could not save her from her fate.

Whatever may be thought of her calling and the sources of her income, there is no doubt about the courage of the woman both in launching herself into independence, and, above all, in facing her end. Her thirty-eighth birthday fell on the 7th of August 1914. When war broke out she was dancing at the Wintergarten in Berlin, and there is talk of her having been seen there dining with a highly-placed German police official, her acquaintanceship with him being one of long standing. She fulfilled various public engagements in other countries, and she first came under the suspicion of the British and French Secret Services when she was dancing in public at Madrid in July 1915, when the Franco-British offensives in Flanders had failed, and the Italians were launching their first attack on the Isonzo.

Her landing in England in 1916 seems to have been partly attributable to the ruthless German submarine campaign and policy of laying mines in the highways of the seas, on account of which it was necessary to bring all shipping into British harbours for examination and allotment of the safest routes to their destination. There is a story of 'Mata Hari' being asked to land with all her luggage and stage equipment by a bashful young boarding-officer; another of her having come to England of her own accord. However that may be, the net result was her examination by Sir Basil Thomson at Scotland Yard, and her complete success in baffling her interrogators. Felstead, one of the most reliable authorities on what went on behind the scenes under such conditions, says that, when taxed directly with being a German spy, she said, with a fascinating glance: 'I have something to tell you, but before I do so, you must send all these gentlemen out of the room.' The room having been cleared, she added: 'I am indeed an agent, but for the Boche—No! a thousand times! It is for France that I act!'

There are reports of her having, on another occasion, tried a similar plan when in Paris, and of the French authorities suspecting her of having sent a French Secret

Service agent in Belgium, with whose name she thus became acquainted, to his doom at the hands of a German firing-party. The net result of her cross-examination in England was that she was sent to Spain, with some good advice as to her future procedure. Had she been less skilful in her defence, it may be that she would have saved her life. Her detention in England as a suspect for the duration of the War might have enabled her to start life again afterwards on the proceedings of her large earnings from her German employers, and, if she was wise, on the savings upon the very high sums that she had received for her other activities.

Most spies who were captured and brought to trial in the War were convicted through documentary evidence, due to their methods of getting reports to their destination. 'Mata Hari's' immunity for a long period in France was due to her personal influence in a certain neutral country which enabled her to use the diplomatic bag of the neutral government concerned for sending her communications, believed to be destined for her relations in Holland, really for the German secret agency. When the correspondence was intercepted her communications were found to be in a cipher that could not be solved. She always succeeded in covering her tracks, even during a visit to Vittel, where a new aerodrome was being made in 1916, though she was purposely allowed a pass, and specially watched, on that occasion.

In Spain, she was much in the company of the German Military Attaché, and her ultimate undoing seems to have been attributable to a message which was sent by wireless by that official telling 'H 21' to call at the neutral Legation or Embassy in Paris for a large sum of money. She was arrested in February 1917, tried by court-martial in July, and sentenced to be shot. The intervening months had been marked by the much-advertised 'Nivelle Offensive' which had failed in its purpose in April with crushing losses in the French Army, followed by mutinies and a wave of defeatism in the country.

Even her most influential friends were unable to obtain a reprieve or a revision, and in October the sentence was carried out in the fortress of Vincennes. Never did woman face her end more bravely. She was described as 'resigned and unafraid' during the last hours in her cell, and as gently shaking a sobbing nun to soothe her. On the day before her execution she is said to have bathed and to have danced, as a diversion from unpleasant thoughts.

As with Eva de Bournonville, sentenced to life imprisonment for spying in England, the ruling passion was strong to the end. She dressed herself carefully in becoming attire on her last morning. When the moment came, she walked proudly past the firing-party and kissed her hand to them and to the priest and others in attendance. So, at the age of 41, her pitiful career was ended.

In his *Air Power and War Rights*, J. M. Spaight gives a list of the other women spies who were condemned to death in France. Their names were Marguerite Schmidt, executed in March 1915; Ottilie Voss, executed in May 1915; Mlle. Lallart, condemned to death in August 1915; Marie Jose de Basi, condemned to death in January 1916; Regina Diane, executed in January 1918; Josephine Alvarez and Victorine Francher, executed in May 1918; and Sidonia Ducret, condemned to death in June 1918. No evidence is apparently available about the exact number of cases in which the sentence was carried out, but Spaight adds that probably they were all executed.

Britain was therefore fortunate, comparatively, in immunity from the need to take stern measures to deal with the activities of women in the sphere of espionage.

CHAPTER XIII

THIRD-PARTY CRIMES IN AMERICA,
1914-1917

SINCE the association of the United States of America in 1917 with the cause of the Entente Alliance, just at a time when Russia was collapsing, was so powerful a factor in the ultimate victory, it will be as well for us at this stage to consider some aspects of the German Secret Service there during the three years which preceded that event.

One of the tragedies in the Great War lay in the ignorance amongst the people in certain countries, especially in the United States and in Great Britain, about the realities of warfare as understood by the European continental school of 'militarists'. The most logical exponents of that school of thought were to be found in Prussia, and it was impossible to induce either the statesmen or the public in the countries mentioned to take them seriously. The theory to which I refer is that, war being an act of violence, and States being bound by no moral or ethical obligations to other States, no limitations whatever need be placed upon war violence. Every act, however ruthless, could be justified by military necessity. 'War', wrote Clausewitz 'is an act of violence that knows no bounds.' . . . International law is a restriction 'hardly worth mentioning'.

The procedure of some of the statesmen of other countries can best be described in words used by Charles Kingsley in his *Water Babies* to picture the attitude of the people of the great land of Hearsay, and how they waged war: 'All their strategy and art military consisted in the safe and easy process of stopping their ears and

screaming "Oh, don't tell us!" and then running away.'
Here is a typical quotation, to illustrate my meaning,
from the German War-Book, the organ of the great
General Staff in Berlin: 'International Law is in no way
opposed to the exploitation of the crimes of third parties
(assassination, incendiarism, robbery, and the like) to the
prejudice of the enemy.' If those words meant anything
they meant that any nation opposed to Germany in war
must take steps to guard against such procedure likely
to be taken by enemy agents, or to be incited by them.

I have described the task which I set myself at the
Admiralty in the years 1913–14, to compile a list of all
places, of importance to the Navy, where arrangements
should be made to cope with the 'evilly-disposed person'
if we should ever be at war with Germany or with any
other European power. Arrangements were made accordingly, and a vast number of troops, besides police, were
employed for the purpose, but our immunity was largely
due to the work of the Counter-Espionage Department
of the Army, who left all the chief German secret agents
free to the last minute (taking the precaution of reading
all their correspondence) and suddenly arrested them
when war was inevitable through the violation of Belgian
neutrality on August 4th, 1914.

I have also endorsed the view expressed by Colonel
Nikolai of the German Secret Service that, although we
were so near the mainland of Europe, our insular position
was a great help to us in keeping out enemy secret agents.
I think that I can add, without fear of contradiction, that
there was not a single case of sabotage due to enemy
agents on land in Great Britain throughout the whole
course of the War. There were, I allow, several explosions
in munition factories, but not one of them was attributable
to that cause, whatever the public might have imagined.
On the question whether some of the explosions in H.M.
war vessels in harbour were attributable to enemy agents
or to their plots, I reserve judgment. They were not so
attributed officially, but the number of such incidents

was to my mind so abnormal that I am not satisfied by the official attitude, especially after hearing about the machinations of German secret agents in the United States. There, and in Russia, some sabotage occurred, and I have never quite understood why, in the early days of American neutrality, the activities of German agents did not cause enough public indignation to bring America into the War, apart from the *Lusitania*, *Sussex*, and other examples of the destruction of the life and property of American citizens on the high seas.

It may be that no one in America had read the German War-Book, or, if they had, that they could not conceive the possibility of third-party crimes being fostered in a *neutral* country, to the disadvantage of a belligerent. If the British, with only the narrow Channel between them and Europe, were so ignorant of the theory of warfare established by Clausewitz for about eighty years, as interpreted in the Prussian War-Book, how much more is it probable, that the American public, separated from Europe by the Atlantic Ocean, should have shared that ignorance?

Not knowing enough about the American Secret Service, I cannot, of course, say what definite proof they had of the responsibility of German agents for sabotage or for fostering strikes in the United States. I do, however, know that a man, obviously of Teutonic race, whom we will call 'I', was carrying on quietly the business of an advertising agent at 60 Wall Street, New York, in those early days. In April 1916 his office was raided by United States Secret Service agents, and this is the remainder of the story as told to me by reliable authority.

When the secret agents appeared, 'I' was standing by a safe bearing the official marks of the German Imperial Government. He was sorting papers, taking them out of the safe presumably for transfer elsewhere; probably, in the light of after events, to the German Embassy. The police agents seized him and his papers, under violent protest, and the safe was removed for examination.

As soon as Bernsdorff, the German Ambassador, heard of 'I's' arrest, he entered a strong objection. The papers seized were official, sacred diplomatic documents. (By an international legal understanding, the precincts of Embassies are ex-territorial—the territory of the countries which they represent.) The obvious reply was that No. 60 Wall Street was a private advertising agency, not managed by any member of the diplomatic service, 'I' being a private person. When the papers which 'I' had struggled so hard to guard were examined in the Department of Justice, there was no doubt about their importance, or about the reason for Bernsdorff's disquietude. They contained abundant evidence of the exploitation by Germany of third-party crimes in the U.S.A., and hence I will retain for a time my imaginings about the real cause of some of the explosions in war vessels of the British and Allied Navies in the war.

On *May* 21*st*, 1915, a fire occurred at sea in the British merchant-ship *Bayropea*. Two small cylinders, two and a quarter inches long and three-quarters of an inch in diameter, were found where the fire had been, and three barrels of alcohol were found empty in No. 4 hold. Holes had been bored in the sides of the barrels. She was on her way from New York to Havre. She was finally lost at sea by fire in January 1917.

On the 10*th of June*, 1915, the British merchant-ship *Kirkswald* arrived at Marseilles from New York. *Nine* bombs were found in her holds on arrival. (The papers bearing on the case are endorsed: 'The man who made the bombs was blamed for their failing to explode. He pleaded that they were amongst the first made, and that they were an experiment.' He had intended the bombs to go off when the vessel was five days out from New York.)

On the 18*th of June*, 1916, a fire occurred in a cargo of sugar, carried by the British S.S. *Ingleside* on a voyage from New York to Hull. When the hatches were taken off, an undischarged rocket was discovered in No. 5 hold. In another British ship (*Saltmarsh*), when discharging sugar cargo, similar evidence of sabotage in vessels leaving the U.S.A. was discovered.

I have discovered amongst my papers a note, made whilst I was serving in Whitehall, that 'the placing of bombs in cargoes has been traced to German agents in so many cases that there can be no doubt that to these advocates of the freedom of the seas must be attributed the loss of many vessels, sailing under neutral flags, reported missing with their whole crews. Three men, described as the last of the most dangerous gang of German plotters in the United States, have lately been arrested and charged with making and distributing bombs which were placed (in 1915) in the holds of thirty merchant vessels'.

In January 1917, the Norwegian S.S. *Gyldempris* loaded at New York. Her after peak was not cleared out until the following July (18th) when, having discharged her last cargo at Naples, she was proceeding in ballast. Two dynamite bombs, fitted with detonators, were then found under the ship's effects in the after peak.

I have notes of other examples, but these will suffice for our purpose, and we will now return to 'I' in New York. He was a man of some importance, entitled to the 'von'. The documents found at No. 60 Wall Street were of various natures. The place was described as a 'clearing-house for crime', through which the German Embassy, more especially the military side, had been in communication with secret agents in all parts of America to exploit third-party crimes.

We will take first the arrangements to destroy civilian life and property (regardless of ownership) in merchant-ships on the high seas. One 'XXX' (Paul Koenig by name) was in correspondence with '7,000' (the German Military Attaché, von Papen). In that correspondence Koenig reported that he had found a man to destroy shipping of the Allies leaving ports of the United States by means of bombs which the man himself was making. They resembled ordinary lumps of coal, and arrangements were being made to conceal them in the coal loaded by Allied vessels. Another document proved that a sample bomb—whether for use in the holds of merchant-ships or in American munition factories I do not know—had been left at the office by one 'O. R.' The document was addressed to '7,000'.

The most conclusive documentary evidence obtained by the U.S. Secret Police was an original cheque, signed by von Papen and dated July 16th, 1915, for 150 dollars, to the order of P. Koenig. The cheque, numbered 146, was drawn on the Riggs National Bank, Washington. It was endorsed on the back 'For Deposit, Paul Koenig' in Koenig's handwriting, and stamped 'Pay to the order of the Philadelphia National Bank—July 17, 1915— Union Trust Co. of New York.' Paul Koenig was ostensibly the manager of an inquiry office, which was really a branch of the German Secret Service. I have a facsimile of his cheque from von Papen for 150 dollars, with its endorsements.

There was more evidence amongst 'I's' papers of his complicity with inventors and research-workers in the making of bombs and infernal machines to be used in neutral America. There was, for instance, a note of a communication dated June 15th, 1915, from one 'G. S. V.' containing an inquiry about bombs and an offer to supply them. The note was endorsed 'Told to send further details.' This 'G. S. V.' did. About four months later there appeared a note of an offer from him to supply picric acid, a well-known ingredient of high explosives. 'G. S. V.' had at one time been editor of a virulent pro-German newspaper in the U.S.A. Another correspondent, W. J. R., put forward proposals for new methods of putting high-explosive mines into ships. Another letter in 'I's' collection suggested a plan for obtaining rooms close to munition-factories in the U.S.A. with the object of blowing up the factories.

The general question of the supply of munitions of war to belligerent governments from privately-owned factories in a neutral country is beyond the scope of a work on Secret Service. I can just remember in early childhood the indignation and soreness which were still being expressed in conversation in England at what was considered the unfairness of the *Alabama* claim award. This must have left a deep impression on my mind as, when I joined the old Naval Intelligence Branch of the Admiralty, one of the first things that I did was to find out what means there were of ascertaining what war material was being made to foreign orders in private factories in Great Britain, with the idea of avoiding future *Alabama* incidents. There was then no machinery at all for the purpose, but I succeeded in its establishment.

When certain countries, in defiance of their solemn obligations, poured arms and munitions into unsettled countries like China in the years after the War, I assumed that the Governments concerned had no machinery like our own for finding out what munitions private individuals were exporting, and that seems to be the situation until this day. Peace is preached by governments, whilst their nationals are exporting arms to countries in the throes of unsettlement. In those circumstances it might have been held by Germans that they were not bound in any way to abstain from exploiting third-party crimes in a neutral country whence munitions were reaching their enemies, but could not reach themselves because their opponents held the sea-communications.

On whatever theory Germany may have acted, her procedure in this matter was clearly disclosed in the 'I' documents, captured in April 1916. One of 'I's' many activities was connected with an organization called 'Liebau's Employment Agency', conducted ostensibly with the object of finding work for Germans, Austrians, and Hungarians resident in the U.S.A. Whatever the German theory of the extension of violence to neutral countries in warfare may have been, the activities incited by the Liebau Agency were not likely to be popular amongst the citizens of the states concerned; in this example, those of the U.S.A. The documents captured from 'I' included amongst their number a report upon this agency. It was addressed to Bernsdorff, the German Ambassador. Amongst other subjects, it disclosed how skilled workers, engineers and others, had been induced to leave munition-factories (which seems to me to be quite a legitimate procedure on their part, if their sympathies were with their Fatherland).

The Liebau Agency, however, did more than that. Having gained the confidence of the controllers of the munition-factories, it supplied them with workmen able to act as spies or to aid in acts of sabotage. A physician helped. Through his position as such he was well able to obtain reliable information about contracts secured by the different factories. The result of investigation was a report that many of the disturbances in such factories, and suspensions of work leading to strikes which lasted for a long time, could be traced to the activities and propaganda of this, apparently harmless, Labour Bureau. Ambassador Bernsdorff, as a result, stated his impression that 'we can disorganize and hold up for months, if not entirely prevent, the manufacture of munitions in Bethlehem and the Middle West'.

Another activity linked with 'I's' organization, for which immunity as a branch of German Diplomatic activities was claimed by Bernsdorff, was subsidizing publishers, journalists, and lecturers. A list was discovered amongst his captured papers of journalists who had accepted sums ranging from £200 to £1,000.

Colonel Nikolai, 'Chief of the German Secret Service in the World War', has since told us that in the first part of the War a very accommodating spirit was shown towards Americans in Germany, where the desire was to maintain American neutrality. It seems, however, that the German Diplomatic service in neutral countries, especially the naval and military attachés, with their network of secret agents and sabotage organization in the United States, paid little attention to the 'accommodating spirit' that was shown by the bulk of their compatriots in Germany.

CHAPTER XIV

THE U.S.A. AND THE GREAT WAR: THE LAST STRAW, 1917

OUR NEXT object will be to describe how the secret department charged with solving enemy ciphers in London came across evidence of German duplicity towards the United States which, of itself, would probably have sufficed to cause a President—though recently elected on a 'Peace-ticket'—to advise Congress to declare war against Germany.

On a momentous day, early in the year 1917, certain jumbles of figures were handed in to solvers of ciphers 'somewhere near Whitehall'. The third group of figures from the end was recognized. 'Hullo!'—we can imagine the recipient exclaiming—'That is Zimmermann [Foreign Secretary in Berlin] pretty busy with Bernsdorff [German Ambassador in Washington]. It must be something important.' We can picture the workers redoubling their efforts to make sense of the jumble. Their laborious and monotonous work was to culminate in one of the most amazing incidents in Secret Service in the Great War.

In my early days as a student at the Army Staff College at Camberley, lectures were delivered to us on the solving of secret codes and ciphers. Few of us realized the importance of the subject in war-time, and most of us came to the conclusion that such work was not in our line. It involved organizing the energies of hundreds of computers in applying systematically various 'permutations and combinations' of groups of figures or of letters. It was sheer toil, of which most of the results were sterile, and about 99 per cent. of it led into a blind alley, from which there was no emerging. One per cent. might lead to the light.

We have a good parallel in Britain of these days in crossword puzzles, to which so many are addicted; some for the stimulation of our intellects and extension of our vocabularies; some for the chance of making our fortunes with a minimum of risk. I once had an interesting experience of the kind. To obtain £1,000 for a shilling offers so attractive a prospect that I tried, during a journey from Salisbury to London, to take advantage of the chance by solving an apparently simple crossword puzzle which promised those results. I found sixty-four solutions before the train arrived at Waterloo (1½ hours) by applying the smattering of knowledge of cipher-solving which I had retained since my old days at Camberley. £1,000 to £3 4s. still seemed to be satisfactory odds to take against what appeared to me to be a certainty.

Then I went to a Club in London for luncheon. It is situated in Bloomsbury, that haunt of the learned, and it is frequented by many skilled mathematicians and by other men of eminence in the academic world whose devoted work for the community is very inadequately rewarded. I explained to them the royal road to prosperity which I had just been so fortunate as to discover. I left a group of them in arm-chairs round the fire discussing the puzzle, and then I proceeded on my occasions. On returning to the Club later in the afternoon, I was hailed by one of my friends with an announcement that instead of the sixty-four solutions (which I hoped were exhaustive) they had already discovered no less than 3,072, and that they were not prepared to guarantee that there were no more.

Cipher-solving involves similar work, and that experience taught me what labour the achievements of the war-time cipher-solvers must have represented.[1] Let us place them in the Adelphi Arches in the Savoy, a spot

[1] Examples of methods of certain cipher-solving will be found in the Appendix.

secure from air-raids, as we are not supposed to know the true locality. A French writer has told us that they worked at No. 10 Downing Street, that house of mystery to foreign observers, but really the private residence of successive Prime Ministers. The private secretaries of one of them in the war overflowed into what we used to call the 'Garden City', in the garden of 'No. 10'. The buildings were of the temporary type, with tin roofs, and one sometimes used to wonder what effect a bomb dropped thereon would have had upon our prospects of winning the War. The decipherers were certainly not there. Like moles, they sometimes showed indications of their activities by throwing mounds up to the surface. The mound produced by solving that Zimmermann secret message reached the dimensions of a mountain produced by an earthquake, and in considering what follows we must bear in mind the names of the actors in the great world-drama who were involved. President Wilson had been re-elected, on a policy of neutrality in the conflict, in November 1916. Colonel House was looked upon by those behind the scenes in European diplomacy as his *alter ego*. Walter Page was the American Ambassador in London. Frank Polk was Secretary at the office dealing with foreign affairs in Washington. Dr. Zimmermann had relieved von Jagow as Foreign Minister in Berlin on November 21st, 1916. Count Bernsdorff was German Ambassador to the U.S.A. Von Eckhardt was German Minister to Mexico. Carranza was the name of the President in Mexico. Mr. Arthur (the late Earl) Balfour had relieved Sir Edward Grey (now Viscount Grey of Fallodon) as Secretary for Foreign Affairs on December 11th, 1916. Sir Cecil Spring-Rice was British Ambassador to the U.S.A. Mr. Hoaller was employed in the British Embassy in Washington.

The best translation of the Zimmermann message from the German is, I think, the one that was made after the War, when the archives of the Foreign Office in Berlin were searched. The sense is the same as that produced by the British decipherers in the War and now published in several versions, minor differences being due only to the translators. I have seen the original German (also published for comparison). Here is the translation:

Secretary of State Zimmermann to Ambassador Count Bernsdorff.

'Telegram No. 158. Strictly Confidential. For your Excellency's exclusively personal information and transmission to the Imperial Minister at Mexico by safe hands.[1] Telegram No. 1. Absolutely Confidential. To be personally deciphered. It is our purpose on the 1st of February to announce the unrestricted U-boat war. The attempt will be made to keep America neutral in spite of it all. In case we should not be successful in this, we propose Mexico an alliance upon the following terms:—Joint conduct of war. Joint conclusion of peace. Ample financial support and an agreement on our part that Mexico shall gain back by conquest, the territory lost by her at a prior period in Texas, New Mexico and Arizona. Agreement as to details is entrusted to your Excellency. Your Excellency will make the above known to the President [of the Mexican Republic] in strict confidence at the moment that war breaks out with the United States, and you will add the suggestion that Japan be requested to take part at once and that we simultaneously mediate between ourselves and Japan. Please inform the President that the unrestricted use of our U-boats now offers the prospect of forcing England to sue for peace in the course of a few months. Confirm receipt.

'ZIMMERMANN.'

German version, as deciphered by Mr. Bell of the American Embassy in London and forwarded to Wash-

---

[1] The intention was to use the German Submarine *Deutschland,* but she was not available.

ington by the Ambassador at 4 p.m. on March 2nd, 1917 (received 10.45 p.m.):

'Auswaertiges Amt telegraphiert Januar 16: No. 1. Ganz geheim selbst zu entziffern. Wir beabsichtigen am ersten Februar uneingeschraenkt U-Boot Kreig zu beginnen. Es wird versucht werden Vereinigte Staaten von Amerika trotzdem neutral zu erhalten. Fur den Fall dass dies nicht gelingen sollte schlagen wir Mexico auf folgender Grundlage Buendnis vor; Gemeinsam Krieg fuehren. Friedenschluss. Reichlich finanzielle Unterstuetzung und Einverstaendnis unsererseits dass Mexico in Texas, New Mexico, Arizona frueher verlorenes Gebiet zuruek erobert. Regelung im einzelnen Euer Hochwohlgeboren ueberlassen. Sie wollen vorstehendes dem Praesidenten streng geheim eroeffnen, sobald Kriegsausbruch mit Vereinigten Staaten feststeht und Anregung hinzufuegen Japan von sich aus zu sofortiger Betrachtung einzuladen und gleichzeitig zwischen uns und Japan zu vermitteln. Bitte den Praesidenten darauf hinweisen dass ruecksichslose Anwendung unserer U-Boote jetzt Aussicht bietet England in wenigen Monaten zum Frieden zu zwingen. Empfang Bestaetigen.

'ZIMMERMANN.'

Unrestricted submarine warfare began on February 1st. The U.S.A. remained neutral, severing diplomatic relations with Germany on the 3rd of February.

Before commenting on Zimmermann's amazing message and the aftermath of its discovery and interpretation by the decipherers we will take account of a further message which followed about three weeks later (February 5th, 1917). It ran thus:

'*Secretary of State Zimmermann to Minister Eckhardt (Direct).*[1]

'Telegram No. 11. In connection with Telegram No. 1, Strictly Confidential. To be personally deciphered.

---

[1] Bernsdorff had been given his passports.

BERLIN, February 5th, 1917. Provided that there is no risk of the secret being betrayed to the United States, will your Excellency take up the alliance questions even now with the President of Mexico. At the same time the definite conclusion of the Alliance depends upon the outbreak of war between Germany and the United States. The President might even now throw out feelers to Japan. If the President were to reject our proposal through fear of later American vengeance, you are empowered to offer a defensive alliance after peace is concluded that Mexico succeeds in including Japan in the Alliance. Wire confirmation of receipt.

'ZIMMERMANN.'

On the 8th of February, Zimmermann, in a secret and stronger telegram, told Eckhardt to contract an alliance with Mexico, and to request President Carranza to adopt the proposed procedure with Japan. To this Eckhardt replied on February 26th that negotiations had been begun. Now let us look at these revelations as they would have appeared to the different actors in the drama.

Zimmermann's outlook was inexplicable. Germany had just issued a peace manifesto, but she was unable to define her war aims to President Wilson. Her losses on the Somme and at Verdun and against Brusiloff on the Eastern Front had been very heavy. Russia was still in the War. The General Staff was beginning to consider the advice of their prophet Clausewitz, that 'Russia can only be subdued by its own weakness and by the effects of internal dissension. In order to strike these vulnerable points in its existence, the country must be agitated to its very centre.' The policy of sending Lenin and Trotsky to see to that was still in embryo. There was no hope of military victory over the Allies, and the ruthless U-boat campaign to knock Great Britain out of the War was intended as a final bid for success. Clausewitz had warned them, and all who invade their neighbours' countries, that there is a culminating point in victory, beyond which the tide turns. There comes a reaction which is greater than the force of their blow. The situation was desperate, and even the hostility of the United States was risked.

Bernsdorff did his best. In a cipher telegram of January 19th he warned Zimmermann that the U-boats would make war with America inevitable. He continued to do his best and reported that President Wilson 'officially, but in the first place privately', had promised to mediate for peace. He welcomed the attitude to the German cause of the Hearst Press, with over 3 million readers of its ten papers, in all parts of the U.S.A. He received from the German Imperial Chancellor himself (Bethmann-Hollweg) this message, sent, it will be noticed, at the time when the intrigue with Mexico was being conducted: 'Please thank President (Wilson) on behalf of Imperial Government for his communication. We trust him completely *and beg him to trust us likewise.*' The message was sent after the communication to Eckhardt in Mexico. Such are the bypaths of diplomacy.

In Europe there had, for some time, been a lack of understanding in public opinion of the American attitude towards the combatants in the Great War. The march of events in the United States had not been followed intelligently. The violation of Belgium, the killing of American women and children in the *Lusitania* (May 7th, 1915), the shooting of Edith Cavell (October 12th, 1915), the torpedoing of the passenger-boat *Sussex* and execution of Captain Fryatt (March 24th and July 27th, 1916) and various incidents bearing upon the Law and Custom of the Sea jealously upheld by American legal opinion had combined to produce the impression that 'too proud to fight' would represent the President's attitude under all possible conditions. Current tales are not a bad indication of popular sentiment and one had been going the rounds, after the heavy sacrifices endured by the New British armies on the Somme, of an interview between an American visitor to Europe and a badly-wounded

British soldier. 'Battle of the Somme? *Some* fight!' the American citizen was represented as saying. 'Some don't!' was the reply of Thomas Atkins.

On February 7th all American shipping was held up by the menace of German U-boats. It was then announced by the Government that no convoy-escorts would be given and the congestion of American ships increased. On February 27th the *Laconia* (Cunard Line) was sunk, and two American women lost their lives in her. On the day before, President Wilson had made his address to Congress proclaiming armed neutrality, and taking powers to arm merchant-ships. On the 9th of March, Ambassador Page telegraphed to Colonel House that British opinion was reaching the conclusion that the American Government would not be able to take positive action under *any* provocation, and that it was holding back the American people until the German provocative incidents towards the United States had been forgotten, and until the British Navy had overcome by its own efforts the submarine peril. On March 12th the American S.S. *Algonquin* was sunk without warning. On the 19th three American ships were sunk within twenty-four hours by U-boats, and in one, the *Vigilancia*, fifteen members of the crew were lost. On March 21st, Colonel House replied to Walter Page, 'We are in the war now, even though a formal declaration may not occur till after Congress meets on the 2nd April,' and that takes us back to the deciphering in London of the Zimmermann secret documents, and how they provided the last straw. Without them it may be that, as we read the *Intimate Papers of Colonel House*, any attempt made by President Wilson to hurry his country into hostilities would have weakened the impression that he had done everything in his power to keep the peace; and that he had accepted war only as a last resort to protect American honour and security. '*It was this impression which led the most pacifist regions to fill their military quotas with enthusiasm, and saved the country from the conscientious objector.*'

169

On the question of how the deciphering of German code and cipher messages, naval and diplomatic, was done, I have nothing to add to what has already been stated in this chapter, about the laborious work involved, and elsewhere about the recovery of clues and keys to secret German ciphers from sunken or stranded German war-vessels.

An 'arresting' story is told in French writings about good work done by an Austrian expert in wireless telegraphy, whose services were commandeered by the German military authorities in Belgium, and of his having, while so employed at the military headquarters in Brussels, copied out laboriously in manuscript the whole of the German Foreign Office codes and the complicated keys to changes therein. I am not prepared to corroborate that story, or that of his escape through Holland to England—still less the dramatic suggestion of his having subsequently been put out of the way by British police authorities. I have only consulted in the English translation the special French book to which I refer. In a message from Ambassador Page to Washington, dated March 15th, Page refers to 'B's cipher telegrams' (meaning Bernsdorff's), and the same French writer states, on that authority, that 'B.I.S.2.' was Bernsdorff's secret signature, so I have not accepted the story.

It is now a matter of common knowledge that the British decipherers managed to collect and to produce the actual wording of the astounding messages sent to Mexico by Zimmermann on January 16th and on subsequent dates. Zimmermann thought the first message of such vital importance that he sent it via Sweden and Buenos Aires and Washington by cable, from Berlin to Washington via the American Diplomatic route, by wireless from Nauen and Sayville (U.S.A.) high-power stations, and for all I know, by other routes. The despatch through the U.S.A. diplomatic channels is not lacking in grim humour, in view of the contents of the document.

Verification and deciphering took some time. On the 23rd of February Mr. Balfour, the Foreign Secretary, handed to the American Ambassador in London an envelope containing an English translation of the Zimmermann message directing von Eckhardt in Mexico to incite Carranza, the President, in the event of war between Germany and the United States, to invoke the aid of Japan (a member of the Entente Alliance) and to invade the territory of the United States. Walter Page at once returned to his Embassy, and at two o'clock in the morning of February 24th he warned Washington that within a few hours he would be despatching a cipher telegram of great importance, intended only for the eyes of President Wilson himself and of the Secretary of State. This message reached Washington at 9 a.m. on February 24th.

Ambassador Page must have sat up for most of the night composing a long cable message containing comprehensive information about the success of the British Government in deciphering German secret cables and in obtaining copies of all the communications between Bernsdorff in Washington and Eckhardt in Mexico. He suggested that the Japanese Government should be let into the secret of what was in store for them [1] from Germany via the Mexican President, and he quoted, in full, the English translation made by the British decipherers of the incriminating cable sent by Zimmermann via the Washington diplomatic channel on January 19th, explaining the reason of the delay in its communication to the United States Government. Page's message was despatched at 1.30 p.m. on the 24th of February and reached Washington at 8.30 p.m.

Let us now cross the Atlantic with that epoch-making message which reached Washington during the night of February 24th/25th. President Wilson was aroused at once, and confronted at last with realities, in place of

[1] The Japanese sent a strong disclaimer to the Allies as soon as they heard of the Zimmermann plot.

theories and propaganda. He referred to Walter Page in London for confirmation, and he asked that a copy of the German code should be sent to him across the Atlantic (the cable was dated February 28th).

On February 26th Colonel House was called to the telephone by Frank Polk from the Secretary of State's office and informed about the exploit of the British decipherers and its result in laying bare the Zimmermann plot, of which he was told the details. On February 27th Colonel House wrote to President Wilson:

'I hope you will publish the despatch to-morrow. It will make a profound impression on the public and on the country.

'Affectionately yours,

E. M. HOUSE.'

(Let us here remind ourselves that American shipping was held up by U-boat outrages, and that the *Laconia* case, to be followed by others involving the loss of American shipping and the lives of American citizens, occurred on February 25th.)

On March 1st Ambassador Page replied that the German secret code itself would be useless to the President. He suggested that he should be supplied with all German cipher telegrams which had passed through the U.S.A. with Bernsdorff's secret signature (which he supplied), and that decipherers in London would supply the meaning which Page would cable back. Finally Page arranged that Edward Bell, First Secretary of the London Embassy, should himself decipher the secret German messages in London. This he did, and on March 2nd Page cabled the result, which was a transcript practically identical with the British one sent on February 24th, of the incriminating Zimmermann messages to Eckhardt in Mexico, of which the text is given above. The Germans were relying upon their belief that their complicated secret codes were inviolate, and it was desirable that they should remain in that belief.

When, on March 1st, the news of the proposed alliance between Germany, Mexico and Japan reached the American public, there followed incredulous amazement, and, in certain quarters, a reversion to the old policy of 'twisting the lion's tail' by certain organs of the Press, attributing the whole story to British invention and prevarication. President Wilson then published the documents themselves, with a guarantee by the Secretary of State of their authenticity. It was announced in the Senate that it would be against the higher interests of the country to publish all the information in the hands of the Government.

Zimmermann himself then confessed to the authenticity of his communications, and he tried, without avail, to discover the cause of the leakage. Bernsdorff had already been given his passports (February 3rd) and he had travelled by a Swedish liner, the *Frederick the Sixth*. The United States of America were at war with Germany from April 6th, 1917.

Meanwhile secret (?) communications continued up to April 13th between Eckhardt and Zimmermann, who still held to his hopes of inciting Mexico to attack the United States, offering money and armaments. On April 14th Eckhardt reported definitely that Mexico would not join in the war; premature disclosure of the secret messages between Zimmermann and Eckhardt had made the projected alliance between Mexico and Germany impossible. The secret about the British decipherers was safeguarded loyally in America and it was kept even from Allied countries. Colonel House tells a tale of one Hoaller, of the British Embassy in Washington, who called upon him on March 9th, 1917, at House's request, to discuss the Mexican situation. We give the rest in House's own words: 'He [Hoaller] asked in the most naïve way how it was that we [the Americans] had obtained the Zimmermann note. I replied, "I think you know." He assured me that he had not the remotest idea.'

Colonel House adds that ' "Blinker" Hall, of the British Naval Intelligence Bureau, was the man who secured, deciphered and gave it to us.' By 'Blinker' Hall he evidently meant Admiral Sir Reginald Hall, the son of my old chief, the late Captain W. H. Hall, whom I helped to start the Naval Intelligence Department in February 1887. Far be it for me to say to what extent Colonel House was right. It rests with Sir Reginald Hall himself to decide when the time arrives for lifting the veil from his activities in the Great War. When he does, what he has to write will be worth reading. In September 1917 Colonel House wrote to Hall calling him his 'dear friend', sending his personal congratulations upon his work, and adding, 'I know of no one who, in the course of the War, has rendered more valuable services than yourself.' In March 1918, Ambassador Page wrote to President Wilson: 'Hall is a real genius. In the whole world you could not find his equal,' and expressed the hope that he (Page) would live until 1938 to read Hall's memoirs and secret documents. Walter Page, alas, did not realize his wish.

Old memories, and recent researches connected with writing a history of the Great War, prompt me to add some personal opinions about the aftermath of the momentous events recorded in this chapter. Far above all controversies and ephemeral writings allotting credit to different nations for 'winning the war', there stand out in my memory certain incidents connected with the United States of America and the participation therein.

First comes the declaration by America of war against Germany on April 6th, 1917, at a time when there was great anxiety in men's minds about the heavy losses of British and neutral shipping that resulted from the depredations of German U-boats from the 1st of February in that year. Free movement by sea (and an adequate supply of shipping) was at that time the very life-blood of the Entente Alliance. Without it the military effort on land would have collapsed, and the people of the United Kingdom would have been reduced to sore straits. On the 2nd of May the arrival at Queenstown of the first American flotilla of destroyers was publicly and very wisely proclaimed. The Chief Naval Censor has told the story of how Dr. Maddick (then Captain Maddick) went to Queenstown, at two hours' notice, with operators and paraphernalia and, nicknamed 'Major Movie' by an American Admiral, took a successful picture and 'This historic incident of the U.S. destroyers coming to the aid of their erstwhile enemy—very erstwhile —is on record.' The film was shown all over the British Isles.

Then came another authorized exploit by 'Major Movie', at Liverpool, where a picture was made of the arrival of General Pershing. On May 19th the U.S. Government announced its intention to send a division of U.S. troops to France at once. That, too, had a heartening effect, following as it did the news that, on May 18th, a compulsory service Act was already in force in America. We had by that time faced such an Act in Britain after we had succeeded, mostly by voluntary enlistment, in placing over two and a half million British Empire troops in the Expeditionary Forces on the different fronts, having lost hundreds of thousands in battle and in other casualties. Compulsory service in the U.S.A. was evidently an earnest of what, in due course, was to be the outcome in the military operations with which General Pershing's divisions were to be 'associated'.

My most vivid memory of the results is one of White-hall, on July 4th—Independence Day—in 1918. The U-boat menace had by that time been mastered. Taking advantage of the freedom of their Eastern Front from further danger from the Russian armies, the Germans had launched in March the heaviest and the most formidable attack in the history of warfare against the British Army covering Amiens. The British line had been forced back nearly to the very gates of the town, and it had bent, but it had not broken. Then, in April, had come the further desperate stand by tired British troops against heavy odds in the Battles of the Lys (April 9th–29th) and Sir Douglas Haig's historic 'Backs to the wall' order of April 12th. Between May 27th and June 6th the French Armies had faced a similar ordeal in the Third Battle of the Aisne.

There was, it is true, engrained in the public mind a grim determination to hold on at all costs for victory, but there was also deep-seated anxiety about the military situation on the Western Front. Military man-power was failing, and Foch's plan for the Mangin counter-attack, which was destined to turn the scale on July 18th, was still in the womb of the future. The recuperative powers of Haig's Army (which was to lead the great Allied offensive from August 8th onwards) were not yet understood. From where was more military man-power to come, to adjust the balance and, in due time, to give the *coup de grâce*?

In view of allegations that, in the opinion of the Allies at the time, the American infantry, which was sent over first by request, should have borne a larger proportion of sacrifice by serving for a time in Allied armies, I will describe my own experience of the moral effect of American participation on Independence Day, 1918. I wrote at the time exactly as I felt, so I hope that it is permissible to recall the words, though perhaps too emotional for peace-time perusal.

'Man-power alone could turn the scale, in time, and all eyes were turned to the West, across the Atlantic. Every office in Whitehall had its map of the Western Front, with its row of little flags showing the constant loss of ground since March. The flags had been moved constantly westward, and it seemed to us that the tide of invasion would never reach its high-water mark.

'I was looking at one of these maps on that July morning. On the way up Whitehall I had passed many tired-looking faces. "We are all tired," Haig had written to his Army, three months before, and part of the nation was showing signs of strain, worn out by nearly four years of sacrifice and disappointment. A new impetus was sorely needed, a new enthusiasm to enable us to endure to the end. Some were getting callous, seeing no light ahead.

'Suddenly, through the open window of my office there came from the distance a sound like the roar of a tidal wave or of surf, mingled with the shrill cries of sea-birds. It mounted in a great crescendo. The pavements filled with people, all heads turned towards the direction of the sound which came surging into my room, mounting to a climax of uproar, until the mystery was solved.

'Hundreds of American soldiers, cheering, yelling and waving flags, were driving down Whitehall in big brakes, smothered with bunting—the Stars and Stripes. The counter-cheers of Londoners, of soldiers, of seamen and of airmen belonging to all parts of the British Empire, resounded from the pavements and windows, and re-echoed from the buildings.

'The Fourth of July. What a memory, and what an outcome! In the presence of the great world-menace a wave of good-will was uplifting, for the time being, the Allied peoples; it carried them forward to their goal, the statesmen balancing their little planks upon its crest.'

Such was the aftermath, to which the monotonous labour early in 1917 of those decipherers (since described by Colonel E. M. House, by Ambassador Walter Page, and others) had contributed, and, after this sample of the far-reaching effect of Secret Service in the diplomatic sphere, we will now return to the fighting forces, to the methods which they employ for ascertaining an enemy's strength and intentions in the field, and to the information which was at the disposal of executive commanders when they arrived at their decision. The dominating impor-

tance of surprise in military operations again emerges—
as it always has in the past—as the outstanding secret of
success. In the most important of the operations it is
possible to trace the methods by which surprise had been
achieved under the difficult conditions which obtain in
modern warfare.

CHAPTER XV

A TRAGEDY OF SECRET SERVICE IN THE EAST, 1917

W E N O W turn our minds to the East, to a tragedy of the Secret Service which again reminds one strongly of the old saw that truth is sometimes stranger than fiction. I shall give the actual facts, only suppressing—for reasons which will be obvious—the names and the exact localities. I hesitated for a time about telling this particular story, but thirteen years have now passed since the occurrence, and with them the bitter war-spirit. A description of the activities of Secret Service officers engaged in field-intelligence work would be incomplete if such a tale were omitted.

Those who took the leading parts in the tragedy were a British Intelligence Officer, whom we will call 'Mannering', and his opponent in the German Secret Service, one 'Fritz'—whom we will ennoble to 'von Fritz' in view of his intrepidity and the sad climax that was caused by his activities. Mannering was serving with certain British Empire troops in the East in the year 1917. It came to his knowledge earlier in the year that the area occupied by that British Army was infested by enemy secret agents, and he pondered over the best method of inciting the troops to take steps to cope with this serious menace to the secrecy of future operations. He reported the danger to the Commander-in-Chief on whose staff he was serving. He also mentioned current rumours to the effect that one 'Fritz', a German, had been constantly behind the British lines in disguise, seeking for information. No proofs of the presence of 'Fritz' had been obtained, and no credence was attached by Mannering to the rumours. Nevertheless, it was decided to make use of the tales for the special purpose of awakening interest amongst the troops in the urgent need to keep a sharp look-out for any Secret Service agents who might attempt to enter—and were believed to have entered—the British war area in disguise.

An order was accordingly issued to all commanders reporting the probable visits of the mysterious Fritz, and urging his detection and arrest. That order had an immediate effect, and great alertness was shown, from the highest to the lowest rank in the Army. Numerous arrests were made, and the bag was varied. It included Mannering himself. He was arrested as a suspicious character, and he was detained until he was vouched for by an unimpeachable authority. The supposed activities of the (non-existent?) Fritz were further described in detail and so was his appearance, for which 'Intelligence' were obliged to draw upon their imagination. All ranks were asked to co-operate in catching the villain, and all ranks did so, with the result described.

About ten days later it fell to the lot of Mannering in the course of his duties to visit a prisoner-of-war camp. His identity appears to have been known in that camp, as the Commandant told him that a certain Greek prisoner, a deserter from the Turkish Army, had expressed a wish to see him. The interview was allowed. The Greek explained the circumstances in which he had effected his desertion from the enemy, and then he surprised Mannering by a statement that he had been in the habit for some time of working for a veritable 'Fritz', hitherto believed to be a mere bogey! The Greek added that, if Mannering would arrange for his speedy release, he would do his very best to help in laying Fritz by the heels.

After some thought, Mannering agreed, but as a precaution he took the Greek with him to the nearest Greek Consul, and they satisfied themselves that the man was a Greek and therefore a neutral subject. The explanation given by the Greek for his desertion from the Turks was that he had had a quarrel with 'Fritz', but nevertheless it would be quite easy for him to go back to the Turkish lines, taking any information with which it was thought desirable to supply him. It must be enough to constitute a guarantee of good faith in the eyes of Fritz and his Secret Service Department. The Greek promised that, if those conditions were fulfilled, he would arrange a meeting-place to which Fritz would be induced to come over from the Turkish lines, and it would then be quite simple to seize his person. The conditions were accepted, and in due course the Greek was supplied with enough (harmless) information to effect his purpose. Then he slipped away, out of ken for the time being.

About five days later the Greek reported that Fritz would be coming within the British lines, in accordance with his usual practice, on a certain day when some troop-movements were to take place. The spot arranged by the Greek as a rendezvous for Mannering was ideal for such a purpose. It was remote and deserted, situated in a dry water-course and only visible at very close range, a romantic setting for such an adventure. During the afternoon of the appointed day Mannering rode out, full of hope, and when he drew near the secret rendezvous, he was rejoiced by the sight of the Greek, standing by his horse, so the man had kept his word. After the usual greetings, the Greek told Mannering that Fritz had come over, and that he and 'an orderly' were within the British lines. They would soon return.

There Mannering remained for about two hours in conversation with the Greek, who produced plenty of documentary evidence to prove that he was still working with Fritz. The Greek asked whether Mannering was armed? Having ascertained that he was, the Greek then advised him to shoot at Fritz at sight, as soon as he arrived. Ample warning would be given of his approach, and thus they waited until, at about 6 p.m., a horseman was seen approaching. 'That is the orderly,' whispered the Greek. 'He is disguised in British uniform. Fritz is certain to be close behind.'

In due course the orderly rode up to the Greek and handed over some papers, telling him (in German) that Fritz, having been chased by some British troops, was making his own way back to the Turkish lines by another route. The Greek appeared to be surprised and disappointed at the orderly's report. He then told Mannering that Fritz would be crossing the lines again in a few days, and promised that another meeting would be arranged. Better luck next time. Mannering saw no alternative but to acquiesce if there was to be any hope of catching the elusive Fritz, but naturally he did not intend to allow the orderly to go back to the enemy. A secret known by three is no secret, so he told the Greek that, in the circumstances, it was necessary to arrest the orderly, who was then standing a few paces away, tending his horse. The Greek saw the point at once and agreed, suggesting to Mannering to look over the side of the gully in order to make sure that the road was clear. 'Then we will hold up the orderly,' he added.

Mannering, with his hand on an automatic pistol in his pocket in case of treachery, led his horse a few yards away and swung quickly into the saddle. As he did so two reports rang out and bullets whizzed past him. Whipping round, he faced the orderly and the Greek, who were both firing at him. The surprise was complete. Mannering's horse bounded about, while he covered his assailants as best he could and opened fire upon them with his pistol. The orderly was hit. The Greek galloped away and was lost to sight, followed by the orderly's horse with an empty saddle. Thus Mannering was left with the orderly, mortally wounded, expiring on the ground.

He dismounted, and he then discovered to his horror that the dying 'orderly', accomplice of the treacherous Greek in the combined attempt to assassinate him, was a woman, apparently German, dressed as a man in British uniform. She soon passed away, a pitiful victim of heroic endeavour in her country's cause, killed in attempting—wearing her enemy's uniform—to help the Greek to assassinate the Chief of her enemy's Secret Service. We can draw the veil over the final obsequies. Mannering did his best. There is no twilight in those regions, and the sun had gone down when he rode homeward in the solitude pondering over the events of the day. With shame at having killed a woman inadvertently, there came the thought of how he had been tricked by the Greek, and then again how could he have acted otherwise? The woman was a German, dressed as a man in her enemy's uniform, and she had done her best to take his life. 'If only I had bagged the Greek instead of the woman!' was his final thought, and there we leave him on his homeward way.

*   *   *   *

There is a sequel to the story. 'Fritz', whom he had tried to capture, was neither a bogey nor a myth, but a formidable reality—probably the most efficient and resourceful German Secret Service agent in the whole of the Great War. The Greek was Fritz himself. The orderly was his wife.

The truth was not known to Mannering until some months after the Armistice, when he knew it on the first-hand authority of Fritz himself, in writing. A year or two later the two were destined to meet face to face in a café in the territory occupied by British troops. They recognized each other, but they did not speak. . . .

We will now pass on to Palestine, a few months later, to the battle of wits between the German Secret Service and the British Intelligence, and here we take note of the point that Secret Service at the headquarters of the German Commander of the Turkish Army in Palestine was run by the Germans, while Field Intelligence (with the troops) was conducted by the Turks themselves.

I do not know whether Fritz, after his pose as a

treacherous Greek in the Eastern theatre of war where he operated, ever again penetrated behind the British lines. After his story few, in comparison, are worth the telling, so I will only mention the fate of a very dangerous agent who had been marked down by our own Intelligence Department with Allenby's Egyptian Expeditionary Forces. Since the lives of British soldiers depended upon the activities of that agent and his like being stopped, the expedient was adopted of sending a letter to him, containing a large sum of money (the amount was about £30) apparently in reward for services that he had rendered to the British. This letter, intended to lead to his being discredited by the Fritzes beyond the Turkish Front, fell as was expected into their hands. Without proper investigation or chances of sifting evidence, they shot their most efficient agent out of hand, on the assumption that he had been serving both sides and was as dangerous to the Turks as he really was to the British.

There is another true tale, told in several of the more sensational spy-books, of a young man dwelling behind the Turkish Front in one of the coast towns of Palestine who longed to see his country freed from the oppressions of the Turk, and decided to throw in his lot as a secret agent with the British. Since the flanks of both armies rested on the sea, and the coastal area was so heavily wired that it was difficult to cross the lines, this youth of nineteen, whom we will call 'B', used to move from one side to the other in a small boat which he owned, landing at a spot some miles to the northward of the Turkish flank and thence repairing to the coastal town containing his house. In that house there dwelt his young sister, who aided him in his work, and in course of time came under the suspicion of the Turks. Her fate was terrible, but no torture could elicit from her anything to incriminate her brother. She did not survive her treatment. I mention her to give an example of extreme heroism in a girl in enduring pain (those acquainted with Turkish methods will best comprehend) rather than betray a trust. We will pass now to other activities of the Secret Services which lay behind Allenby's wonderful campaign in the Holy Land, and no Old Testament story of triumphs in warfare surpasses them in dramatic interest.

CHAPTER XVI

ALLENBY IN PALESTINE, 1917

WHEN we ponder over the grave disappointments that were suffered by the Allies in the year 1917—the Nivelle failure on the Western Front, followed by mutinies in the French Army; the ordeals of Haig's Army ending in the mud of Passchendaele; the collapse of Russia and of Rumania; the grievous wound to British sea-power by the ruthless U-boat campaign, and the Italian disaster at Caporetto—it is refreshing to turn our minds to Allenby's operations in Palestine, undertaken at a time when the cause of the Entente Alliance was overshadowed by the gloom of repeated failure. In March and in April 1917 two unsuccessful battles had been fought by British Empire troops to force their way into Palestine by the usual coastal route, through the gateway of Gaza, a town which had been developed into a formidable fortress.

We pass now from the thought of mud and monotony of the lice-infested trenches of France and of Flanders to the Third Battle of Gaza (October 27th to November 7th) and to the open warfare which followed in Palestine. The tale of the intelligence work which preceded that battle affords an opportunity of describing a brilliant bit of Secret Service in which an unassuming and traditionally 'stupid' Englishman got the better of the 'wily' Turk and his German advisers and taskmasters. In connection therewith we shall renew our acquaintance with 'Mannering', the intelligence officer whose battle of wits against 'Fritz' the German (and its tragic ending) I have described. Though my only personal knowledge of Palestine was gained many years ago during a ride from the coast to Jerusalem and to other parts, in the days before the incongruous railway-whistle desecrated the peace of the Holy Land, sufficient memory of the nature of the country remains, and eye-witnesses have helped me in my effort to tell a story to which it is difficult, even with such assistance, to do proper justice.

Lord Allenby (then Sir Edmund) arrived in Egypt from the Western Front in July, 1917, and this is the problem with which he was faced. The Turks were very strongly entrenched in a position that extended from Gaza on the sea-coast for about 30 miles inland, as far as Beersheba. Gaza and the coastal sector was aptly described as 'a strong modern fortress, heavily entrenched and wired, offering every facility for a protracted defence', and there were formidable groups of works standing about a mile apart as far as the Hareira Group. Then there was a gap of about $4\frac{1}{2}$ miles, and then another series of works which covered Beersheba. The most elaborate defences were those nearest to the coast, on the Turkish right flank. Their left flank, inland, was more vulnerable, but the difficulty of getting there in sufficient numbers was almost prohibitive in so waterless a country.

Allenby's front extended from the coast opposite to Gaza for a distance inland of about 22 miles, to a place called Gamli. Water was his greatest difficulty. The supply at the Gaza end of the line was comparatively easy. It came all the way from Egypt in a pipe, so the old Arab prophecy that the waters of the Nile would flow some day into Palestine was in process of fulfilment. The difficulties in conveying water to distant troops will be realized by all who have had experience of desert warfare. A gallon a day represents a man's normal requirements for cooking and for drinking, without allowing any for washing, and every gallon weighs ten pounds. That figure enables one to imagine the tremendous weight which represents the daily requirements of tens and perhaps of hundreds of thousands of men, and of animals which drink about six gallons a day if they can get it. Storage adds to the difficulties, because of rapid evaporation in a dry atmosphere.

I remember, in one of the Sudan campaigns (in 1884), undergoing an experience in the desert with a force in which the daily allowance of water was two pints per man. That, when on the march, meant tongues drying, cracking, bleeding and swelling at the back of the throat. I do

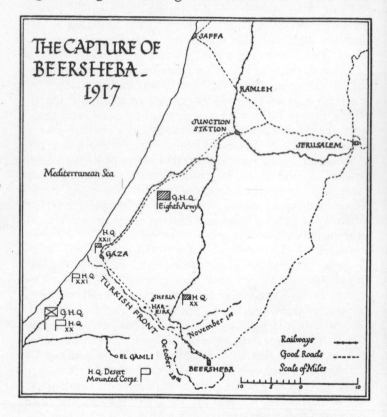

not know what the Desert Mounted Corps on Allenby's right flank was allowed, but I do know that in order to send water and other requirements to his troops between 15 and 20 miles from railhead he had to use all his camels (30,000 of them), besides other transport.

In spite of these grave difficulties, Allenby decided that surprise was essential, in order to avoid the holocaust of slaughter, with uncertain results, which would have been involved by undertaking another big and decisive attack upon the barbed-wire entanglements and elaborate defences of the Gaza sector. If, by any possibility, the Turkish left flank could be turned, the Gaza defences would perforce be evacuated. If the physical difficulties could be overcome, Allenby foresaw several advantages in striking from his right against the Turkish left about Sheria and Hareira, where the defences were less formidable, but first of all Beersheba must be taken. At Beersheba there was water.

With the water-supply of Beersheba in his hands, the advance in sufficient force against Sheria and Hareira would be much more easily arranged. Beersheba must be taken, and at every cost the secret must be kept. The Turks had quite good roads behind their position, which they could use to reinforce their left flank, but on Allenby's side the communications were bad. The ground was much broken up by nullahs and clefts in the land, with steep sides that no transport could negotiate. The troops on Allenby's right were provided with their requirements by long strings of pack-camels.

This was Allenby's plan. An attack would be made upon Gaza supported by a bombardment from the sea, in order to deceive the enemy. On the other decisive flank (inland) Beersheba would first be taken by *surprise*, and then, helped by the wells of Beersheba, the troops for the main attack could assemble on the high ground north and north-west of the place. 'Secrecy first' was the motto, and while secrecy meant almost certain success, discovery might mean costly failure.

It is at this stage that we renew our acquaintanceship with 'Mannering' of the Intelligence Department, and we find him engaged on his problem of deceiving the Turk. He had plenty of time; the web of deception that he proposed to spin began to grow in September, or even earlier. The 31st of October was to be the fateful day for the surprise attack upon Beersheba. The object was to convey two misleading impressions; one of these was that there would be no serious attack until late in November, and the other was that the attack, when it did come, would be made against the Gaza position on the extreme Turkish right.

September was spent in creating an atmosphere by various methods, such as sending misleading messages by wireless telegraphy in a code which the Turks, by various ruses, had been taught how to solve, without realizing the situation. So valuable were these British disclosures believed by the Turks to be, that one of their wireless receiving stations was specially allotted the task of listening-in on the British wave-length, so that nothing should be missed. Numerous messages were sent, some to official destinations, and others taking the form of private 'chat' between wireless operators, for instance: on one occasion an operator asked his friend, as a favour, to find out 'when the Chief goes away, and for how long'. A certain Colonel had asked for the information. In due course, back came the reply: 'Chief (Allenby) leaves for Suez on October 29th, and returns on about November 4th.' (It will be noted that those were to be the most critical days.) Then there was a message to the Desert Mounted Corps on the extreme right, conveying the impression that a report on the hilly country as impassable to cavalry had been corroborated from other sources.

Later messages, at a time when parties of patrols examining the ground round the Beersheba flank might create suspicion, indicated that the activities in that area foreshadowed only a British reconnaissance, not any serious operation. The most dramatic part of the story is to come, but if that tale only were told the impression might be conveyed that field-intelligence work consists of a string of such exploits, whereas success in it really means a hard and constant grind, as it does in every other form of human activity. It was known in due course that, from

September 26th onwards, hard work was being done by the Turks upon the Gaza defences, which were doubled in strength between that date and the end of October.

Early in October 'Mannering' decided to make a final effort to deceive the enemy, and this brings us to his *pièce de résistance*, and to the Tale of the Baited Haversack. Deceivers of fish with artificial flies have made great advances in the art of deception by remembering that it matters not at all what the fly looks like when seen in the hand of the angler. What does matter is its appearance as seen by the fish, probably against the light, through the medium of water, and it has come to my knowledge that Mannering is a keen fisherman. On this occasion he determined to deceive the Turko by losing a specially baited haversack, under conditions that would avert all suspicion of a ruse. In deciding upon the nature of the bait the impression that was likely to be conveyed upon the German and Turkish minds was the main point.

Firstly, suspicion must be averted. The Turk of that time was notoriously addicted to *baksheesh*. There was little that money could not buy before the days of reform. Bribery and corruption were rampant, but money was only given for value rendered in exchange, and for any-one to drop money about in large sums on purpose seemed to be inconceivable. Mannering put £20 in notes into a note-book, which went into the haversack. That note-book was a certain 'Army Form', and it contained abundant evidence that it was the property of a staff officer serving at Allenby's General Headquarters. It was a genuine note-book, with plenty of old entries of interest (though not of value) to the enemy, but the latest entries and enclosures were calculated to mislead.

Then there followed a more intimate human touch. What could be of more value to a husband than a letter from his wife in England reporting the arrival of a first-born son? Would he be likely to part willingly with such a possession? No man could write such a letter; only a woman could do so, and Mannering knew of one who could be trusted to provide the document. She rose well to the occasion. This is what she wrote (I have altered only the address, which was a real one):

> '36, BALHAM GARDENS,
> 'LONDON, S.W.
> '*August* 21*st*, 1917.

'DEAREST,

'How I wish you were here now! I am simply longing for you and would love to show you our dear little baby son. I am *so* proud of him! He is such a splendid little fellow and so good——

'You must not worry about either of us, as I get stronger every day and baby, the doctor says, could not be better. Richard is the name we are giving him—I know it is the one you always had in mind, and I chose it, as I felt you would be glad I had remembered it.

'All your sisters came and Alice wanted to adopt him at once.

'I sent you a telegram as soon as baby was born, and your reply arrived three days later. If it had been you arriving instead of the telegram, how lovely it would have been. Darling, you *must* try and come to see your little son. Don't smile if I say that to me he already has a look of you. He is such a darling, and you will love him so.

'I heard the last raid but no bombs were thrown anywhere near. Poor baby! Fancy coming into the world to find this awful war going on and Germans dropping bombs all over London. Louis had a narrow escape in the office, for some of his windows were broken.

'Good-bye, my darling!—Nurse says I must not tire myself by writing too much—so no more now but I will write again soon and then it will be a longer letter than this. Take care of your precious self! All my love and many kisses.

> 'Your loving wife,
> 'MARY.

'Baby sends a kiss to Daddy.'

I have read that document several times, hardly believing that it could be only a 'fake', intended to delude an enemy and not to cheer and inspire a husband. Then I tried to add some comments. It is better left as it stands, so we will get back to the War.

The letter, much worn by repeated handling, went into a pouch in the pocket-book. So did another letter, dated the 6th of September from a place near the right of Allenby's line, signed by an officer stationed there with his regiment. Its object was to convey the impression that there would be no attack until late in November. It began on a note of depression at the projected offensive having been 'postponed again'. Then there followed some caustic comments upon conferences at Allenby's Headquarters (the agenda for such a conference and 'faked' orders on the subject were also put into the pocket-book). The writer adds: 'I thought Allenby was a good enough man to chance these things himself without having a round-table conference!' He goes on with a note of resignation; if the business was really settled, there was no use in grumbling. At the same time it was silly to start the offensive at a date when the rains were sure to be at their worst. The writer (who, be it remembered, was stationed in the arid part, where water-supply governed the possibility of moving large bodies of troops) adds in a conversational strain that they were fed up about the transport for officers' messes having been cut down to one camel. 'Doesn't leave much room for luxuries, does it?' The letter closes with (apparently) indiscreet references to the proposed naval effort north of Gaza; with mention of the great strength of the Gaza defences; and with notes of a few trifling occurrences. It went into the note-case to join the letter from the happy wife.

To them was added a copy of a general order, issued early in September, calling attention to the fact that a new practice trench-system had been constructed at a place called Abu Sita, and that this was an exact model of the defences of an enemy's position near the sea-coast. Every officer and non-commissioned officer in the force in that area was directed to make a special study of that trench, and there would be plenty of time to master it during the many weeks which would intervene before the offensive.

Various maps and sundries were added, and also a copy of a telegram from Allenby's Headquarters to the Desert Mounted Corps about a proposal to send a staff officer out in front of Allenby's right flank to confirm the news that physical obstructions on that flank were too formidable for an enveloping movement round the Turkish left to be a practical proposition. Also a few rough notes on a cipher which was intended to help the enemy to solve bogus messages sent in that cipher.

On the 10th of October, 'Mannering' added a parcel containing luncheon to the contents of the baited haversack, mounted his horse and rode off into No-Man's-Land with a small escort. Leaving the escort behind, he crossed the Wadi Ghuznee and rode from thence to the north-west towards Sheria, in the Turkish main system of defence. He was well mounted on a fast horse. On approaching a place called Girkeir, he found a Turkish mounted patrol, which at once gave chase. Mannering fled for about a mile, when the Turks pulled up. Then he dismounted and opened fire upon them at a range of about 600 yards. This was too much for them and they resumed the chase, blazing away at him without doing any harm.

That gave Mannering his chance. He mounted hastily, and in so doing he loosed the straps of the baited haversack, his field-glasses and water-bottle (precious in those parts). He also dropped his rifle, first smothering it with fresh blood (from a slight cut on his horse, sustained by grazing a rock). Those little final touches were calculated to give the impression of disorderly flight.

Judging that he had done enough to achieve his purpose, and that the Turks were near enough to see the

194

little stage asides, Mannering then made off, rolling about in his saddle as if wounded. He dropped his stage properties as he went full speed for the British lines, confident of success, and intending to make assurance doubly sure by sending plenty of cipher messages confirming the incriminating (?) documents in the lost haversack, which he had seen a Turk pick up.

The next morning (October 11th) a notice appeared in the orders that were issued to the Desert Mounted Corps stating that a note-book had been lost by a Staff Officer on patrol, and that the finder was to return it at once direct to Allenby's Headquarters. An officer who then went out with a patrol towards the Turkish lines was stupid (?) enough to wrap his luncheon in a copy of those orders, and to drop it near the enemy. The stupidity of the English is proverbial. A small party of mounted men was sent out to search the country for the pocket-book. Really, it was said, these brass-hats are the limit in the tasks that they set to the troops through their idiotic habits. Such was the sowing, and now for the harvest.

Work on the Turkish trenches about Sheria, Hareira and Beersheba at once began to slacken, while efforts to strengthen the Gaza defences were redoubled. Reinforcements from the northward were brought up and they were sent to Gaza, not to Sheria. The last Turkish division (the 19th) to arrive was still completing its assembly behind Gaza, when Beersheba was attacked on October 31st, and the Turks' general reserve, of two divisions, was concentrated near the coast in rear of Gaza, far away from the critical eastern flank. Fifty aeroplanes were railed from the northward in packing-cases to the coastal sector. They were still being unpacked leisurely when Allenby struck his blow—they were all captured or burned.

On October 27th, Turkish cavalry came in force towards Karm and attacked the outposts, probably in order to find out what was behind them, but Yeomanry put up a good fight until infantry came up in support, and the Turks retired. On the same day, and again on October

30th, warships bombarded Gaza, thus confirming the impression conveyed by the documents in the note-book. During the night of October 30th–31st all the troops that were destined for the attack upon Beersheba reached their appointed stations. The first advance took place fifteen minutes after midnight. I do not know how Mannering spent that day. If he was at headquarters in the evening, I can imagine his feelings when this message, addressed to 'G' (General Staff) and 'I' (Intelligence) arrived: 'Beersheba occupied at 1940 by 4th L.H. Brigade who galloped in. A.A.A. Estimated captures include 250 prisoners 9 field-guns one machine gun A.A.A. Water reported plentiful in Beersheba. DESCORPS. 2030.' And that was the climax of our story, for the time being.

From the evidence of captured documents we can now follow the fortunes of the baited haversack after it fell into the enemy's lines.

In a Turkish official summary of the incidents of October 10th and following days we read that the documents which were discovered in the captured note-book were taken at once to von Kress (the German Commander) himself, and that he had them examined under his own supervision. In a copy of the orders issued by von Kress, found at Beersheba on November 1st (the day after its capture), there was a description of the incident of the baited haversack, containing 'a note-book which gave the enemy's strength, which evidently belonged to an officer of the enemy's headquarters. . . . In the note-book which gave the enemy's strength, there was some very important information about their intentions and operations.' The order concluded with special thanks to the Turks who effected the capture, and the moral was pointed by a warning to everyone concerned on the Turkish side not to make such an appalling mistake as to drop secret documents about for an enemy to capture.

On the 8th of November a copy of the orders that were issued on the subject to the XXth Turkish Army Corps was captured at Gaza. The order described graphically the incident of the haversack, adding that the fortunate non-commissioned officer into whose hands the document fell had been handsomely rewarded. Then comes this paragraph:

'The information contained in these documents is of such great value to us that we have been able to ascertain the date of the enemy's offensive, and it will enable us to forestall him in that all our reinforcements will now be at Gaza in time for us to crush the arrogant English.'

With that evidence of its effectiveness, we can close the tale of the Baited Haversack, the best bit of bluff that I have come across in Eastern warfare outside the tales of the Old Testament.

By successful surprise a very strong position, vitally important for further operations, was taken with trifling loss. 2,000 prisoners and 13 guns were captured, and the Turks left 500 dead upon the field of battle. Allenby reported: 'This success laid open the left flank of the main Turkish position for a decisive blow. . . . The Turks at Beersheba were undoubtedly taken completely by surprise.'

The decisive blow was then struck from a concentration area about Beersheba on November 5th, the impression having been conveyed that the Beersheba operation was a strong reconnaissance, rather than a prelude to a decisive attack upon the main position. The Turkish Eastern flank, resting on Hareira and Sheria, was driven in. Gaza fell on November 7th, and the Turkish Army was in full retreat. By the 14th of November, Allenby's advanced troops were at the important junction station where the line from Gaza meets the line from the coast to Jerusalem. On the 16th they reached Jaffa. On December 9th Jerusalem was surrendered, and on the 11th Allenby entered the Holy City on foot by the Jaffa Gate.

There we can take leave of him for the present in a theatre of war reminiscent of Old Testament memories and the wars of the Crusades. In a later chapter we shall return to find him preparing again to mystify and mislead the enemy before the decisive Battles of Megiddo on September 19th to 25th, 1918, which broke down the Turkish resistance and were followed by the destruction or surrender of the whole of the Turkish armies.

CHAPTER XVII

THE FIFTH BRITISH ARMY IN MARCH, 1918

NINETEEN HUNDRED AND SEVENTEEN, as we have already noted, had in the main been a year of grave disappointment for the Entente Alliance in the main theatres of war. The much-advertised Nivelle offensive in April, with its heavy losses, had been followed by a wave of defeatism in France and of mutinies on a large scale in the French Army, and the ruthless U-boat campaign had taken so heavy a toll of the merchant-shipping of all countries, hostile and neutral, as to bring Britain nearer to her knees than she had been since the eighteenth century. In April the United States of America had declared war upon Germany, but the weight of the American troops was not expected to be brought to bear against the German Army, the dominating factor in the situation, for many months. The collapse of Russia and of Rumania had rendered possible the blow which German and Austrian troops had struck at Caporetto in October (Twelfth Battle of the Isonzo, October 24th to December 26th).

On the other side of the balance, as sops to the Cerberus of public opinion, could be put the occupation of Baghdad in March, the defeat of the Turks at Gaza in November, and the occupation of Jerusalem in December.

None of these incidents had tended to ease the situation of the Entente armies which were facing the main German Army in France and in Flanders, and they took away manpower and munitions, thus weakening the lines defended against the impending crisis. Where would the next blow fall? Some said against Italy, to knock her out of the war once for all. Opinions in the Supreme War Council of the Allies (which had been established after Caporetto) were divided, and no clear guidance was forthcoming from that supreme authority during several weeks of the New Year, when time was priceless. Before that time of emergency arrived, the British Intelligence Department on the Western Front had received news about new German methods of attack. The information had come from other theatres, from the Russian and from the Italian fronts.

The situation in Russia was becoming clear, and doubt had been turned gradually to certainty; from a military point of view, Russia had collapsed. Under the Lenin-Trotsky régime (fostered by Germany), military discipline had fallen to pieces, and the ruthless dictators who had seized by main force the reins of government had decided to take no account of the Russian solemn obligations to the cause of the Entente Alliance. National honour had been cancelled by anti-national and by world-wide ambitions. After the great Brusiloff offensive in 1916 (which, with the British attacks on the Somme, did so much to aid the French Army in its gallant defence of Verdun) and after heavy fighting on the Eastern Front during the next year, the Russian Army suffered its final great defeat in the Battle of Riga (September 1st–5th, 1917). Von Hutier commanded in that attack.

Thenceforward there was little danger to the Germans from the east. Russia could safely be left to the process of disintegration, to the effect of rottenness in high places and to the disruptive forces of internal dissension and of popular ignorance. With no national sentiment in Russia, national loyalty to other nations became a negligible quantity, and there was worse to follow for the cause of the Allies. The Russian collapse, serious disaster as it was, did not entail weakening the French or the British Armies on the Western Front. With the best will in the world, neither the French nor the British Governments could take troops from their armies there to send them to aid Russia to hurl back the German invasion. There was no route by which they could have reached the Russian front in time to be of any avail. It was otherwise with the formidable attack upon the Italians. The enemy's triumph there was due partly to victory in the field, partly to the poison of propaganda amongst certain sections of the Italian people. When the blow at Caporetto was struck on October 24th, 1917, it drove the Italian Army back to the line of the Piave. The line was stabilized there by the aid of French and of British troops, who might, had they been able to remain on the Western Front, have made the brilliant attack of the British Third Army at Cambrai in November far more than a sop to Cerberus. Von Hutier was credited with the plan of attack at Caporetto.

The main feature of the method was to mass an immense number of divisions on an extended arc, with forward routes converging to a narrower frontage. Only a skeleton force was put in the front line in the first instance, say one battery out of each brigade in the artillery, and the other arms in proportion. Thus, for some time before the battle, no indication was given of the impending hammer-blow. The isolated batteries of the skeleton force in front would range upon their targets and reconnoitre, and the information so obtained would be used by the great masses of artillery when they came up to reinforce. The bulk of the reinforcements were kept three marches away until the starting-lever was put over and the great human machine awoke into motion to overwhelm its enemy. The final advance was preceded by a terrific bombardment to destroy obstacles and to beat down all resistance. Such was reported to be the plan of von Hutier, the organizer of victory.

Let us now, in January 1918, go to the headquarters of Sir Hubert Gough, Commander of the Fifth British Army in front of Amiens. On January 10th his army was holding, in sufficient strength, about 12 miles of the Allied front line (North of Gouzeaucourt to the River Omignon). Within the next two days, that Army took over the frontage of one French Army Corps on its right. Between

January 26th and February 3rd the frontage of another French Army Corps was taken over, and the right of Gough's line was thus extended to Barisis, beyond the River Oise. The total front measured 42 miles. Thus, while the German Army was being strengthened every week, the British line, especially that of the Fifth Army, became thinner and thinner.

Haig's Army, as a whole, was weaker by 180,000 in March 1918 than it had been in March 1917, and it held a longer front, so Haig could spare no more troops for Gough. If the line should be forced to bend back before a German attack in overwhelming force, then it was thought that the bulge had better be made on the Fifth Army front than elsewhere, as there was more room for manœuvre behind it. Further to the northward, to be forced back might spell disaster, since the attackers were so near the coast. The Kaiser was waiting behind the German lines for his victorious entry into Paris, and the name 'Kaiser-Battle' was being applied to the great operation which Ludendorff had inspired. German prisoners had called it the final call for sacrifice, the final bid for victory.

Haig had done his best to obtain reinforcements wherewith to strengthen Gough, but the Supreme War Council apparently did not realize the imminence of the danger. Opinions there were divided. Lloyd George had plans for still further weakening Haig's Army, and for finding easier roads to victory than those which crossed the lines held by the main German Army; and for the first time in the War such projects were being supported by a responsible military adviser, so Haig's request for more troops received no adequate response. Gough must do his best.

Great events in war sometimes hinge upon small incidents, and this is the story of how a small provincial paper in Germany gave away, by an apparently harmless statement, the German plan for the heaviest attack that had been launched in the history of warfare, an attack which, given surprise, it was believed that nothing could withstand.

To Gough, lacking so sorely in strength, intelligence of the enemy's plans was vital. He obtained information, not only that the great blow was coming upon him, but, in due course, the actual day upon which it was to be expected. He was not taken by surprise, and he was well served with intelligence. Every possible use was made of his scanty resources, and above all of the time that was available to improve the defences which he had recently taken over. The secret of how Gough obtained his information has never, to my knowledge, been made public, and this was the position.

Gough had 11 Divisions on the front line, and the rifle-power of 4 more behind them in support. He was holding 42 miles of front. In Byng's Third Army to the north-ward (on Gough's left) there were 10 Divisions in the front line and 7 in support, holding 26 miles of front. To the eastward, facing those two British armies, there were 67 enemy Divisions arranged on a great arc of which the radii—for the bulk of the masses—measured about the distance that they might cover in three night-marches, as occurred before Riga. The new system of tactics had succeeded twice, especially against Russia. Britain was now bearing the main burden of the War in all spheres, moral, naval, military, air, economic and financial, and the German attempt to knock the British Empire out by the ruthless submarine campaign of 1917 had failed. It had brought America into the War, and something must be done as a last resort against 'England the enemy' before the masses of American troops could arrive. Would that something be a tremendous blow, stronger than that which had been struck at Riga, directed against the principal British army? And would it fall upon the thinnest portion of the British line, held by Gough?

Let us take note of a special local factor. When the Supreme War Council decreed that Gough should extend his line to the southward to relieve the French, account was taken of an argument that much of the frontage there was secured by marshy ground, easily held by a handful of troops. 'General Mud' is a potent commander in war, as Napoleon discovered to his cost on the day before the Battle of Waterloo. So had Haig, at Passchendaele, but in March 1918 there was no mud in those marshes, in front of the Fifth British Army. In one of the driest winters on record (the weather had been dry since December) the marshes had dried up, and even the River Oise itself presented but little obstacle to movement.

Gough, facing these conditions, issued a moving order to his higher commanders in January, warning them of what was probably in store for them, and then he received news which turned conjecture into moral certainty. During January 1918 a young German airman left for the westward his aerodrome behind St. Quentin, on what was to prove to be his last flight. He was brought down in the Fifth Army area, grievously wounded, shot through the chest. He was respected by his enemies as a gallant lad, and every effort was made to save his life, without avail. He died in hospital and he was given a military funeral with the honours appropriate to his rank. He was laid to rest in an honoured grave.

The scene now changes to Switzerland. There on that patch of neutral soil surrounded by combatants, the newspapers of all the belligerents circulated freely. Exchanges of inter-Allied and of enemy intelligence departments were established. As was only natural, the agents there of the Entente Alliance searched carefully for war news in the German papers, and special care was devoted to scrutinizing small provincial journals which came from places where censorship was likely to be less expert, and less strict, than it was in more populous centres producing organs with a wide circulation in other countries. An intelligence agent of the Allies was glancing one morning through a small Baden journal when he came across a letter to the editor from the proud mother of the young airman who had given his life for his Fatherland in the area of the Fifth British Army. The poor woman, in pride at its reception, quoted also a letter from an officer of high rank, the Army Commander in the St. Quentin area. The editor, seeing no harm in so doing, published that Army Commander's letter. It was signed von Hutier.

Never before that time had von Hutier, organizer of victory at Riga and elsewhere, been located on the Western Front. The news of his arrival at St. Quentin—a secret as jealously guarded as that of the arrival of Nelson off Cadiz in October 1805—soon reached the Commander of the Fifth British Army, via Switzerland, and it was thus that his conjectures were changed to certainty. On the 3rd of February Gough impressed upon his commanders that the storm was soon likely to break upon them. He added that the River Oise sector must not be deemed immune, in spite of the arguments which had been used elsewhere to that effect. (I well remember watching a situation-map in Whitehall in those days, noting the River Oise and its surroundings, and thinking that that obstacle should stop the enemy's advance. I did not know that the river was nearly dry.)

Gough pointed out how the Battle of Riga had been opened by the crossing of a river by von Hutier's troops. A month before the attack orders were given for about 350 bridges to be prepared for demolition if the army should be driven to bend back by overwhelming force (when the occasion arose, the bridges were destroyed). A rigid holding of one line would be fatal; if a break-through were achieved, that would spell disaster, it would be like the breaking of a cast-iron bar. The thin line must bend, like supple steel, not break, so arrangements were made accordingly. This general deduction was drawn (on February 3rd): *The main German attack may be expected against the Third and Fifth British Armies, with Amiens for its objective.*

Such, then, was the result of that German mother's pride in the son whom she had lost, and of the indiscretion of the editor of her small local journal. Surprise, that potent factor in warfare, was not achieved. The artillery in every Corps in the Fifth British Army received directions to create well-defined gaps in sections of roads and other communications behind the German lines, and air photographs were constantly taken of those gaps. When the Germans began hastily to repair them it was evident that the great attack was coming. On March 12th the order, 'Prepare for Battle', was issued. Then, on March 20th, the order, 'Prepare to man Battle-Stations'; and, a few hours before the actual attack, 'Man Battle-Stations'. An officer, just returned from leave, visited the Fifth Army Headquarters in the evening of March 20th. He was given a good meal and told to join his unit at the Front during the night, in order to be ready for the battle in the morning (in which he lost his life). The remainder of the story, as it first appeared, is well known.

The thin line of the Fifth Army was bent back almost to Amiens; not quite, because by bending it did not break, and Ludendorff's great plan failed. The Kaiser did not ride into Paris. Lord Milner, hastily sent to Doullens from England (where the situation was thought in high places to be desperate), took upon himself on March 26th the responsibility for committing the British Government to agree to the appointment of Foch to co-ordinate the efforts of the Allied Armies. This was intended to ensure mutual reinforcement in future grave emergencies, and the decision was warmly welcomed by Haig. Gough, with whose handling of his attenuated force no fault could be found, praised by Haig his commander in the field, was offered up as a scapegoat to a public not acquainted with the circumstances. The truth for a long time remained obscure, as Haig's dispatch was not published for many months.

We have referred elsewhere to popular rumours amongst those who are deprived of information in war, and to their effects, and the tale of Gough's arrival in London is worth telling in that connection. I was present when he came into the smoking-room of a certain London

Club. His bearing was cheery. There was no vestige in his manner of bitterness at the cruel blow which had fallen upon him at the summit of his military career. He was full of a story which had just reached him of tea-table talk in Kensington, and I will give it as nearly as possible in his own words:

'Have you fellows heard what they are saying about me in London? One dear old lady in Kensington said, "*Have* you heard about that *dreadful* General Gough? . . . He was *asleep* during the great Battle!" Sleep!' he added, 'of course I slept. The battle lasted for five days. I slept like a baby when I had a chance.' Hearing that, it did not seem to me to have been wise to 'unstick' (as the French say) a higher commander of that type whilst Haig's Army was still being faced by an ordeal needing fearlessness and cheeriness in adversity, but independent historians can be trusted to put these things right in course of time.

Official historians (a contradiction in terms) are however faced with considerable difficulties, as they are not permitted in the public interest to write freely on political matters. Events are too recent, and the reputations of the living are involved. The best of them in pre-war days (Colonel Henderson, author of *Stonewall Jackson*) devoted the first volume of his history of the Boer War of 1899–1902 to its political origin, including some personal aspects, and the volume was ordered to be destroyed and the type to be broken up. There have been later examples. There is a story, in somewhat similar connection, against a writer who was believed to be subservient to Government influence. He was attending, in full evening dress and decorations, an official reception that was given some years ago by the Vice-Chancellor and the Senate of the University of London. Two learned scholars were standing close to me at that gathering and I could not help hearing this scrap of their conversation: A. 'I never trust a decorated historian.' B. 'No more do I.' The story illustrates the attitude of independent historians towards all suspicion of control by Governments or others over the publication of what they deem to be historical truth, even when they are engaged upon writing 'contemporary history'. Some, far from the scene of conflict, have claimed prescience about the impending attack of March 21st, 1918: I have relied upon the evidence of the men on the spot about what was actually known there through secret services, and I hope that this evidence will be of value to future historians.

There remains the need to fill a few gaps in our notes about the days and hours that preceded von Hutier's great massed attack, with von Marwitz conforming further to the northward, upon the thin line of Gough's Fifth Army. During the nights of March 18th and 19th information was collated from German prisoners and deserters, two of whom, as Ludendorff has since confessed, gave away news of the impending attack. Then there followed an ominous calm, and intense expectation of the storm shortly to burst. In order to verify the news of the imminence of the great attack a raid was launched late on March 20th against the German trenches near Fayet. Thus it was discovered that three German regiments (nine battalions) had just been massed upon a frontage, which, up to that time, had been occupied only by three battalions. Fifteen prisoners were taken, and it was thus ascertained for certain that the attackers would arrive within about six hours. The news was conveyed, as fast as possible, to the British and to the French commanders who were most likely to be affected.

Then, as is common in those regions, a thick early-morning mist closed down upon the scene. It was described by a regimental officer in the front line as a 'dense ground-mist and a light north-west wind'. 'Variable light airs' would be a true summary of descriptions which emanated from all parts of the line. Up to past 4 a.m. the complete silence, reported by so many as 'tense' or 'impressive', seemed to be further intensified. Was that mist an advantage to the attack or to the defenders? The reports which were most current at the time amongst those who were not subjected to the great ordeal all agreed that the attack was favoured, and that surprise was achieved.

This I believe to be unjust to the Fifth Army. In the light of my information about what was known concerning the impending attack, and about the strenuous work that was done in the short time available after taking over the extra frontage, I believe that if visibility had been better the slaughter of the German troops from British machine-gun posts would have been terrific. Other matters must be considered, such as artillery-fire, gas, counter-battery work, also the organization and control of the attacking masses. Ludendorff summed up this question of fog inconclusively. Sir Hubert Gough's views are more interesting. In a private letter (to Mr. Shaw Sparrow) he considered the question of the relative advantages of the fog to each side to be 'a thorny point'. Gough's final opinion is worth quoting *in extenso*:

'My opinion is that at first, say for a couple of hours, fog was a great disadvantage to the defence. Had it not been present, many of our machine-guns, very skilfully hidden, would have taken a terrible toll. It is possible—but considering the immense superiority of the German numbers, hardly probable—that this toll might have repulsed the attack. But as soon as the foe had broken through the first lines of resistance and was pushing on, he must have found that command, co-operation, and communication became increasingly difficult. Then—so I think—it is quite true that fog was a serious hindrance to the enemy. How could he go ahead for a decision—a big decision, and a rapid one? In war, when all is uncertain, and where so many influences are unceasingly at work, it is foolish to be dogmatic; but my summing-up is this: If the day had been clear and the attack had got through the first line of defence, losing hugely more than it lost in the fog, the German skill in the movement of masses of men would have had opportunities to exploit rapidly the first gains. Ludendorff's object was not a

209   o

limited one; it was unlimited and supported by enormous pushing power backed by vast reserves; and in all unlimited war-aims, swiftness in execution is necessary throughout an attack. Can we be certain that the Germans would have been stopped by their first losses on a clear day? Their numbers and their training make it impossible for us to say Yes to this question. *On the whole, then, it may be said that the fog favoured our Fifth Army.*'

At 4.40 a.m. all who were not already on the watch were awakened by a terrific bombardment. As one writer has described it, 'Earth and stones and volcanic smoke spouted into the fog as big new craters were scooped by explosions in and between many thousands of old ones.' Then, behind a creeping barrage, the hosts came on for what, according to prisoners' accounts, they had been led to believe was to be the final bid for victory, the last experience of slaughter. By that standard the outcome must be measured.

'It was bitter' as Gough wrote afterwards 'to the officers and men of the Fifth Army, but more particularly to the families of those who gave their lives in those dark days of struggle, to hear the misconceptions which were so freely bandied about of their action and their conduct; and the hard judgments that were passed upon them.' They can take cheer, now that reports from the other side show that their terrible losses, suffered in stemming the heaviest attack in the history of warfare, ended not in defeat but in victory. The line was bent, it was not broken, and Ludendorff's plan for a final victory was by his own showing a failure. The morale of the German Army and of the patriotic nation behind it, upheld by high promise, began thenceforward to deteriorate. Through the discovery in good time (through the comparatively small incident which I have described) of the arrival of von Hutier at St. Quentin, the Fifth Army was not surprised, and the weeks of strenuous preparation did much towards averting an irreparable disaster. I quote, in conclusion, a report by one who knew the true state of the morale of the survivors of the Fifth Army after their tremendous battering, and their success in defeating the enemy's object:

'By the night of March 25th the tide of the great advance towards Amiens had been stemmed. The Army Commander had been able to report to G.H.Q. that all that he wanted was some fresh divisions, and that with them he would be able to roll back the invaders. The army was proud of its achievement, and congratulations poured in from comrades elsewhere. Fresh troops not being forthcoming, all that could be done was to hold on. Small counter-attacks were successful. They showed that the enemy's advance had reached its extreme limit. When the news arrived of the grave anxiety in high places about the situation, and then of the supersession of the Army Commander, the first idea was that it must be a somewhat ill-timed joke. Assurance of its reality was received with dismay.'

Time is a great healer. Let us hope that the truth as I have written it will, in due season, supersede the impressions formed in minds in high and in low places— far from the scene of action—in those momentous days of what was freely described as 'Disaster', but which in fact was a great achievement, preceded by a success in the work of Secret Service which secured notice of the great attack which was impending.

AUTHOR'S NOTE.—In the foregoing chapter the German plan is purposely described in the light of information known to the Fifth Army at the time. The rôle of von Hutier was really subsidiary to that of Marwitz, and Amiens was not the original objective. (See *The Real War*, pp. 418–19, 424, and *passim*.)

CHAPTER XVIII

THE RAID ON ZEEBRUGGE, 1918—I

ALTHOUGH small in scale in comparison with the major operations of the War, the raid on Zeebrugge on St. George's Day, 1918, was the most dramatic incident of all, and it came at exactly the right moment.

Nearly four years of heavy and apparently fruitless sacrifice seemed to offer no prospect of victory for a just cause which had been embarked upon with zeal and high hopes. Influential voices had even been raised in favour of peace by compromise, and though the general feeling amongst the British people and the British 'Commonwealth of Nations' could be described as a dogged determination to hold on for victory at all costs, the disheartening events of 1917 had been followed by the terrible ordeal of Haig's Armies on the Western Front in March and in the early weeks of April 1918.

In addition to these depressing features of the war on land, the ruthless U-boat campaign, launched in the early months of 1917, had brought home to the people of Britain once more the old lesson that they depended upon the secure movement of merchant-shipping to and from the United Kingdom for their very existence, a lesson taught by every great war in history, and sometimes forgotten. Even foreign invasion was feared by the authorities, if we can judge by the number of troops that were kept in the United Kingdom.

For a parallel in history we must go back to the summer of the year 1805, to the months that preceded the Battle of Trafalgar, when the bogey of invasion by Napoleon's Grand Army overshadowed the land. Barham, that fine old seaman, had written to Pitt, the Prime Minister, immediately after taking over the office of First Lord of the Admiralty from Melville: 'If our Fleet is not kept in motion . . . we must sink under the preparations that are making against us. . . . Something must be done, and that right soon; defensive operations . . . must end in bankruptcy.' He advocated a sudden descent upon Minorca, then held by the French as a base for warships which were a thorn in the side of the naval authorities responsible for the security of the route to Malta and to other ports in the Mediterranean.

An American naval officer[1] recently quoted, in direct reference to the Zeebrugge venture, the opinion which was expressed at an earlier period by Wolfe, the hero of Quebec:

'In particular circumstances and times, the loss of a thousand men is rather an advantage to a nation than otherwise, seeing that gallant attempts raise its reputation whereas the contrary appearances sink the credit of a country, ruin the troops, and create infinite uneasiness and discontent at home.'

As a member of the Secretariat of the War Cabinet in those critical days, I can vouch for the fact that there was some uneasiness in Whitehall, and a tendency in the country to think that the limit of apparently fruitless sacrifice of the lives of British Empire troops in Flanders and in France had been reached. No prospect of decisive victory over the German Army was expected to be in sight until trained American troops had arrived in the front line in sufficient numbers to turn the scale.

Britain, the mainstay of the Entente Alliance, had nearly been brought to her knees in 1917 by the ruthless submarine campaign, at the time when the United States, newly 'associated' with the same cause, was preparing a colossal army to take part in the conflict. Had Britain

[1] Lieut.-Commander H. H. Frost, U.S.N. (United States Naval Institute *Proceedings*).

then collapsed, the American Army would never have reached the scene of carnage and decisive conflict, and, though the peril at sea was steadily diminishing, the difficulty of safeguarding helpless transports arriving in European waters still seemed to be almost prohibitive. Many UB boats using torpedoes and UC boats sowing mines broadcast were based upon the coast of Flanders. They were causing a large proportion of the sinkings of merchant-shipping—23 per cent. of the losses from the torpedoes and guns of UB boats, according to a German authority (Admiral Scheer). We do not know what proportion from the mines of UC boats, but we know that it was serious. Up to the end of 1917 those German submarines, of both classes, were passing up and down the Channel in spite of the Dunkirk-Goodwin barrage of nets. (That barrage was abandoned, and a Folkestone-Gris-Nez barrage was substituted, on January 1st, 1918.) Defensive measures had proved ineffective. Could a blow be struck from the sea against the Flanders bases? However desperate such an attempt might appear, it would at least fulfil the conditions laid down by men like Wolfe and Barham in days of old.

Several proposals had been put forward for such a blow, but no action had been taken upon them. Meanwhile every month of delay had added to the difficulties of the task. Time had been given to the enemy to construct formidable fortifications along the coast and these forts contained by 1918 no less than 136 heavy guns of 6-inch and of greater calibres up to 15 inches (including 6 of this largest size, 4 of 12-inch and 31 of 11-inch calibre), and 90 smaller pieces. Admiral Sir Lewis Bayley had been one of the first to suggest offensive action against the U-boat bases. On November 25th, 1916, Commodore Reginald Tyrwhitt at Harwich had also put forward proposals, and he had repeatedly returned to the charge. Then, on December 3rd, 1917, the Plans Division of the Naval Staff at the Admiralty drew up a definite plan to block the outlets to the Zeebrugge and Ostend canals which was sent to the Vice-Admiral commanding the Dover Patrol (Sir Reginald Bacon). He came to the Admiralty about a fortnight later (December 18th) with a modified scheme of his own, involving the use of Army troops and of monitors with gang-boards overhanging the bows. The monitors were to ram the Zeebrugge Mole end-on and they were to be held in that position against the long-shore current while the troops landed. The proposal for such an expedition was approved in principle by the First Sea Lord (Lord Jellicoe), but he left the Admiralty a few days later, being succeeded by Sir Rosslyn Wemyss (afterwards Lord Wester Wemyss).

On the 1st of January, 1918, Sir Roger Keyes, Director of the Plans Division at the Admiralty from which the proposal to take definite action without further delay had emanated, was appointed to command the Dover Patrol, and he was given a free hand by the Admiralty to make and to carry out a plan to block the entrances to the canals. We can now turn to the definite problem that had to be faced, and to the measures which were taken to ensure the secrecy upon which the prospect of success depended.

The main feature of the plan was to run blockships into the entrances to the sea canals at Zeebrugge and Ostend which led to Bruges, the German base for submarines, destroyers, and other light craft. It will be worth our while to follow the whole story at some length, comparing it in our minds with the 'worst-kept secret of the War', the Gallipoli landing three years before, described in a previous chapter. The outstanding features of that campaign were lack of preparation and premature publication.

The first decision, to ensure secrecy for the Zeebrugge raid, was to put as little as possible on paper. Meetings had been held at the Admiralty in December and plans had been discussed, so more than the proverbial three people, in whose hands a secret is said to be no longer secret, knew what was on foot. One feature of the plan was to use certain vessels (*Iris* and *Daffodil*) of light draft plying as ferry-boats in the River Mersey, and the Chief Naval Censor, Sir Douglas Brownrigg, has stated that he thus got to know about the plan in a curious way. He has not given the exact date, but he puts it 'very early in 1918'.[1] He was sitting in his office at the Admiralty with his assistants when he heard a Lieutenant-Commander ask one of them, just behind him, what newspapers were printed in Liverpool. Brownrigg asked why the applicant wanted the information, and he was told that the reason was secret. It appeared, from the appointment held by that Lieutenant-Commander (presumably in the Plans Division?), that something important was in the wind, so Brownrigg promised to do what was necessary with the Press, which was his own particular concern.

Then he told the Deputy-Chief of the Staff at the Admiralty the story, and he heard from him that the ferry-boats *Iris* and *Daffodil* were wanted for a raid, which must at all costs be kept secret. Brownrigg pointed out that it would be useless to take only the Liverpool papers into the confidence of the Admiralty; the absence of the ferry-boats would concern millions of people, not only in Liverpool but in Birkenhead, Salford, Manchester, and other places publishing journals in which complaints might appear. It was then left to the Chief Naval Censor to do his best in any way that he thought fit, so he took the Directors of the Press Bureau into his confidence. The result was a decision to tell not only the group of local newspaper editors but the whole Press, in confidence, trusting them to be patriotic and to keep the plan secret. This was done, and Brownrigg adds: 'Never a sign or trace of the news got out. Not the vaguest reference was ever made, and the Press, as was invariably the case when it was told what was expected of it, loyally carried out the wishes of the Admiralty.' He also states that he visited the Speaker of the House of Commons and told him the secret. The Speaker agreed to see any Member who wanted to ask a question about the two ferry-boats being

---

[1] *Indiscretions of a Naval Censor* (Cassell).

commandeered, to explain to him what was happening, and to ask him not to put the proposed question.

Brownrigg guarantees that nothing leaked out through the Press. Nevertheless, it is certain that there was talk on the subject in the military camps for some weeks before the event, and here is a report, dated the 12th of March, from one camp: 'A rumour is current in this camp to the effect that the Admiralty are about to send four or five old ships filled with cement to the entrance of one of the channels off Zeebrugge, there to engage the enemy and to allow these loaded ships to be sunk in the channel in order to block it and to prevent submarines from emerging from their base. It is said that volunteers were called for to man these ships and that there was a ready response. The volunteers were granted a few days' leave of absence prior to embarking on the venture, and the rumour apparently emanates from these men when proceeding on leave of absence.'

That may have been the case, but I doubt it. I think that I can vouch for the volunteers from my own old corps, the Royal Marine Artillery, which I had commanded until late in 1917. I met a party of them at Waterloo Station on their way to their destination and I had a long talk with non-commissioned officers, whom I knew well. They were most discreet, and they took care not to give anything away, even to their old C.O., and they certainly had no official knowledge themselves. (I have since ascertained that they had no knowledge at all, so they, at all events, could not possibly have gossiped during their last leave of absence.)

Sir Roger Keyes apparently foresaw some leakage, and decided to issue 'very secretly' something to account for the preparations that were being made to fit up old vessels and to train seamen and marines for some mysterious venture. Gossips must be fed with something plausible. The diaries of the late Sir Henry Wilson disclose the state of anxiety that prevailed from March 1918 onwards about the possibility of the German Army reaching the Channel ports and taking Dunkirk and Calais. Use was made of the supposed military situation to circulate secret rumours that Dunkirk and Calais might have to be abandoned; that steps were being taken to block their harbours (special vessels being prepared for the purpose); and that Marine Artillery were being trained at Shoeburyness and Light Infantry at Deal for special services to cover the operation. Secrecy about these matters was enjoined.

The Adjutant-General of Marines was naturally taken into the confidence of the authorities concerned, since the aid of the Royal Marine forces was needed for the proposed landing on the Zeebrugge Mole, and for manning mortars and machine-guns in the *Vindictive*, the vessel which had been chosen to carry the bulk of the landing-parties. The true story was communicated to the late Sir David Mercer (the Adjutant-General) by the 8th of January.

The work of preparation began at once, and on the 24th of February Sir Roger Keyes came to London and explained his plan, which by that time had taken shape, to the Board of Admiralty. One of its important features was to use a smoke-screen, laid by small craft, and the discovery had been made that the chemical which had been adopted by the Dover Patrol authorities before Christmas, 1917, was unsuited to the purpose, because fire appeared when the smoke was projected. The need was for white smoke, like sea-fog, to be laid without attracting the attention which would be caused by projectors which showed flame. The nature of the whole operation, the further leakage of information, and the success attained in securing a surprise must form the subjects of another chapter.

Aᴼᴛᴇʀ reading every book on warfare to which he could obtain access, the late Marshal Foch was appointed to lecture in his younger days at the *École Supérieure de Guerre*, the French Staff College. He then had to prepare a course of lectures of far-reaching importance, which would frame military opinion in France at a time when the new French Army was rising from the ashes of the old régime which perished in the bonfire of experience of German invasion in 1870. Foch, by much reading and study, had so bewildered his brain that nothing clearly established—upon which he could build his lectures—would emerge. He buried himself at Eastertime in the woods of his estate in Brittany and, at last, after much wrestling of the spirit, a simple little question emerged from his consciousness. *'De quoi s'agit-il?'* What, after all, is the definite problem to be solved? That little question points the way to success in warfare as in all other forms of human activity. 'What is the problem?' Cast everything else out of your mind and concentrate upon that.

I have often tried to put myself in the position of Sir Roger Keyes, whom I had known for many years, at the moment when, on New Year's Day in 1918, he was given the responsibility of carrying out the proposal which, as Director of Plans at the Admiralty, he had put forward on the 3rd of December for blocking the canal exits (at Zeebrugge and at Ostend) from the German U-boat base at Bruges, remote from the coast and out of reach of naval attack. It is one thing to put forward academic proposals, another to bear the responsibility for carrying them out yourself. I remembered him chiefly as a hard rider with the Staff College Drag Hounds in the days when I was a member of the Directing Staff there, and I also remembered a letter which he wrote afterwards from Rome, where he was Naval Attaché, rejoicing in the height of the huge post-and-rail fences which were the feature of the country hunted by the local foxhounds.

'What, on this occasion, was the problem?' First and foremost to block the canal-exit at Zeebrugge, because

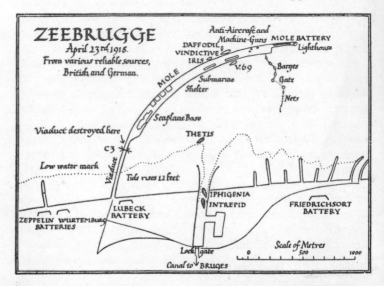

that canal was the biggest and deepest (8 miles to Bruges, 230 feet wide, 25 feet deep). Ostend was 11 miles from Bruges, and the canal much smaller. What were the difficulties to be overcome by blockships on their way to plug the entrance to the Zeebrugge-Bruges canal? In order to realize them properly, it is necessary to consult a diagram.

Zeebrugge, like all other ports along the coasts of Belgium and of Northern France, is a tidal harbour constantly subjected to the silting up of mud, needing dredging to keep the channel clear. The rise and fall of tide is about 12 feet. From a point on the coast to the westward of the canal-entrance there runs a long iron viaduct above the waters. It leads to a huge mole made of concrete blocks. This mole curves round gradually to form a harbour. Its length is about a mile, its width 75 yards. At the seaward end there is an extension of stone, 5 yards wide, the level of this extension being the same as that of a rampart, 8 feet wide, running the whole way along the seaward face of the Mole, and on that rampart there was a parapet, 3 feet high and 2 feet wide. The whole rampart stands 14 feet above the Mole itself. There is a lighthouse at the extreme end of the extension.

There were important buildings on the Mole. Beginning from the shore end we come first to the German seaplane base, with large shed (No. 1), then to a row of hangars for aircraft, then, tucked away on the harbour side of the Mole, secure from sea-bombardment, to a shelter for submarines, then to sheds Nos. 2 and 3. Then, stretching right across the 75-yard width of the Mole, to a protected machine-gun position, from which the bare concrete surface of the Mole to the westward could be swept with machine-gun bullets. Those machine-guns protected from any attack from the westward a battery of four guns of 4·1-inch and two of 3·5-inch calibre on the extension. Blockships attempting to pass round the end of the Mole extension to get to their destination, the canal-entrance, would be under the point-blank fire of those guns, which had an all-round arc of training. They must also pass round an obstruction formed by anchored barges running southward from a point on the Mole near the inner end of the extension. Beyond the most southerly barge there was an entrance gate to the harbour, and beyond the gate a net-obstruction extending to water too shallow for the blockships.

I have already mentioned the formidable array of batteries of heavy guns along the fortified Belgian coast-line between Nieuport in the west and Sluis, on the Dutch frontier, to the eastward. The nearest of these batteries to the Zeebrugge canal-entrance were, to the westward of that entrance, the 'Zeppelin' battery (four 5·9-inch guns), 'Wurtemberg' battery (two 4·1-inch guns) and, just inside the iron viaduct leading to the Mole, a battery of four 37-millimetre machine-guns. To the eastward of the canal-entrance, enfilading the line of barges and nets, was a more formidable 'Goeben' battery, with four big guns of 9·2-inch calibre, and further inland more guns and entrenchments. The whole coast-line of sand-dunes was entrenched, on both sides of the canal-entrance, from the viaduct to the 'Goeben' battery.

That, then, was the definite problem which faced Sir Roger Keyes, apart from the great navigational difficulties involving alterations of course under difficult conditions, to get the blockships, still afloat, past the defences of the deep channel which led to the canal. Another, and changing, factor to be considered would be the German destroyers and submarines which might, on the date selected, be found alongside the inner face of the Mole, sheltered from sea-bombardment. In order to avoid too many complications, we will take the problem piecemeal, bearing always in mind that the need for secrecy and surprise was the basis of the whole plan.

Partly to distract attention from the all-important blockships, and partly to overcome the defences, it was decided to land a force on the seaward side of the Mole itself *to the eastward* of (behind) the machine-guns mentioned, which faced westward, and swept the surface of the Mole. The old cruiser *Vindictive*, and Liverpool ferry-boats *Iris* and *Daffodil*, were selected to carry this storming party. The *Vindictive* to take two companies and a machine-gun section and four Lewis guns, a trench-mortar section, two 7·5-inch howitzers, one bigger howitzer of 11-inch calibre, two pom-poms and two fixed Stokes mortars. All these units to be marines, Royal Marine Artillery and Royal Marine Light Infantry, each allotted to appropriate duties for which they were specially trained.

The *Vindictive* also to carry the naval landing-parties, two companies of seamen, a demolition party, and an experimental party with flame projectors. The *Iris* to carry a company of marines, two mobile Stokes mortars, and a company of seamen; the *Daffodil* to carry a demolition party of seamen. On arrival at the Mole, the storming parties would land, the marines sweeping westward along the Mole, covering from that direction the storming and demolition parties of seamen who would work havoc amongst the guns on the extension and amongst any hostile craft tied up inside the Mole.

The danger of reinforcements reaching the Mole by the Viaduct from the shore to face the marines was realized. Old submarines (C1 and C3) filled with explosives were to ram the viaduct, to be abandoned by their crews, and to be blown up, thus cutting off communication between shore and Mole. It was all magnificent, but was it war? Time only would show. The American naval officer to whom I have already referred reminds us of Wolfe's writings after he had had experience of failure in such an enterprise. First Wolfe writes that no time should be lost, when once such an attack is launched, in idle debate or 'in consultation when the sword should be drawn': 'Pushing smartly on is the road to success and more especially in an affair of this sort. . . . Nothing is to be reckoned as an obstacle to your undertaking that is not found really so on trial. . . . In war something must be allowed to chance and fortune, seeing that it is in its nature hazardous and an option of difficulties.'

Before we turn to the actual execution of the plan, let us take the advice of Foch and concentrate upon the real problem, to which all else was accessory. Some, in their zeal, have thrown the limelight upon the heroic storming of the Mole. That was valuable in so far as it helped in the main plan. *De quoi s'agit-il?* What was the problem? To get the blockships into the canal-entrance. Two out of three of them got there, led inside the Mole and speeded on their way by the destroyer *Warwick*, flying the Vice-

Admiral's flag of an intrepid commander, but I must not let my pen run away with me to the climax on St. George's Day, 1918. Our subject is secrecy, and Secret Services that achieve surprise.

I once heard a Field-Marshal address a Brigadier-General who had delivered an oration, to the officers of a battalion, about what the great masters of war would have done in such a situation. The Field-Marshal said: 'The success of that battalion in war would have depended upon whether the C.O. had covered a long trek over the veld, making sure that everything needed—machine-guns, ammunition, and so forth, was at hand when they reached their destination. That, under the conditions, would have depended chiefly upon care of their mules. Let us have a look at the mule-harness.'

Getting the blockships to their destination depended upon secrecy, first over the preparations, and finally upon details, especially a smoke-screen. That depended upon a certain chemical, of which large quantities were needed. That again meant special plant, which in its turn meant delays that nearly wrecked the whole enterprise, as will appear in due course. We can now go back to the 24th of February, 1918, when sufficient advance had been made in the preparations for the plan to be explained by Sir Roger Keyes to the Board of Admiralty.

Up to the 16th February, and maybe up to a later date, Keyes hoped to have everything ready for the 19th March, when the tide and other essential conditions would suit. Moonlight would be a disadvantage that could be predicted and avoided. For the smoke-screen to be effective a gentle sea-breeze to blow the smoke landwards was hoped for. One can take note of the extraordinary combination of favourable conditions that were needed for such a venture to offer any prospect of success, and we can also remember how good fortune has sometimes favoured the boldest plans. Nelson's scheme in the old sailing days (1801) for dealing with the Danish Fleet at Copenhagen was the most outstanding example of its kind that I can remember. He proposed with his little squadron to sail *southward* through the Straits, anchor, reorganize, reconnoitre the difficult channels, and then sail *northward* through another channel to his destination. That needed a northerly wind for the first stage, and a change of wind to the southward for the second stage. The change of wind that he wanted came exactly at the right time.

Keyes discovered by experience the immense amount of detailed staff work that was needed for his purpose. The Sea Lords of the Admiralty approved of his plan on the 24th of February. On the 4th March he was obliged to agree to a postponement for two reasons, the fitting of the blockships (*Thetis*, *Intrepid* and *Iphigenia* for Zeebrugge, *Brilliant* and *Sirius* for Ostend) took longer than had been expected. They were of 3,600 tons displacement; they had concrete for ballast; their masts were removed, but a few guns were retained, and some smoke-producing apparatus. The training of the bluejackets and marines had begun in February. A model of the Zeebrugge Mole was constructed for their use in training. Every detail of scaling and assault was studied.

Another cause of delay was the difficulty in obtaining the necessary chemical in sufficient quantity (62 tons) for the smoke-screens. These were designed by the great firework firm of Brock, one of whom held a commission in the Air Force. I do not know whether I am at liberty to explain the exact nature of that chemical, so I will remain on the safe side, only mentioning that the highest Government authority, the War Cabinet, had to be appealed to in order to obtain the supply in time. A certain by-product, which we will call $X_2Y_5Z_7$ to conceal its real nature, was useful for making sugar, so the balance had to be struck between the importance of the Zeebrugge adventure and the supply of sugar! With such problems the highest authorities in the land were constantly faced in the Great War, and this form of dilemma could hardly have been foreseen in pre-war preparation. I only quote this as an example of the many details and vexatious delays

P

which had to be overcome, and to remove the impression, which still exists, that success in bold ventures under modern conditions is a matter of brilliant improvisation followed by immediate action. A long period of preparation precedes what Wolfe styled the road to success 'pushing smartly on' when the issue is once joined. The longer the period, however, the greater the difficulty of achieving the all-important surprise, and we know from the previous chapter that by the middle of March the true purpose of the blockships was being discussed in military camps.

The 4th of April saw the collection at the West-Swin Anchorage, off the Essex coast about 8 miles south of Clacton-on-Sea, of the bulk of the armada. There, accommodated in the *Hindustan*, were the landing-parties destined for the *Vindictive* and other craft. They were only allowed to communicate with their relatives by the prescribed postcards. The officers were all let into the secret. At the Swin there were also collected the blockships both for Zeebrugge and for Ostend, the *Vindictive* and the Liverpool ferry-boats *Iris* and *Daffodil*.

On the 7th of April, Keyes visited the men to be engaged in the enterprise. All was now known to them, and he issued a circular containing the words: 'I am very confident that the great tradition of our forefathers will be worthily maintained and that all ranks will strive to emulate the heroic deeds of our brothers of the Sister Service in France and Flanders.'

Expectation was becoming intense while awaiting the day, between the 9th and 13th April, when conditions of tide, moon, and it was hoped wind, would be favourable for the attempt. I take the next few days from entries in a diary.

April 9th. Stood by. Weather not suitable.

April 10th. Ditto.

April 11th. Started at 4 p.m. When within 16 miles of destination, at 0.45 a.m. on April 12th, the operation cancelled. 'Wind dead against us.'

There we get an interesting touch—the moral courage required in a responsible commander who cancels an enterprise at a moment, at so late a stage, so near success, when conditions which rendered the risk justifiable no longer exist. Success was deemed to depend upon the smoke-screen, and with the wind unfavourable the screen could not be effective. The precedent of Teneriffe ('afraid to turn back') as a hopeless operation occurs to our mind.

And so they returned, with the loss of one of the coastal motor-boats (the use of those vessels will come into our account of the final operation) which accompanied the blockships intended for Ostend. She ran on a mine; her crew was lost. It was not known at the time that her hull drifted ashore to the eastward of the entrance to Ostend harbour. I have since seen a German account that, from the wreck of that 'C.M.B.', they retrieved a chart which gave interesting details of the object of the abandoned raid. The chart was No. 125 'Ostend Roads'. On it was endorsed in black ink 'No. 33 Boat chart. April 9, 1918', and, in red ink, various notes including 'Motor launches making smoke and sending smoke-flots' to cover the approach of blockships. To that the writer added that it was possible to deduce that a similar attack, not only upon Ostend but also upon Zeebrugge, would be made when the conditions of tide, *moon* [sic], and wind would be favourable, adding that such would be the condition on the night of the 22nd of April. I fear that I have come to the conclusion that that report must represent wisdom after the event. The night of April 11th/12th was a dark one, without a moon. Under ordinary conditions, the night of April 22nd/23rd would be one of brilliant moonlight.

And now we go back to the armada, returned to its bases, and to Keyes. Another false start was made on the night of April 13th, but again conditions were unfavourable, and the venture was again abandoned, on that occasion after about three hours. The moon, the tides, and perhaps the wind, might offer a favourable opportunity again on about the 10th of May. The Admiralty were not prepared to contemplate a pause for three more weeks. It was too much to expect that secrecy—upon which the all-important surprise depended—could be maintained for so long. All the enterprise, all the thought, and all the careful training of the officers and men seemed to have been thrown away.

Post nubilia Phoebus—after clouds the sun—was one of Nelson's favourite mottoes, and he, of all others, with his five years of unemployment, out of favour with the Admiralty, knew the need for some such thought in days of adversity. Keyes represented that there was no need to wait for three weeks. He would be ready to try again in ten days, when the moon would be full. The enemy would think that no one but a fool would choose such a date, and if the enemy thought that, there would be all the better chance of a surprise. The Admiralty gave permission. The result is not likely to be forgotten in the English-speaking world. The tale has often been told but never, to my knowledge, with the exploits in their true proportion, so the events of St. George's Day, 1918, and its Eve on the 22nd, will form the subject of the next chapter. It is a tale worth telling.

In the actual achievements, it is important to bear in mind that the landing on the Mole, as it was planned, was intended partly to distract attention from the all-important blockships, but primarily to capture or to destroy the guns at the Mole-end, which could engage the blockships at point-blank range, and menaced their safe passage.

CHAPTER XX

ST. GEORGE FOR ENGLAND!
APRIL 22ND–23RD, 1918

HAVING dwelt, of set purpose, upon the long weeks of preparation, of overcoming obstacles, of attempts to secure secrecy to ensure surprise, and of days of disappointment when tide and darkness suited the venture on April 11th and only the wind failed, we pass to ultimate achievement. We are familiar with the object of the commander and organizer of the whole project—to get block-ships into the exits from the Bruges canals at Zeebrugge and at Ostend; three (*Thetis*, *Intrepid*, and *Iphigenia*) for Zeebrugge, two (*Sirius* and *Brilliant*) for Ostend. The alternative of ramming the lock-gates at Zeebrugge as a primary purpose had been considered, but rejected on the plea that, if this were done, it would be possible for an enemy rapidly to re-create a channel by blowing away the upper parts of the blockship, and forming a way through which the U-boats could pass at high tide.

We have dealt with the main features, the blockships, and with the Zeebrugge Mole and shore batteries, but not with all the accessories. The uses of the other craft, of monitors, destroyers, motor-launches ('M.L's') and coastal motor-boats ('C.M.B's') will appear in the course of the narrative, as will the functions of the naval aircraft. We will concentrate on Zeebrugge. During the preceding weeks the monitors had bombarded Zeebrugge at regular intervals and at regular times. The 'evening hate' had become a routine, the idea being that when a similar bombardment occurred on 'The Night' it would convey the impression of nothing abnormal. The aircraft had been indefatigable in taking photographs and in raiding.

On April 22nd the conditions of tide were favourable. Meteorological conditions were obligingly broadcasted from the German wireless station in Belgium. There seemed to be no risk of an off-shore night-breeze which would blow the smoke-screen away to windward. If the night was clear, there would be a bright moon, but that was to be risked. (As matters turned out, the night was cloudy and rainy. This cut out the part to be taken by aircraft from Dunkirk in the venture, but it had a screening effect over the sea-surface.)

From 1.10 p.m. onwards the different portions of the armada began to leave their respective bases. From Dover there came three destroyers (*Velox*, *Morris*, and *Melpomene*) to reconnoitre northward of Zeebrugge. Also *Attentive* (light cruiser), a flotilla leader and three destroyers to a position about 15 miles from Zeebrugge, their mission being to beat back enemy patrols which might otherwise discover the main body, and also to keep intact the aids to navigation which marked the channel of approach. From Dover came also the destroyer *Warwick*, flying the flag of Vice-Admiral Roger Keyes. With her were 9 destroyers, the 2 submarines charged with explosives to blow up the viaducts, 1 minesweeper, 18 coastal motor-boats and 33 motor-launches; the functions of the light craft being to lay smoke-screens, pick up survivors, and raid the hostile craft sheltering inside the Zeebrugge Mole. From the West-Swin Anchorage there came all the blockships. Also *Vindictive*, *Iris*, and *Daffodil* with the landing-parties. All assembled at a rendezvous and at a quarter before 9 p.m. Everyone knew that, this time, there was to be no turning back. '*St. George for England!*' was passed as a final inspiration from *Warwick* flying the red cross of St. George in her Vice-Admiral's flag.

At five minutes to 10 p.m. the main force lay with stopped engines about 17 miles from Zeebrugge, covered by the *Attentive's* screen. Until daylight failed (7.30 p.m.) the 61st Wing and Scouting planes from Dover had provided an air escort. Meanwhile the Harwich Force of

23 pennants lay off the coast of Holland to guard against the risk of interference by a hostile force from the German North Sea bases. The time had come for the supernumeraries to leave the blockships, about 30 from each. They pleaded to remain, and they were allowed to do so. Final arrangements were completed and all knew the details of the plan. The minutes dragged on until, at ·10.30 p.m., the time for action at last arrived.

Had the secret been kept? And would surprise be achieved? It seemed so. No enemy patrol-boats had been encountered. No minefields had been found. The night was dark, the sea calm. Only the dim shapes of the motionless vessels could be distinguished as blurs in the rainy mist. A gentle sea-breeze was favourable for the smoke-screen. There was stillness over the waters, not broken until 10.30 p.m. when the whole armada began to move towards the shore. Monitors *Erebus* and *Terror*, with their destroyers, parted company to carry out their routine bombardment. Three destroyers, *Whirlwind*, *Myngs*, and *Moorsom*, altered course to port to join the *Velox* patrolling north of Zeebrugge. Two more destroyers, *Trident* and *Mansfield*, towing submarines C1 and C3, charged with explosives, bore away to starboard towards the viaduct joining the base of the Zeebrugge Mole to the shore. A little picket-boat went with them.

Led by *Warwick*, the *Phœbe* and *North Star*, *Vindictive*, *Iris*, and *Daffodil* with their landing-parties steered for the head of the great Mole, at 10 knots. Following them, at 8 knots, came the cause of all the dispositions—blockships *Thetis*, *Intrepid*, and *Iphigenia*, each escorted by a motor-launch. In front of all were 24 motor-launches and 8 coastal motor-boats to lay the screen of smoke, 9 more coastal motor-boats to attack with torpedoes the hostile craft in the harbour. (According to official German authorities there were 7 German destroyers and 7 coastal (A) torpedo-boats in Zeebrugge harbour; 3 of the destroyers and 4 of the A-boats were tied up inside the Mole.) For fifty minutes the procession moved slowly shorewards in the darkness. We now follow events by the clock.

11.20 *p.m.* The monitors opened fire—their normal procedure for several nights.

11.40 *p.m.* The small craft laid their heavy clouds of smoke, blown shoreward towards the Mole by light airs from the north-east. The breeze died away, and then the wind came from the southward, rolling away the smoke-clouds. Helped by destroyers, the small craft went in closer, nearer and nearer to the guns which had now opened fire from the Mole, to lay more smoke.

11.56 *p.m.* *Vindictive* emerged from the smoke-screen a cable and a half (300 yards) from the battery on the Mole-extension, and then there came desperate and determined action, the climax to months of preparation. Every minute counted. *Vindictive* opened fire on the shore targets. We cannot picture the scene better than it was described afterwards in the Press:

'It seemed to those in the ship as if the dim coast and the hidden harbour exploded into light. A star-shell soared aloft, then a score of star-shells; the wavering beams of the search-lights swung round and settled to a glare; the wild fire of gun-flashes leapt against the sky; strings of luminous green beads shot aloft, hung and sank; and the darkness of the night was supplanted by the nightmare daylight of battle fires. Guns and machine-guns along the Mole and batteries ashore awoke to life.'

0.1 *a.m.* On *St. George's Day*. *Vindictive* increased to full speed and instead of striking the Mole by the battery on the extension, behind the line of machine-guns which defended that battery against an advance along the Mole, she bumped over 300 yards further to the westward, the fenders on her port side pressing against the Mole, one minute after midnight.

0.4 *a.m.* *Daffodil*, from the seaward side, presses *Vindictive* against the Mole. *Iris* goes alongside the Mole ahead of *Vindictive*, but there the Mole cannot be scaled by the landing-party. Assaulting parties from *Vindictive* storm the Mole, but they have been set an impossible task. Little progress could be made towards the battery on the Mole-extension across the 400 yards of flat surface swept by machine-gun bullets. Though material results were small, moral effects were tremendous, and the heroism shown by seamen and marines on the Mole was repaid. The object of distracting the attention of the defenders from the approach of the all-important block-ships was largely fulfilled.

0.15 *a.m.* Submarine C3, running on the surface at 6 knots, covered the last 3,000 yards to the base of the viaduct, striking the right spot though blinded by search-lights ashore. Wurtemberg Battery of 6-inch and 4·1-inch guns opened fire on her, but for some unexplained reason ceased fire. She fulfilled her mission. Fuse lighted, her crew leave her, and then came a tremendous explosion which destroyed 100 feet of the viaduct, and cut off communication between the shore and the Mole. That drew attention to that flank, and seemed to confuse the defenders, who are said to have mistaken the blockships approaching the harbour entrance for friendly vessels. The survivors from C3 reached the picket-boat.

0.25 *a.m.* Escorted by 3 motor-launches, blockship *Thetis* ran the gauntlet past the uninjured guns on the Mole-extension and the batteries on shore. She rounded the end of the barge obstruction, and struck a net which fouled the propellers and stopped her. She took the ground eastward of the canal-entrance, succeeded in backing off, and grounded again westward of the entrance, holed on the water-line by the Mole-extension guns. The survivors reached an escorting motor-launch.

Blockship *Intrepid* passed her. The order was that if three blockships got in, the first was to ram the lock-gates, the other two to block the canal-entrance outside them. *Intrepid* was sunk there. *Iphigenia* followed. For the first time in history, blockships succeeded in fulfilling their mission under such conditions. Motor-launches and the destroyer *Whirlwind* saved the survivors. M.L. 110 was sunk. M.L. 282 having saved over 100 men, all the members of her crew wounded and some killed, was dangerously overloaded when she met *Warwick* just outside the harbour and spent half an hour in transferring her load, including many wounded. During the critical period, destroyers and the light craft had helped, continuing to keep up the smoke-screen. Destroyer *North Star* was sunk inside the harbour, *Phœbe* saving her crew. The coastal motor-boats came in and attacked the hostile craft alongside the Mole.

0.50 *a.m. Daffodil's* siren sounded as a signal to the landing-parties on the Mole to re-embark. *Iris*, having failed to land her party on the precipitous Mole, had just ranged alongside *Vindictive*, but too late for further operations.

During the withdrawal, in spite of gallant attempts by a motor-launch to screen her with smoke, *Iris* was riddled by heavy fire as she withdrew, losing 77 killed and 205 wounded out of the total casualties (176 killed, 412 wounded, and 49 missing) suffered by the British force, compared with far lighter German losses.

Wolfe had written in the eighteenth century that the loss of 1,000 men to a nation in such a venture, launched at the right moment, was 'rather an advantage to a nation than otherwise', for the great raising of morale in a whole nation and in its fighting forces. Were those conditions fulfilled? In Whitehall, at the hub of affairs, where I was serving at the time, they were. All over the United Kingdom and Empire they were; and tributes poured in from foreign countries. From Haig's main British Empire Army—still with 'backs to the wall', stemming the German avalanche pressing its way towards the Channel ports, there came this message: 'On behalf of the Army in France please accept for yourself and all ranks engaged our most hearty congratulations on the success of your operations against Zeebrugge and Ostend. St. George's

Day was indeed a fitting date for such a daring feat of arms.'

As a matter of fact, the Ostend venture had failed, partly because the Germans—probably on account of the warning received from the contents of the 'C.M.B.' that was washed ashore on the morning of April 12th—had cleverly removed the light-buoy marking the entrance channel more than two sea miles eastward of the proper position. My inference is that, had they known beforehand of the Zeebrugge raid, they would have been equally well prepared, and that surprise, the object of Secret Service, was successfully achieved.

Partly, it seems to me, out of sheer bravado, Roger Keyes sent the old *Vindictive* into Ostend as soon as the tide served in May, and there she lay in an honoured grave for some years. *Warwick* picked up the survivors of the *Vindictive's* crew from a sinking motor-launch off Ostend and returned from that enterprise, with her stern shattered by a mine (in tow of *Whirlwind* with *Velox* lashed alongside to steer her), flying a large Vice-Admiral's flag. That exploit was also welcomed by Haig on behalf of his Army, as witness this message of the 10th of May: 'The whole Army has learned with enthusiasm the good news of your action at Ostend. We all send to you, and to all ranks and ratings who took part, our congratulations on their skill and courage.'

Whatever the material results may have been, there is no doubt that surprise was achieved at Ostend on that second occasion, and that secrecy was successfully maintained. I have dwelt at length with these exceptional episodes in sea-warfare since they bring out, in an unusual degree, results that can be attained by secrecy beforehand, by careful preparation and by bold leadership at the last moment.

On the material side, the Germans managed to pass A-boats (small coastal torpedo-boats of light draft) and a small UB submarine past the sterns of the *Iphigenia* and *Intrepid* at high water. Ultimately the two piers on the western side of the canal were removed and a channel was dug through the silt on that bank of the canal. Great iron girders were driven in to mark the channel, and between these the destroyers and larger submarines, which were shut up at Bruges for some ten weeks, were warped at the top of high water. So it remained until Zeebrugge fell into British hands in October 1918. In 1920, after nearly two years' work, the Liverpool Salvage Company succeeded in removing the blockships and cleared the channel.

The Admiralty, in a general order to the Fleet of April 27th, described the first operation as 'An exploit high in the annals of the Navy and Royal Marines. . . . A proud memory for the relatives of those who fell.' But, to put patriotic bias on one side, we had better conclude with an opinion from the U.S.A., that of Lieutenant-Commander H. H. Frost, U.S. Navy, from whose historical writings we have quoted before: 'The British losses were a cheap price to pay for its immense moral effects. Exploited by world-wide propaganda, the heroism of British seamen and marines in those gloomy days created a tremendous impression in Allied and neutral countries, perhaps even in Germany. As a *beau geste* it was superb. It showed that Britons still knew how to die! It proved that the Royal Navy had reverted to the Nelsonic idea of warfare. That old-time aggressive fighting spirit gave heart to soldier and civilian when hopes fell low. The attack will ever be ranked as one of the most heroic and spectacular exploits in the history of war. As such it was of distinct value to the Allied cause.'

My object in devoting three chapters to the raid upon Zeebrugge has been to show the results which can be obtained in an amphibious operation provided that three conditions are fulfilled—secrecy, careful preparation, and bold leadership, and I will add a few last words. Was the venture worth while? Was there no glamour over the Great War? Do sentiment and high purpose count for nothing?

On the 11th of April of this year (1930)—the twelfth anniversary of the time when the limit of endurance and sacrifice seemed to be approaching in Flanders and Haig issued his 'Backs to the wall' order—*The Times* published a moving leading article upon the recent spate of war-books, protesting against the recall of the depths into which some of the lowest natures fell, while omitting mention of the heights to which the majority rose. These things seem to be a question of individual outlook, best illustrated by a parable.

Near the north-west windows of my home in the country there is a farmyard, evil-smelling, and beyond it a view of sunsets and of broad expanses of sky over ever-changing downlands. It is possible to imagine some men, standing in that farmyard, paddling ankle-deep in the dung and sniffing its aroma. It is also possible to imagine the attention of others being fixed upon the beauty of the downlands, upon the roseate reflection of the dawn, or upon the glories of the sunset sky.

CHAPTER XXI

THE CLIMAX ON THE WESTERN FRONT, 1918

FROM the inspiring theme of Zeebrugge we now turn to the climax which followed the four years of patient endurance, the suffering of supreme sacrifice under monotonous conditions, and the constant but disappointing endeavour to win the war decisively against the main German Army on the Western Front in France and in Flanders; and here we remind ourselves of Britain's proclaimed purpose in sending an army across the Channel in August 1914: 'To assist the French Government in preventing or repelling the invasion by Germany of French and Belgian territory, and eventually to restore the neutrality of Belgium, on behalf of which, as guaranteed by treaty, Belgium has appealed to the French and ourselves.'

The British Empire Army on the Western Front had reached in 1917 its maximum strength of over 2,044,600 (including 141,000 Canadians, 140,000 Australians and New Zealanders and 7,000 South Africans) during the month of August, by which date native labour corps numbering some 90,000 had also been provided from the British Empire. By the end of the year, when 760,000 battle casualties had been suffered and reinforcements had been sent to Italy, the numbers had sunk to 1,828,600, with 142,000 in the native labour corps. The German Army had been strongly reinforced from their Eastern Front and the bulk of it faced the British line, which had been considerably extended. The inevitable result, the forcing back of the Fifth British Army towards Amiens, and the work of the secret and field intelligence departments in connection therewith have been dealt with in a previous chapter, where the point clearly emerged that success in these services under the conditions that obtain upon a 300-mile front, held by immense masses of troops with secure flanks, involves the sifting of huge piles of evidence coming in from numerous sources, and upon drawing the right deductions.

It would be impossible, even within the compass of a whole book, to deal adequately in detail with the activities of Secret Service and Field Intelligence that lay behind the events between the great 'Kaiser-Battle' attack upon Gough's Fifth Army in March 1918, and the break through the Hindenburg line by British Empire and American troops which gave the *coup de grâce* to the cause of the Central Powers by compelling Germany to sue for an Armistice on any terms that could be obtained. Before we come to that event, however, it will be well to add a few notes in order to connect the story of the main events on the Western Front between March and the end of September 1918.

Having failed by the 5th of April in their attempts to break through the British Fifth Army to Amiens, or to force a wedge between the British and French Armies, the German High Command attacked in April the British line in Flanders, to which some of the tired British divisions had been sent from the Amiens front. It was on that occasion (April 12th) that Haig issued his famous 'Backs to the wall' order. The Battle of the Lys died away on the 29th of April, the Germans having again failed to achieve their purpose, and from thenceforward Haig's Army was left time for rest and replenishment until August, when the attack by Rawlinson's Fourth Army was launched under conditions to be described in due course.

Marshal (then General) Foch had been appointed to co-ordinate the operations of the British and French Armies on March 26th. He had been made Commander-in-Chief over the British, French and American Armies

on the Western Front on April 14th, and soon he appealed
to Haig to send some of his tired divisions to relieve
French divisions on the French Front. Foch's object was
to take these fresh divisions out of the line in order to
form a reserve for a counter-stroke in due course. Only by
such means could he wrest the initiative from the enemy.
Haig complied, and sent the IXth British Army Corps.
Acting in good faith, Pétain put that Corps in a part of
the French line that was heavily attacked from the northward in the Battle of the Aisne (May 27th to June 6th),
which forced the French portion of the line back to form
a sharp salient with its apex at Château-Thierry on the
River Marne.

This 'Third Battle of the Aisne' came upon the French
as a complete surprise. Information, based upon first-
hand authority, shows that until May 26th nothing
definite had been reported by Pétain's headquarters about
the storm that was about to burst. Foch was asked on
that evening whether he thought that a great German
attack in that area was brewing. He replied that he did
not think so, and he added that reports of impending
attacks were reaching him every day from all parts of the
line. (It is interesting to compare this with the exact
intelligence about the enemy that preceded the attack
upon Gough in March 1918.)

Colonel F. G. Piggott has published[1] the story of a *coup*
'towards the end of May' (the exact date is not given) by
a British patrol who took prisoner a German non-commissioned officer carrying a bag which contained his company's letters. There followed at Headquarters of the
British Second Army a long and monotonous search
through the contents, and the searchers were rewarded.
They discovered the famous 'Laon postcard' which
furnished a topic for conversation in British intelligence
and other circles for many weeks. In Colonel Piggott's
words: 'A German pioneer Sergeant . . . writing from
near Laon to a friend in his former unit in Flanders,

[1] *Army Quarterly*, Vol. IX, No. 2, p. 239.

mentioned the heavy and important work in which he had been engaged, and he informed his correspondent that the results would soon be seen. *This was the first indication of the sudden blow which fell upon the French front on the Chemin des Dames on the 27th of May.'*

It is a great pity, from the historical point of view, that the exact date when news of the impending attack was received is not given, but however that may be, reliable French authorities state that the Germans succeeded completely in deceiving their Field Intelligence and Secret Service Department about the intention to launch that heavy attack on the 27th of May, 1918. A very few German prisoners had been taken on the French front during the month of May. The principal information which was obtained from the prisoners was that constant warnings had been issued to them of an impending French attack. These warnings were doubtless given in order to explain any abnormal activities, improvements in communications and so forth, that German soldiers might observe.

Another method that the Germans employed to ensure secrecy, was to forbid all movements or visits to other areas, and more especially all attempts to approach near enough to marching columns to obtain identifications of the troops therein. There is a story, told by French prisoners who escaped and reached their own lines, that they were fired upon by German troops when near one such marching column as a caution to keep out of its way. It was thus that up to the afternoon of the 26th of May (the day before the big German advance began) the 'Third Bureau' at French Army Headquarters had only collected enough information to cause the deduction that all was normal along the German front. There was no indication of an impending attack on a large scale. At that period the discipline on the German side must still have been excellent; regulations enjoining secrecy and forbidding visits to other areas were not only issued, they were strictly obeyed. It seems evident also that the lack of information about the arrival of extra guns was due to the von Hutier method (used at Riga against the Russians in 1917 and against the British Fifth Army in March 1918) of keeping only a skeleton force in the front line and reinforcing it at the very last minute.

Passing now to the 26th of May; on that date two prisoners were taken. One of them was a cadet-officer, the other was a private soldier. The cadet-officer at once volunteered somewhat suspiciously the (false) information that no German attack was contemplated in that area. The private soldier, examined separately, disclosed enough to enable his examiners to deduce that an attack was impending, and that it would come very soon. The cadet-officer, when re-examined, let out more of the secret. From that, and from further information based upon French sources, I can add with confidence that the French Intelligence Department had not received enough definite information to warn the higher commanders of the impending attack until 3 p.m. on the afternoon of May 26th. Hence the attitude of Foch.

The nights of May 24th, 25th and 26th were not very clear, so reconnaissance from the air was difficult. Good reports of movements in the back areas seem to have come from the air on the 23rd, but apparently nothing very definite arrived after that, although we now know that heavy columns, certainly more than 20 divisions, were marching southward to form up for the attack. The deduction is that the attack came upon Foch as a surprise, because the Germans succeeded in concealing their intentions well enough to deceive the staff at French Headquarters. On May 27th the enemy advanced and penetrated the French line for five kilometres; on the 28th the River Aisne was crossed on an 18-mile front; Soissons was lost on the 29th, and by the 31st the enemy was on the River Marne from Château-Thierry to Dormans. During the first two days of June a violent battle developed on the River Ourcq, but Allied troops, including Americans, had driven the enemy back over the Marne by the night of June 3rd, and the tide was stemmed.

I have been obliged to dwell at some length upon these operations as the failure of the Secret Service caused a climax in the unified command, and they bear very strongly both upon the subject of Secret Service and upon recent revelations about the relationship between Foch and Clemenceau. Clemenceau's version has just been published. What, on first-hand evidence, I believe to be Foch's version, is described in my life of the late Marshal (pages 225–226). He was never so much admired by British observers who were in intimate touch with him as he was in that critical battle. The strain upon him must have been tremendous. His command, his reputation, and the success of his plans were all at stake. Either through faulty information, or through deliberate determination to keep the front line weak so as to form a reserve of fresh troops for a counter-stroke, he seemed to have failed.

He had the enemy in his front, and the Supreme War Council, full of apprehension, behind him. He had to stop the advance of the one, and to reassure the other. He did both, and even if a feeling of tension did last for a time, it did not prevent Haig from responding to further appeals from Foch for British divisions to reinforce the French portion of the line. Haig sent him the XXIInd Army Corps in July. The main events in that month were the next German bid for victory by another blow to the southward, struck on each side of Rheims on July 15th, and Foch's great counter-stroke on July 18th (with the fresh reserves which he had steadily accumulated under Mangin) against the western face of the Château-Thierry salient. We have given full value to the success of certain British commanders in achieving surprise through keeping their preparations secret. If the performance of Haig and Rawlinson during the days preceding the Battle of Amiens in August were to be the best-kept British secret in the War, these leaders were set a good example by Foch in his preparations for that Mangin offensive which turned the scale on July 18th. He did not take even Haig into his confidence. It may have been a pity that he did not do so, though previous experience proved that he was right in keeping the secret from his own Government.

Foch, as we have seen, had been taken by surprise by the great German attack on the French line on the 27th of May. In July he was better served, and the only error was in the exact date of the impending attack. Foch expected it on July 14th, but it did not come. Access to the original documents of French Field Intelligence are essential to anyone who wants to get to the bottom of that question, but these are not available. Foch received some valuable information from the British Air Force (the R.A.F. had been established in April 1918, and a small independent Air Force was being formed). Some British night-bombers noticed a line of lights, probably from bivouacs, which moved southward on each night before the attack was launched. It may be that Foch relied upon their reports.

Much hinged upon that error of twenty-four hours in General Foch's expectations of attack, as it nearly caused a rupture between him and Haig. On July 12th Foch told Haig's Chief of Staff (Haig being in England) that he wanted Haig to send two more divisions south of the Somme. On July 13th Foch asked Haig to send four divisions and the headquarters of an Army Corps to the French Front at once, the entrainment to begin at 4 p.m. on the 14th. Four more British divisions were to be held in readiness.

Prince Ruprecht's reserves were still waiting to attack the British Army, and Haig was entitled, should he so desire, to protest to his Government against such a demand. He complied with Foch's wishes, but he wrote a letter asking the reasons for the change of view about the situation. (It should be borne in mind that, so far, Foch had only the unfortunate bulge in the French line, made between May 27th and June 2nd, to show as his record.)

Foch was waiting for the attack on July 14th to launch his counter-stroke. The attack did not take place. He then sent a message to Haig to arrange a meeting on the next day (July 15th). He knew that he might not be able to go if things went badly, and in that case he meant to stop Haig from starting for the rendezvous. If the enemy attacked early on the 15th, as Foch hoped, the appointment could be kept. The Germans did attack, early on the 15th, and Foch met Haig, but, even then, he only gave him an inkling of his plan. It was not until the 17th that he sent Haig a message to tell him of the projected counter-stroke, to be launched on July 18th. Haig wished the British IXth Corps to be returned to him, and after he had written another letter on July 17th, the incident was closed by a verbal message from Haig to Foch saying that, if British troops were wanted to exploit a success, they would, of course, be available.

The Mangin counter-stroke of July 18th turned the scales. It transferred the initiative once for all from Ludendorff to Foch. Thenceforward the British Intelligence officers on the front covering Amiens began to find signs of a loss of morale amongst the German troops, as will be explained in the succeeding chapter on the Battle of Amiens of the 8th of August. Personally, I am sure that the Mangin attack would have come equally as a surprise if Foch had taken Haig into his confidence earlier, but the error, if error it was, was on the right side. The result of Foch's secretiveness provides us with another example of the supreme importance of surprise, and of secrecy as the road thereto.

AUTHOR'S NOTE.—Since this chapter was written, the fact has been published that the Intelligence Department of the U.S.A. Army drew the deduction on May 14th that the attack upon the French on May 27th would take place. (See *The Real War*.)

CHAPTER XXII

A WELL-KEPT SECRET OF THE WAR, 1918:

AUGUST 8TH, 'THE DAY OF MOURNING OF THE GERMAN ARMY'

THE 'Mystify and Mislead' of Stonewall Jackson (now a cliché in the British Army), the 'Violence and Cunning' of the German War-Book, the proverb 'All's fair in love and war'—all these point to secrecy and surprise. The commander who can keep his plans secret, and find out those of his enemy, is like a boxer who can see fighting a blind opponent. We have noted some of the most glaring examples of the results of giving away secrets in the Great War, such as those afforded by the failure of the Dardanelles expedition in 1915 and of the Nivelle offensive on the Western Front in 1917. Whoever were responsible for the leakage of information on those occasions, were they soldiers, camp-followers, Cabinet Ministers, or society or street tattlers, bear the responsibility for the wholesale slaughter of their fellow-countrymen in the fighting forces and for the failures that followed.

A most striking lesson in the value of secrecy was afforded by the achievement, described in an early chapter, of the British Counter-Espionage in August 1914; Allenby provided another example in the Third Battle of Gaza, which opened in October 1917, and the one in the Battles of Megiddo in September 1918.[1] Sir Roger Keyes another one at Zeebrugge in April 1918; and Marshal Foch excelled in secrecy before the Mangin counter-stroke of July 18th, 1918. The late Lord Rawlin-

---

[1] See Chapter XXV.

son, by similar methods, won the Battle of Amiens, which began on August 8th, 1918, 'the Day of Mourning of the German Army', to which this chapter will be devoted.

In a war of movement it is easier to secure secrecy than it is in a war of positions. A force can be located (say) at nightfall, but it is difficult for an enemy to predict the direction of its future daily or nightly movements. In trench warfare, on the other hand, many months of experience with the masses on the Western Front had proved by the summer of 1918 the extreme difficulty in keeping secret the preparations for a great attack. Nevertheless complete surprise was achieved in Rawlinson's Fourth Army until the actual moment of advance.

This is not a story of the adventures of secret agents; they were only employed by higher authority. It is a story of Army, Army Corps, Divisional and Brigade Commanders and their Staffs; of Administrative officers and their assistants on the lines of communication; and, perhaps above all, of all ranks in the units in the front line, from commanding officers to private soldiers who played up to the Army Commander and avoided the temptation to gossip. 'The regimental officer and man played up extraordinarily well,' writes a friend who was in high place in that Fourth Army. 'They entered into the spirit of the orders that had been given, and this is proved by the information that we obtained from Intelligence Summaries that we captured from the Germans after the attack had taken place.'

Not even the troops of the nearest British Army (the Third) on the left flank of the Fourth had any idea of what was in store, even after the attack had actually been launched. This I can illustrate by another story. An officer from the nearest brigade of the Third Army (on the immediate left) happened to call at the Fourth Army Headquarters on his way to England on leave. Hearing heavy firing, he asked what the firing was about. He had no idea that anything unusual was taking place, although Rawlinson had put forward on July 16th to Sir Douglas

Haig his proposal to attack as he did, and had then been told to carry on with his preparations. Marshal Foch had approved the plan, after amendment, on July 26th, and he had fixed the actual date (August 8th) on the 1st of August. Rawlinson's Corps commanders knew on July 21st, the divisional commanders on July 30th, the brigade and battalion commanders not until a day and a half to two days before the attack was actually launched.

Coloured notices enjoining secrecy generally about operations were posted up all over the Fourth Army area. In addition to that, a warning of the danger of talking too much was pasted into the pay-book carried by every man in that army. The tale of how the secret was kept from others on the Western Front, outside the Fourth Army, is worth telling, but we first will take note of further steps that were taken to keep it from the Army generally.

Not even the War Office was informed. On July 22nd Sir Henry Wilson, Chief of the Imperial General Staff, obtained only an inkling of what was afoot and wrote in his diary: 'Met Rawly at Abbeville, 8 a.m. He wants Douglas Haig to give him 5 or 6 Divisions and tanks, and let him push out from Villers-Bretonneux; and this is certainly worth thinking about.' (The plan had been drawn up on July 16th and Rawlinson's Army Commanders had it on July 21st.) Then Henry Wilson visited Foch and added: 'I told him of Rawly's proposal, which we discussed and which pleased him.' (Foch had known all about it from Haig since July 17th.)

It is difficult in these days of peace-strengths, when a whole brigade of infantry hardly catches the eye during army training on Salisbury Plain, to recall the appearance of those immense masses of men and material that went to form the war-strength armies of the Great War. To illustrate the difficulty of secrecy when preparing to launch those great masses upon the enemy, we will take one example, the need of large-scale maps. No less than 160,000 of these were required for the advance in the great Battle of Amiens. They were produced by the

Army Printing and Stationery Service and by the Field Survey Battalion. Large quantities of such special maps were always ordered of an area that was to be attacked, and the map-producers were able to form their conclusions accordingly. The fewer people outside the Fourth Army who knew the secret, the better would be the hope of secrecy, so preparation of maps for attacks by other armies were undertaken by the Field Survey workers in the Fourth Army, and the work of preparing the maps which the Fourth Army wanted for its own attack was distributed amongst other armies, so as to avoid mass orders. The results proved that the ruse was effective.

Then again, there was always the possibility that prisoners who were taken in the trench warfare might give away something inadvertently to the enemy. Special lectures were given on this subject to all ranks, and the comparative quiet on the British Front from the end of April to the beginning of August gave opportunities for the lessons to be widely spread. On the 6th of August, two days before the attack, over 200 British prisoners were taken in the Morlancourt sector by the enemy. They were put through a stiff examination. The written account of that examination was captured from the Germans a few days later, and it was found that no information about the projected offensive had been given away. An intelligence officer of my acquaintance tells me that at that stage of the War he could obtain from a group of German prisoners minute details of the trench organization to which the prisoners belonged, including the positions of the headquarters of their platoons, companies and battalions. The information derived from examining larger groups of prisoners would include the positions of batteries, divisional headquarters, and organizations behind the front line.

He also tells me a story, which can well come in here, of various methods that were adopted to ensure secrecy by using extemporized codes and ciphers for messages. Here is one example of a code for which a certain specialist department was responsible. The message when it was coded ran : '*Please send Nettie's drawers—Elsie's drawers are too short.*' It referred to some special requirement in munitions at the Front. Higher authority, lacking in a sense of humour, asked the Army Commander concerned whether he authorized the dispatch of such highly improper messages.

These few notes will suffice to give an impression of how secrecy was achieved in the Fourth Army itself, but in this as in other operations in the main theatres the danger of leakage did not lie with the front-line troops as much as it did with those on the line of communication, at the base, or with gossipers in civil and in military circles at home. I have given an example, from my own experience, of gossip at a luncheon-table in Knightsbridge when the important secret bearing upon our losses at Jutland was given away. That leakage might have done much harm, although it was after the event: to give away the secret of a projected massed attack in the trench warfare on that 300-mile front in France and Flanders simply meant failure. Preparations had to be carried out for weeks. If they were observed by the enemy he had plenty of time to move his reserves nearer to the threatened part of the line, and it was principally for that reason that most of the costly attacks failed to achieve decisive results.

Foch, when he had in his mind the Mangin offensive of July 18th, had been given a bad time by political and other authorities, from the Supreme War Council downwards, during the preceding weeks. He had kept his own counsel even from Haig, upon whom he relied nevertheless to lend British troops to put an extra force into the blow. To previous information we can add Haig's message (in writing) to Lloyd George, just before the Mangin attack, as an example of loyal co-operation by a high commander, kept in the dark by a colleague. Haig wrote: 'I take the risk: and I fully realize that, if the dispositions of (Foch) prove to be wrong, the blame will rest on me. On the other hand, if they prove to be right, the credit will lie with Foch. With this the Government should be well satisfied.' (The full story is given in my recent biography of Marshal Foch.) I can vouch for the fact that nothing was generally known in Whitehall, even when the Fourth Army attack had actually been launched on the morning of the 8th August, 1918. My personal belief is that the Prime Minister and War Cabinet knew nothing, at that time, of the project, but for that I can quote no definite evidence.

When I had the temerity about twenty years ago to perpetrate instructions on the conduct of warfare to Staff College students, I remember having made the suggestion that an Army staff should always contain at least one example of each of the following types: (1) A Fool. All orders should be referred to him, to make sure that they are too clear to be misinterpreted. (2) A Gossip, not to be trusted with real secrets. (3) A skilled Prevaricator, in the confidence of the Commander, to provide No. 2 with suggestions likely to be spread abroad. Whether Rawlinson's Fourth Army Staff was so provided I do not know, and I have not studied the names of the officers serving at his headquarters in order to try to identify the types from amongst my former students. I can, however, give some idea of the false impressions that were purposely conveyed to others outside the Fourth Army. Four or five of these false reports were the subject of current gossip.

It was confidently believed that the Canadian Corps would shortly be engaged in an attack upon Mount Kemmel, a key position which the French had lost to the enemy in April. That rumour was so widely believed that King Albert of the Belgians felt hurt at not having been let into the supposed secret. Another rumour referred to the XXIInd Army Corps which Haig had recently sent to reinforce the French Army at Foch's request. For the 8th of August attack, a Cavalry Corps, the Canadian Corps, and numbers of tanks and batteries of artillery had to be assembled behind the Front. It was universally believed, and I believe that the rumour was deliberately started, that this force was put there to take the place of the XXIInd Corps. Then there was another rumour that the real reason why the Fourth Army was strengthened was because it had received orders to extend its right in order to release French troops to reinforce their own Army in the Argonne country. I have good reason to believe that all these plausible statements emanated from the Fourth Army.

I have written enough, I hope, to show how secrecy was maintained during the weeks before the great battle which was the main factor in starting the great offensive which brought victory to the Allied and Associated Powers in 1918, at a time when all statesmen and nearly all soldiers had given up hope of decisive success before 1919. We have two more aspects with which to deal, one being the secrecy that was maintained during the last hours, while masses of men and material were being crowded into a small space, offering a deadly target for a gas bombardment which would have upset the operation altogether; the other being the methods that were employed to discover the enemy's most secret dispositions, apart from the use of secret agents and spies by higher authorities. In the next chapter we will take the last point first, reserving the concentration as a prelude to the climax.

CHAPTER XXIII

A WELL-KEPT SECRET OF THE WAR, 1918

(Continued)

SINCE both sides were living underground, personal observation by scouts was of little value for gathering intelligence. The most valuable information that was obtained in the Fourth Army about what was going on behind the enemy's lines was obtained from prisoners and from air photographs. Every infantry regimental officer and man who had experience of trench warfare on the Western Front will probably agree that no order was more loathed by the troops in the front line than one to raid a trench and to capture prisoners. Careful preparation was needed, and for some, at all events, of the raiding-party the operation meant certain death, however careful the preparations. It may, however, be some consolation to the survivors to know that the value of their work could not be exaggerated. The information that was obtained from prisoners on this occasion gave the positions of machine-guns, of trench-mortar emplacements, and of many headquarters. When the big attack came, the artillery concentrated their fire upon those vital targets, and so saved the lives of thousands who were engaged in a big attack.

Amongst a large batch of prisoners there would always be a good proportion who were both intelligent and talkative, and apparently they liked showing off their knowledge. It was on the authority of prisoners that the enemy's 'order of battle', the actual enemy units facing the Fourth Army's front, was built up, but not much information could be obtained from their direct state-

253

ments about enemy divisions that were in reserve in areas behind. Air photographs were of great value, both to check what prisoners said, and also for use when a prisoner was being examined, so as to find out what something shown in the photograph represented on the ground. Sometimes batteries were dug during the night, and carefully camouflaged. Prisoners afforded the only information about these batteries.

The morale of the enemy was another important point that was ascertained from prisoners: from their attitude, appearance and conversation, and from their documents. There is no doubt that morale had deteriorated considerably, especially since the Mangin counter-stroke launched by Foch in July. Instructions had been issued from Haig's Headquarters to pay special attention to the categories to which the prisoners belonged, and it became evident that man-power was at last beginning to fail, judging from the extreme youth of some of the lads who were captured. Then again, the absence of barbed wire in front of the German defence-line, months after an offensive had been launched from that front, was taken as a proof of slackness and depression. (It might possibly, with equal probability, have been due to a plan which had been made by Prince Ruprecht's reserves to attack the British again, if the thrust on both sides of Rheims on July 15th towards Chalons had succeeded. That move, as we know now, had been countered by Foch's attacks from July 18th onwards, which drew reserves in that direction to extricate the Germans from an awkward salient south of Soissons.) The knowledge of the absence of wire, whatever the true reason may have been, had a heartening effect upon the Fourth Army. They could hardly conceive that they were opposed by the same enemy whose wire-defences, upon which an immense amount of labour had been expended, were the envy and despair of the British troops who had attacked in the First Battle of the Somme in July 1918.

An astounding amount of information about the situation of the reserves behind the German front line was obtained from captured documents, mostly private letters. News was thus obtained about divisions in the back areas when men belonging to them wrote to their friends in the trenches announcing their arrival. Such information from the enemy's side sometimes arrived only a few hours before a projected raid, so the news reached Headquarters 'red-hot'. Anyone who retains memories of the monotony of trench warfare will recall the fact that it was expecting almost too much of human nature to be certain that all men would leave their private correspondence behind them in back-billets when they were sent forward to the trenches. Some intimate letters were far too precious to be abandoned, and the Germans probably obtained much valuable information in the same way. Documents that were taken from the German prisoners at that period showed that the loss of morale applied, not only to the troops, but also to the civil population in Germany, whose letters were full of complaints of the shortage of food and the difficulties of life in general. Secret Service agents behind the German lines doubtless sent in a good deal of information to Haig's General Headquarters about the divisions in reserve there, but with that we are not concerned when describing the intelligence policy in the Fourth Army.

The general result was that Rawlinson had ascertained from his Intelligence Department that he would be opposed by six German divisions. As matters turned out, the night of August 7th/8th had been chosen for certain reliefs, which slightly raised the total number of divisions encountered in the front line. That was really to the advantage of the British. 'Never relieve during a battle' was Foch's maxim, and perhaps the Germans would have followed it if they had known that there was to be a battle. The result was that neither relievers nor relieved were at the disposal of the German Headquarters as a reserve for emergencies.

The general result of the Secret Services in the Fourth Army before the decisive Battle of Amiens of August 8th, 1918, was that its massed attack came as a complete surprise, and that the Fourth Army Commander had at his disposal an extraordinarily accurate detailed estimate of the strength of the German forces in his front, and of their distribution. This estimate showed 52 battalions in the enemy's forward areas, and 20 battalions in the back areas, a total of 72 battalions with 17,000 rifles, 1,400 light machine-guns and 870 machine-guns.

'How' it may now be asked 'could Rawlinson's masses of tanks, batteries and troops have possibly been brought into a crowded area close behind the front of the Fourth Army, exposed to gas bombardment if discovered, without giving any indications to the enemy?' To the answer to that question we will now turn. Some idea of what the secret concentration of such masses may mean can be gathered from a few special notes. By long and careful preparation the speed of a concentration can be greatly increased, and during the last few hours before a great attack, speed means secrecy.

During the week preceding the advance, 290 special trains (230 for reinforcements and 60 for extra ammunition) were run into the Amiens area. No transport was allowed to move eastward by daylight in the Fourth Army area, and aeroplanes constantly watched to see whether any abnormal movements were going on behind the enemy's lines. That watch was kept up until the night of August 7th/8th. The Canadians, destined with the Australians to take a leading part in the advance, did not take over the front line until about 2.30 a.m., zero hour being 4.20. During the preceding days they had been kept far in rear, and the Germans had no idea that they were anywhere in the neighbourhood. (The Canadians had arrived in the night of July 30th/31st.) Reconnoitring officers were warned to go about only in very small parties, and to forgo the habit, all too common, of waving conspicuous maps about in the front line. Newly-arrived batteries were forbidden general registration of ranges to their targets.

The actual concentration began during the night of July 29th/30th. A thousand extra guns then began to arrive and to take up their positions. This work was completed on the night of August 5th/6th, with liberal dumps of ammunition close at hand. There were 600 rounds for each field-gun and 400 for the big howitzers up to 8-inch bore. Even the huge 12-inch pieces each had 200 rounds. 456 tanks, including 96 whippets, were concentrated in the area. They began to arrive during the night of July 31st/August 1st, and they were all ready by dawn on August 5th. Some had come on their own tracks; most of them had come on railway trucks.

The mass of cavalry presented special difficulties. Experience had proved the fatal effect, from the point of view of secrecy, of sending masses of horses to water the (same, of course, applied to the horse-artillery). The presence of the cavalry was kept secret by keeping it far away, near Auxi-le-Château, until the last moment. Thence they came in three night-marches, and they were just west of Amiens on the night of August 6th/7th. They marched through the town on the night of the 7th/8th and they were ready on the open plain at zero hour next morning.

We can picture to ourselves the hushed multitude during that night of August 7th/8th, with its atmosphere of tense anticipation, and of wonder whether the great secret had really been safely guarded, a question of life or of death for thousands. Fulfilment of the hope to crown with achievement those days and nights of elaborate preparation and ceaseless labour seemed too good to be true, but the German morale was known to be low. In addition to the intelligence reports already mentioned, there had been some corroborative evidence. The Australians in a surprise attack in the Hamel area on July 4th, had sent forward 6 battalions on a front of about 4 miles, supported by 60 tanks, and they had taken 1,500 prisoners.

On the other side of the balance must be put some disturbing and more recent events. During the 3rd of August, only four days before, a small party of Australians (a sergeant and four men) had the bad luck to be captured by the enemy on the Roye road, east of the River Luce. Had they given anything away? Certainly not intentionally, but they might have been overheard talking to each other or they might have been tripped up in examination.[1] Then, on August 6th, just before the final day, a heavy German attack was launched before the 18th Division, north of the River Somme. It was then that the 200 prisoners, mentioned above, were captured. The attack was a heavy one. It was intended to fall upon the Australians as a reprisal for their former attentions, and it was carried out by the 27th Wurtemberger Division, which consisted of special storming-troops, sent there for the purpose and supported by no less than 96 batteries and by 32 mortars. It seemed hardly possible that nothing had been disclosed to the enemy by so large a body of prisoners.[1] The situation on that night has been described to me by a senior officer in the Fourth Army as 'disturbing'.

So the dark hours passed, in expectation and in wonder whether complete surprise was really to be achieved, for nearly the first time, by a British Army on the Western Front. Rawlinson's original plan had been changed by Marshal Foch. Experience of Allied attacks had proved to Rawlinson that, difficult as it was to keep a big British attack secret, it was hopeless with Allied attacks because arrangements for them had to pass through so many channels that the news invariably reached the enemy in plenty of time for reserves to be moved towards the threatened part of the line. Gossips on the lines of communication and at the base were always looking out for stories to display their knowledge of what was going on

[1] Further details will be found in Chapter XXIV.

at the front, and every military secret that reached the inter-Allied political sphere was as good as told to the enemy. Nivelle had learned that to his cost in his big attack in the spring of 1917 that was to end the War out of hand. For this, and for reasons based upon greater military effectiveness, Rawlinson's original intention had been to make the Battle of Amiens an affair for British Empire troops alone. The French, he hoped, would make a simultaneous attack in force from the direction of Montdidier. After some discussion, however, Foch's plan for a French Army Corps on the British right to participate in the attack was adopted.

The audacity of the plan, and the reliance that was placed upon the effect of secrecy, can be gathered from the figures which follow. During the tremendous attack by the Germans upon Gough's (Fifth) British Army, launched on the 21st of March—with a screen of dense fog giving the attackers the benefit of complete cover from view—40 German Divisions attacked 14 British Divisions and 3 cavalry Divisions, who were reinforced the next week by only one single Division (the 8th), 40 German Divisions against 15 British. In the Amiens battle of the 8th of August, 11 'British' Divisions (4 of them were Canadians and 4 were Australians), backed up by 3 cavalry Divisions, attacked the German Second Army (Marwitz, whose acquaintance we made in describing the retreat from Mons) which contained 15 Divisions, two of which were attacked by the French XXXIst Corps, on the British right. During the next three days 12 more Divisions reinforced the German side and only 3 Divisions reinforced Rawlinson's Army. The net result was that Rawlinson's total of 14 Divisions and 3 cavalry Divisions encountered, in four days' fighting, 25 German Divisions, many of which they destroyed.

Such was the Battle of Amiens, the 'Day of Mourning of the German Army' (Ludendorff). When the battle began on the 8th of August, the Crown Prince Ruprecht, in command of the group of armies to which that of

CHAPTER XXIV

INFORMATION FROM PRISONERS:
GERMAN MORALE IN 1918

WHEN one examines original documents showing the information that was gathered by the British Empire Armies in France and Flanders, few points strike more than the completeness of the reports about the enemy hidden away on the other side of 'No-Man's Land'. Nearly every hostile division was correctly located in the later stages, whether it was in the front line or in reserve. Intelligence maps, constantly kept up to date, show the lines of defence that were held, the positions of important headquarters, batteries and communications. The system of obtaining the information had gradually been built up after many months of experience in the almost static warfare of the trenches.

The principal sources of information, as obtained by the field-intelligence, were prisoners' statements and documents, refugees from areas occupied by the enemy, air-observation and photographs, listening-sets, survey-posts and artillery sound-ranging sections, and wireless communications generally. Streams of information emanating from these varied sources poured into 'Intelligence' ('I' of the General Staff) at Army and at Army-Corps Headquarters. There it was all checked, compared and co-ordinated in statements which became more and more accurate as experience was gained. These statements were passed on to 'Operations' ('O' of the General Staff). The reason why the recording and co-ordinating was done as far back from the front-line as Corps Headquarters was that in operations on such a huge scale the division became a tactical unit, constantly relieved in the front line, while the Headquarters of higher informations were seldom moved.

Going back to July 1st, 1916, the opening day of the Battle of the Somme, which provided the baptism of fire of the New British Armies, the records show that within a week of that momentous day the Intelligence Department was dangerously in the dark. Troops had been seen behind the enemy's defence-line, but few deductions could be made about the significance of the movements that had been observed. Raids upon the enemy's trenches had failed, and the few prisoners who were captured were either ignorant or reticent. Then the preliminary bombardment opened, and the opportunity was seized to launch raiding-parties by night to ascertain how far the gunners had been successful in cutting paths through the wire entanglements, whether the enemy's troops in the front line had been reinforced, and whether he was expecting the impending attack.

The result of these raids was immediately apparent and 'I' was able within a few hours to tell 'O' the exact number of enemy divisions that were likely to be met with in the front line and in immediate reserve. Complete information on these points was disclosed in letters and in documents taken either from prisoners, from raided dug-outs, or from the dead. At first there had been a tendency amongst the troops to retain some of the documents as 'souvenirs', but this tendency was soon overcome, and the number which reached their proper destination—'Intelligence' at Corps Headquarters—rapidly increased. The disclosure of German mentality was particularly helpful, especially the almost universal habit amongst German soldiers of keeping intimate private diaries and their craving to be photographed in uniform, often in groups.

A captured diary showed what the man who kept it did, thought and hoped; what places he had visited, what route he had followed, how long he had stayed in each place, what he had had to eat and drink, and information in abundance that was of value to his enemy. The censorship of field-postcards was strangely remiss on the German side in those days. The cards showed the addresses of the men to whom they were sent, and the name, regiment and address of the sender. Picture postcards of groups of men (indications on the uniform showing the unit to which they belong) showed on the postmarks the place of origin and date, from which valuable deductions could be made. Many definite examples of the use to the Intelligence officers of documents that were found on German soldiers could be given. I select two, the date being September 1916, and I suppress the details which would make exact identification possible if the men concerned are still alive.

On September 7th a deserter from the enemy near Delville Wood carried on his person a battalion order which showed that the regiment to which the battalion belonged would be relieved by another by a specified route at a stated time. The opportunity was taken to bombard the main communication trenches at the critical moment, and the relieving regiment suffered such heavy casualties that it was only left in the front line for two days. During the same month, a soldier who was taken prisoner near Martinpuich carried on him a copy of a regimental order which stated the time at which the regiment would be relieved. It also gave instructions for the guides who were to meet the advanced parties at a small specified village, and information that motor-buses would meet the troops at a certain church.

Even dirty old envelopes and postcards that were picked up in trenches and in dug-outs sometimes gave information of infinite value to the higher commands. Soldiers' pay-books showed, by disclosing the history of each man, the rate at which the German reserves were being used up, and the age categories from which the last contingents were being drawn. The importance of all the collecting and sifting and of the examination of prisoners thus becomes obvious, but not the difficulties which had to be faced when prisoners came in by the thousand. The Provost-Marshal's department, in whose charge they were, naturally wanted to rush them through to the rear as fast as possible to avoid administrative difficulties over supply, provision of escorts and so forth. Proper examination entailed the provision of special systems of 'cages', sorting out different ranks, selecting the most promising subjects for cross-examination and many other details. All these things meant delays, which were reduced as the result of experience. Each man's documents were tied up in a packet for which labels were kept in readiness to show names, dates and places of capture.

The Germans also learned by experience, as can be gathered from the foregoing account of the methods by which they completely deceived the French Army Field Intelligence in the attack of May 27th, 1918, which forced the defenders back to the Marne, but after the tide had been turned by the Mangin offensive of July 18th in that year, and German prisoners in larger numbers began again to fall into the hands of the Allies, the same troubles recurred and a strong circular was issued on the subject. It began with typical propaganda clauses, intended to frighten men inclined to surrender by stating that, if they fell into enemy's hands, they would be subjected to 'unexampled brutality of treatment' and to 'being slowly tortured to death'. A confession followed to the effect that the War had provided many instances where prisoners' statements, unfortunately only too accurate, had had disastrous effects for their own comrades. The success of German attacks had thus been imperilled; the issue of the War might be jeopardized, and the whole Fatherland might be gravely injured. As an inspiration for others, the name was quoted of a young German soldier, 19 years old, who in August 1917 had pleaded his soldier's oath and refused to give any information. The circular of July 1918 concluded with a warning to prisoners who did give away information, threatening them with criminal proceedings after the War, and with 'great unpleasantness for their relatives (parents, brothers, sisters, wife and child)'.

In the preceding chapter we took account of the anxiety lest prisoners taken before August 8th, 1918, from the 18th Division and from a small Australian patrol should have given away the secret. Five officers and 231 other ranks of the 18th Division had been captured in the heavy attack which was intended as a reprisal against the Australians who until recently had occupied that portion of the line. The captured Australian patrol had consisted of five men under a sergeant. Reports of their examination on the 6th of August were captured from the enemy during the Fourth Army's successful advance.

The officers and men of the 18th Division gave away no information about the preparations, then reaching a climax, for the great attack, and the report of the examination of the Australian patrol speaks for itself:

'The prisoners are young men, 21 to 31 years of age. They give one a good soldierly impression although their military knowledge is limited.[1] The sergeant, who was the only one who had served a long and unbroken period with the troops, refused to make any military statement and could not be shaken in his resolve by any means employed. The remainder were, some a short time with their battalion, others, on account of wounds, a long time in hospital or convalescent. Whether their statements are pretence or truth there is no means of proving. All were reticent.

'Their general feeling was confident. They speak a great deal of the American assistance. . . .[2] No reports could be got from them about lights, air-service, meteorological service, Verey lights, dirigible balloons, captive balloons, butts for Lewis gun, long-range shooting,

[1] By their discretion in not disclosing it?
[2] A point of interest for those who minimize the moral effect of American participation.—AUTHOR.

attachment of guns to mechanical limbers, bombing of back areas, or defence against yellow cross gas.'

That patrol earned special mention in Australian Corps Orders. Nearly all the headings on the German examination form were marked 'No information' or 'Nothing of importance'.

During the second week in August, 1918, an escaped British prisoner (a Company Sergeant-Major in the Coldstream Guards) who had been in German prison camps from November, 1914, to March, 1918, furnished a valuable report about German methods of eliciting information from prisoners which, with other reports, were embodied in full instructions on the subject from Haig's Headquarters. As with us, documents and letters were examined, and to that were added verbal examinations both formal and under cover of casual conversation. Agents, disguised as British or Allied Officers or soldiers, mixed with the prisoners in their camps or in hospitals. Sometimes these agents simulated wounds. Listening apparatus, to tap private conversations between prisoners, was installed in the rooms or in the camps in which they were confined.

I have before me, as I write, the German account, dated the 6th of September, 1918, of the number of British Empire and Allied Divisions on the Western Front on that date. The total number (211 and 10 cavalry divisions) is correctly estimated. The errors cancelled each other. The number of new American Divisions was under-estimated by four, the number of other Divisions was over-estimated by one. Two British and one French Division that were shown were not present. In their estimate of the number of divisions in the front line the Germans paid the British the compliment of counting as 18 the 11 divisions south of the Scarpe opposite to the 17th German Army.

Of the total of 211 Allied Divisions, 17 were wrongly placed in the front line, and 42 were wrongly placed in stantly under supervision, and resistance was to be broken by armed force.

We read in prisoners' reports of the morale amongst officers being bad, of complaints against orders that were issued by higher commands; of troops from the Russian front and drafts for the front line in the West being in a state of revolt; of the effect of the loss of ground, captured at great cost in March and April, upon the troops; of numerous desertions, and of general insubordination amongst formations in rear; of arrests upon a large scale; of men cheering when important headquarters were heavily shelled by British guns; of dismay when the extent to which divisions in reserve were being used up in August was realized; and of the effect which the opinions of soldiers on leave had upon the morale of the civil population. Complaints have been made by German military authorities since the War that the defeat of the German Army was attributable to lack of support, due to loss of morale, in the German nation. The evidence of prisoners and of captured secret documents during those days shows that the boot was undoubtedly on the other leg. It was the defeat of the Army, superimposed upon the sea-blockade, that caused the loss of morale in the nation. This was definitely indicated by Ludendorff himself, in an order which he issued on the 3rd of September, in which he referred to the increase in the number of complaints received from Germany that men on leave from the Front were creating an unfavourable impression by making statements that bordered on high treason and incitement to disobedience. He added that 'Instances such as these drag the honour and respect of the individual as well as of the whole Army into the mud, and *have a disastrous effect upon the morale of the people at home.*'

Late in August and during the first three weeks in September there were further indications that the avalanche was beginning to slip (down an inclined plane and increasing in speed, as Marshal Foch put it afterwards), and we come across in captured documents frantic appeals by higher commanders to their troops to hold their ground. Machine-gunners and artillery seem to have been little shaken by the prevailing spirit, and they continued to offer a formidable resistance. A report of examination of prisoners who were captured on August 30th and 31st states that there appeared to be little actual desertion amongst German soldiers in the front line; that surrender when attacked was looked upon as safer, and was freely indulged in by non-commissioned officers and men. The officers themselves were steadfast, but could not control the wholesale surrenders amongst other ranks. Respect amongst men with years of army experience for young officers without it was constantly decreasing.

By the 27th of September the conclusion arrived at at Haig's Headquarters was that the failure of the great German attacks upon the British portion of the Allied line in March and upon the French portion in July, followed by Allied successes on the Western Front and upon other theatres, had caused considerable depreciation in the German morale. Still, however, there remained in front of the British Empire Army the great 'Hindenburg Line' of defences, believed to be impregnable, upon which over two years' labour had been expended.

Some of the secret services whereby information was gained about that Hindenburg Line will form the subject of a future chapter. Meanwhile we will return to the subject of surprise in open warfare, as practised by Allenby in his campaign in Palestine and in Syria.

on the Jaffa flank to cross the formidable obstacle of the Nahr El Auja, a river which runs into the sea north of Jaffa and is only fordable in places. Nor need we take into account the attempt by fresh Turkish troops to recapture Jerusalem, except to note that 'Intelligence' gave good warning of that attack, which was repulsed.

There followed an advance into Mount Ephraim, the descent in February into the Valley of the Jordan, the occupation of Jericho, various raids, the crossing of the Jordan at the end of March, and then, in April, the dispatch of a large proportion of Allenby's Army to the Western Front in Europe, where, as can be gathered from previous chapters, they were sorely needed. The period from May to September was occupied in holding the ground that had been gained, in reorganization and reinforcement, and in preparing for a final advance. This was the position early in September. Allenby had wrested from the enemy the whole of the country south of a line running from a point on the coast rather more than 10 miles north of Jaffa, to a point on the Jordan nearly 20 miles north of the Dead Sea and some of the country beyond. Eastward of the Jordan and Dead Sea the Turks still held the Hedjaz Railway as far southward as Ma'an (60 miles south of the Dead Sea), and they possessed a railway which ran from behind the Jaffa flank to El Afule and to Haifa on the coast. From El Afule there was also a line which ran along the Jordan Valley to the southern end of Lake Tiberias, and thence to join the Hedjaz Railway at Deraa.

Away in the Desert, about 70 miles eastward of the point where the River Jordan runs out of the Dead Sea, and about 50 miles eastward of the Hedjaz Railway, an Arab Northern Army had its headquarters. Of the doings of those Arabs controlled by Emir (now King) Feisal, Colonel Lawrence has written an epic tale. We will not trespass on his preserves. We will return to Allenby, to his plan for defeating the whole Turkish Army, and to the way in which that plan was kept secret. He decided

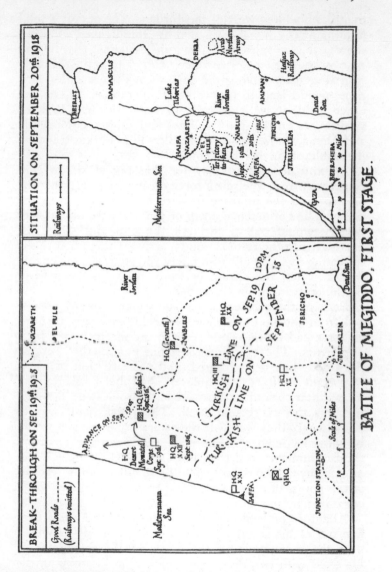

SITUATION ON SEPTEMBER 20ᵗʰ 1918

Railways ———

BEIRUT

DAMASCUS

Arab Northern Army

DERAA

Hejaz Railway

Lake Tiberias

River Jordan

AMMAN

HAIFA

NAZARETH

EL FULE

NABLUS

Sept. 20ᵗʰ 1918

JERICHO

Dead Sea

Mediterranean Sea

JERUSALEM

JAFFA

GAZA

BEERSHEBA

5 0 10 20 30 40 Miles

BREAK-THROUGH ON SEP.19ᵗʰ 19-8

Good Roads - - - -
(Railways omitted)

NAZARETH

EL FULE

River Jordan

ADVANCE ON SEP.19ᵗʰ

HQ (English) Sept.26th

HQ (Seventh)

NABLUS

HQ XX

1.0 P.M 18

HQ Desert Mounted Corps Sep.9th

HQ XXII Sept.18th

TURKISH LINE ON SEP.19

TURKISH HQ.III

TURKISH LINE ON SEPTEMBER

HQ XII

JERICHO

JERUSALEM

HQ XXI

JAFFA

GHQ

JUNCTION STATION

Scale of Miles
10 0 5 10

Mediterranean Sea

Dead Sea

BATTLE OF MEGIDDO, FIRST STAGE.

to strike his blow west of the Jordan. The enemy's total fighting strength was estimated by 'Intelligence' at 4,000 sabres, 32,000 rifles, and 400 guns. Against that he had 12,000 sabres, 57,000 rifles, and 540 guns. Purely frontal attacks, driving the enemy back a few miles each time, would lead to interminable operations. If, on the other hand, it were possible to burst through to such vital points on the Turkish lines and supply as El Afule and Deraa, a *débâcle* would result. The Turks would be incapable of further resistance.

Allenby decided to play for that big stake, to concentrate an overwhelming force on his left, near the sea, and to send the infantry forward to make a gap in the enemy's line of defence north of Jaffa. There the mass of cavalry would gallop through the gap and strike far northward to the critical points, arriving there before the retreating foe. Cut off from safety and supplies, the enemy would be left the option between death on the field of battle, starvation, or surrender.

Perhaps the greatest advantage which Allenby possessed from the point of view of intelligence was that his air force had by that time secured the mastery over their opponents. The hostile aerodromes behind the Turkish lines had thus been located, and the situation of every important military headquarters had been ascertained. The military headquarters were left unmolested; 'fattened up' was the expression used. The great point was to know where they were. If they were bombed they would be moved elsewhere. The plan was to leave them until the last moment, and then to bomb them intensively out of existence. The result would be to cut communications at the points of convergence and to paralyse the enemy's organization and command.

Allenby's general plan was to concentrate no less than five out of his seven infantry divisions on his left flank near the coast, holding the whole of the remainder of his front with two divisions. Behind the infantry on the left the cavalry divisions were to be massed, and Allenby believed that, if a gap were made at once for them to get through the wire, it would not be too much to expect the cavalry to move up 45 to 60 miles and to reach as their destinations El Afule in the Plain of Esdraelon and Beisan in the Valley of Jezreel. For this to be possible, the cavalry must move fast enough to anticipate the retreating enemy before he could reach the hills of Samaria, or their extension towards Mount Carmel on the coast. Those must be crossed before the Esdraelon Plain or the Jezreel Valley could be reached. With such names constantly in evidence it is not surprising that there was a great demand for copies of the Old Testament in Allenby's force.

The coastal plain north of Jaffa is about 10 miles wide. The Turks had two systems of defence, one 14,000 yards long and 3,000 yards deep; the other, 3,000 yards behind the first, easy to hold with a few men, as much of the ground was marshy. There could be no half-measures. All the eggs must be in one basket to make sure of success, so on this (Sharon) front there were to be 35,000 rifles against 8,000 Turks, and 383 guns against 130. In order to achieve this, the Jordan Valley and the hills north of Jerusalem where Allenby's reserves were stationed had almost to be denuded of troops. It was necessary to make sure that the two cavalry divisions and the Australian Mounted Division were not appreciably delayed. Surprise was essential. When the cavalry had established themselves behind the line the infantry were to make a further advance and drive the enemy into their hands. Such was the plan, and now for its execution. The 19th of September was chosen for the main advance.

Olive and orange groves were available behind the line to conceal the infantry divisions massed on the left flank. To these positions they moved silently by night, without being observed. The cavalry, far away in the Valley of the Jordan, presented greater difficulty. In our study of the massing, in a small area near Amiens, of Rawlinson's army that was destined to strike the blow on the German Army's 'Day of Mourning', the most difficult arm to conceal was found to be the cavalry. Their masses of horses had to be sent to water, and observers in the air could easily spot the horses, even when little dust was raised.

The routes that led from the horse-lines to the water in the Jordan Valley were deep in soft, impalpable dust. Dust and flies in Palestine and Syria took the place of the mud and lice in the trenches in Flanders. When horses went to water dense columns of choking dust rose in the air. The animals were knee-deep in it. The scene can be imagined by anyone with experience of the dust-clouds that were raised by columns of troops moving across the veld in the South African War. Such columns could be seen for 30 miles or more, but there was nothing in South Africa to equal that dust in the Jordan Valley.

The enemy saw great clouds of the dust every day on Allenby's right flank when the cavalry were sent to water. If at any time there were no such clouds, the deduction would be obvious. The cavalry must have moved elsewhere. Secrecy therefore hinged upon dust. The cavalry could move by night, but not the whole way from one flank to the other, on the night of September 18th/19th, and arrive with horses fresh ready for the great ride over the hills of Samaria and across the Plains of Esdraelon and Jezreel. They must move some nights beforehand, and rest concealed somewhere till the moment came for the great adventure. The dust-columns would be missed directly they left the Jordan Valley, so there was only one solution—artificial dust.

From the morning after the cavalry had slipped away from the right flank there were to be seen, going up and down to water by the tracks generally used by the cavalry horses, team after team of mules dragging great branches of trees and every possible device to stir up the impalpable dust-clouds. These rose in great columns at the appointed hours and led the enemy to believe that nothing unusual was happening. That he was deceived was proved by the following incident.

When the Headquarters of the Yilderim Army Group at Nazareth fell into the hands of Allenby's troops an intelligence 'Disposition Map' was captured. It was issued on the day before the Battle of Sharon. It supported reports received from the air that 'No essential changes had taken place in the disposition of the British Forces'. On the whole, that map was extraordinarily accurate in representing what that disposition *had* been. The only important mistakes were made in placing (with a query) the 6th Poona Division of Indian troops (which had gone to Mesopotamia), in omitting Allenby's real Headquarters, and in misplacing by 11 miles the Headquarters of the Commander of the XXIst Corps (Sir E. S. Bulfin), which was to lead the advance.

In the modest official account of this campaign that was prepared locally we read (September 18th):

'The way in which the preliminary concentration was carried out and concealed from the enemy was one of the most remarkable achievements of the whole operations.

'A hostile aeroplane reconnaissance on the 15th September reported as follows: "Some regrouping of cavalry units apparently in progress behind the enemy's left flank; otherwise nothing to report."

'And this at a time when three cavalry Divisions, five infantry Divisions, and the majority of the heavy artillery of the force were concentrated between Ramleh and the front line of the coastal sector, there being 301 guns in place of the normal number of 70.

'On the same date the enemy Intelligence Staff was advised in another aeroplane report that General Allenby's Headquarters at Bir Salem was an "infantry camp, two battalions." '

On the appointed day Bulfin's infantry burst through, making a gap for the cavalry. Much depended on the occupation of Megiddo, the main gateway through the hills. It was only by speed and by making the most of the opportunity created by the infantry for the horsemen that a handful of Indian cavalry [1] anticipated—by only half an hour—a whole battalion of Turkish infantry which were seen moving up from the lower ground to occupy and hold the pass.

Two days before the battle (September), Allenby's air force had bombed the important railway junction at Deraa, where the railway-line from the coast at Haifa joins the Hedjaz railway to Damascus. On both sides of Deraa the Arabs, from their base 50 miles away in the Eastern Desert had made the railway-track impassable through their demolitions on September 17th and 18th. Defeat was turned into a rout. The nearest Turkish armies to the west, the Seventh and Eighth, became a rabble. At Nazareth Marshal Liman von Sanders, the German High Commander, only escaped capture by minutes. At the first alarm, it is said that he left his bed clad in pyjamas and equipped only with an electric torch to seek his fast motor-car, but he had time to return for a few minutes to his headquarters to dress before he fled. A German aeroplane landed on a captured aerodrome far behind the lines, the pilot not realizing its loss.

Their communications cut, the retreat of the IInd and IVth Turkish Corps beyond the Jordan and Dead Sea was inevitable, but they also were involved in the disaster. The IInd Corps surrendered; the IVth was destroyed. Damascus fell on October 1st, Beirut on October 8th, Aleppo on the night of October 25th. An Armistice was granted to Turkey, left defenceless by the destruction of the main army. It came into force at noon on October 31st. In the meanwhile the War had been won by the defeat of the main German Army on the Western Front where, according to reports from German sources, the breaking of the Hindenburg Line was the decisive factor.

[1] Preceded by armoured cars.

CHAPTER XXVI

THE FINALE ON THE WESTERN FRONT

URING the closing weeks of the Great War unful-filled promises of German victories resulted in strong reaction. Loss of morale in the Army was reflected amongst a people suffering acutely from the slow pressure of Allied sea-power.

One of the strongest impressions left upon the mind when studying naval and military history, is the impotence of words, in the long run, to counter the results of deeds. The War was ultimately won by the fighting men of the Navy, Army and Air Forces, of whom a million in the British Empire alone lost their lives as battle casualties; by 'Unknown Warriors' sometimes in spite of, rather than with the help of the men of spoken or of written words. It was through the fighters that openings were made for the propagandists whose business it was, through secret and other channels, to infect bodies politic and fighting forces with decay, to hasten an enemy's collapse in the days of impending defeat, or to cheer their own nation in adversity. It is desirable here to make a short digression on the subject

One sort of war propaganda—the least effective in the long run—took the form of direct falsehood, of which an example from history has been given in connection with Nelson's victory at Trafalgar. It was through the use of such methods that the expression 'To lie like a bulletin' became proverbial in the Napoleonic era, and bulletins lost their force. I gained my own first experience of that form of propaganda immediately after the Anglo-Boer War in South Africa, where I had just been for a long trek with a mounted column composed of British Yeomanry, Canadians, West Australians and New Zealanders. It had fallen to my task as chief staff-officer of the column, to examine all claims that were made by the civil population against the troops. I had received only one, during a long trek of five or six hundred miles. Someone's pet dog had followed one of the units in our column on the march, and it had been treated so well that it had not returned to its home. That experience was typical of the behaviour of British Empire troops in other similar columns in that war, but subsidized propaganda in the European Press invented imaginary horrors perpetrated by British soldiers against a defenceless people. One paragraph described with gusto how women, stripped naked, were driven into cattle-kraals. Such deliberate falsehoods were not subtle enough to be effective.

There must be some substratum of truth, however small, as a basis for propaganda, even if facts are distorted and the truth twisted. I came across an example of that form of propaganda when the Germans evacuated Lille in 1918 in their final retreat. Two papers were placed upon my table in the War Cabinet office in Whitehall on the same day. One of them stated that, when British troops arrived at the outskirts of the town, the idea occurred to the General in command that the people of Lille, after having been under the heel of the invader for nearly four years, would probably like to greet their own victorious fellow-countrymen first. The nearest French troops were 8 miles away. The British were halted until they could arrive to head the column. The other paper contained the account of the same incident that was published broadcast by German wireless. There I read that the French had insisted on sending their own troops on ahead, in order to protect the women of Lille from the British soldiers. Such is propaganda, in its baser (and less effective) forms.

Here is an example of a more effective twisting of the truth in order to produce a desired effect. Sir Douglas Brownrigg, the Chief Naval Censor, tells us how, in the early days of the War, a film was taken of the Grand Fleet at Scapa and of the activities of British seamen, of which little was known to the public. The picture was called 'Britain Prepared'. It was sent across the Atlantic. There it fell into hands notoriously unsympathetic with the idea of goodwill between the English-speaking nations, and the title was altered to '*How* Britain Prepared'.

I can only recall two examples of deceptive British propaganda in the Great War. One was the circulation of the human corpses story, that the Germans (whose respect for the dead is well known) were sending trainloads of corpses to be boiled down for their fats. I have been told that the exploitation of that story was due to the linguistic ignorance of the circulator, who thought that the German word *Kadaver* (dead body of any animal) had the same meaning as the French word *Cadavre* (a human corpse). It was a pity that the error was not promptly confessed. The other was an example of suppressing a truth likely to do harm in the opinion of naval authorities. The battleship *Audacious* struck a mine which had been laid by the Germans off the north coast of Ireland in October 1914. The incident was watched by the passengers in the *Olympic*, on her way to New York, and they took photographs of her in a sinking condition. Her loss was not admitted by the Admiralty until the end of the War, four years later. The attempts to keep her loss secret were made at the instance of Sir John Jellicoe, commanding the Grand Fleet, because owing to repairs and other causes he had only 17 effective battleships, 5 battle cruisers and 42 destroyers at that time against 15 battleships, 4 battle cruisers and 88 destroyers with the High Seas Fleet. The German Admiralty must have been puzzled for some time as a New York paper published a picture of the *Audacious* as she *rejoined* (!) the Grand Fleet, describing the work that had been done upon her in dock at Belfast, where the men were said to have worked in day and night shifts. However effective that ruse may have been at the time, it did not score in the long run. It shook the confidence

283

of the British public and of foreign nations in the *bona fides* of British announcements, and it gave the Germans useful help in their own propaganda until they made a similar mistake over their Jutland announcement, of which they, too, felt the recoil.

One of the best comments on propaganda in war that reached me after I had joined the War Cabinet office early in 1918 was contained in a remark by Raisuli, the Moor, that he would be ready to believe in the victories constantly claimed by one side when they were acknowledged as defeats by the other.

By that date British propaganda was being dealt with by a number of different authorities, and I was charged for a few weeks with the task of co-ordinating their efforts behind the scenes. The Admiralty and the War Office both dealt with propaganda, and the Foreign Office had its 'Political Intelligence Department' which undertook similar work. So, to some extent, did the Colonial Office, and throughout the War there had been a committee of members of Parliament, presided over by the Chief Whip, on which all shades of political opinion—including those with a tendency to pacificism—were represented. The result was rather a discordant chorus, so I arranged a weekly meeting of representatives of the different propagandist authorities at a round table in my office in Whitehall Gardens. While we were getting into our stride a system was adopted that the Parliamentary committee should cover the United Kingdom (a special arrangement being made to deal with Ireland), that Lord Northcliffe should deal with propaganda in enemy countries, and that Lord Beaverbrook, who had joined the Government as Minister of Information, should deal with Allied and neutral countries.

I then received a visit from a representative of Lord Northcliffe who explained a new proposal to form a 'Propaganda Policy Committee', to take over the work upon which I had been engaged. I was a member of that committee to keep its activities in touch with those of the

War Cabinet. The only change that was made in the system described was that Lord Northcliffe took over propaganda in one Allied country, Italy, and Lord Beaverbrook became responsible for Turkey, an enemy country.

The activities of that Propaganda Policy Committee have been described in a book by Sir Campbell Stuart, who took the chair in Lord Northcliffe's absence. I can only recall having taken an active part in the deliberations of the committee on two occasions. Once I raised a question—I thought with sufficient cause—whether the committee held that Propaganda should govern Policy, or that the Policy of the Cabinet and the country should govern its Propaganda. On the other occasion I expressed doubt about the wisdom of accepting the 'Freedom of the Seas' clause in President Wilson's schedule of 'Points' affecting peace proposals. Although there was a representative of the Admiralty present, the committee was in favour of acceptance. The Government did not agree.

The matters that interested me most in connection with propaganda were those that affected the prospect of an Allied victory in France and Flanders, the only area, in my opinion, in which decisive victory could ever be secured.

I remember being amazed at the impression which I gained that many Frenchman had really been induced to believe that, if we occupied the coastal sector with our Army, we should want to stay there after the War. I commend to attention the amazing disclosures on that subject that are contained in Adam's *Treason and Tragedy* (p. 59). He describes the bitter anti-British propaganda in France and he states that Duval (editor and manager of a propagandist publication, and prime mover in Germany's interests) was the man 'who so energetically spread abroad the idea that the British, once having occupied Calais, and the Channel ports, would never evacuate them, and incredible though it may appear in British ears, this subtle fable obtained wide credence in the country districts of France.'

Soon after the Ministry of Information had been established under Lord Beaverbrook in 1918, a representative of that department came to ask for my help in dealing with a report which had reached him from Paris that the common gossip there was that we had only 400,000 soldiers in France and that we were leaving the French to their fate (at a time when we were bearing the main burden of the war on land as we had in all other spheres from the outset). The obvious answer to the rumour was that if the whole of Haig's Army was only 400,000 strong, the portion of it that prevented about a million and a half of the enemy's Army from reaching Amiens must be pretty good men. What usually happened in connection with Allied propaganda in those days was that when the line was pressed back, mud was thrown, and after a successful advance, bouquets.

During the weeks that followed the turning of the tide I was specially anxious to enforce upon the German soldiers the 'logic of events' by countering the frantic appeals that were being made to them to stand fast, reinforced by promises of victory and misrepresentations of the economic and military situation. Sending showers of hundreds of thousands of leaflets, revealing the truth, across the lines, attached to little balloons, was a good idea of Lord Northcliffe's propaganda department. I wrote one of the leaflets to persuade 'German Michael' that it was a mistake to believe that ruthless destruction of the world's economic resources was either a good way to win a war or to ensure future prosperity. At the same time 'economic expansion' was being put to the fore as a German war-aim. The only other piece of propaganda in which I took a personal part was the design of a poster entitled 'The Grave of the Red Cross Nurse', showing a red cross in the sky above an empty blue sea, the scene of the sinking of a hospital ship. The artist treated the subject with dignity and in good taste.

Hindenburg has thrown some light [1] upon the influence

[1] *Out of My Life.* Translated by F. A. Holt, 1920; pp. 314, 392.

of such propaganda upon the German Army. He wrote that: 'In the shower of inflammatory pamphlets which was scattered by enemy airmen our adversaries said and wrote that they did not think so badly of us; that we must only be reasonable and perhaps renounce something we had conquered. Then everything would soon be right again and we could live together in peace. . . . What a blessing peace would be after all the fighting. There was, therefore, no point in continuing the struggle. Such was the purport of what our men read and said. The soldier thought that it could not all be enemy lies, allowed it (the truth?) to poison his mind, and proceed to poison the minds of others.'

We left the Western Front during the period of depreciating morale in the German Army which followed the Battle of Amiens on the 8th of August and subsequent successes of the British and Allied Armies, and we now come to an incident in the Secret Service which lay behind the climax, the reaping of the harvest after years of laborious endeavour.

While public attention, and perhaps public belief, treats wars and 'Intelligence' connected therewith as matters of brilliant improvisation, they have another quite different aspect. Somebody once defined genius as an 'infinite capacity for taking pains'. However it may be with genius, the definition exactly fits the requirements for successful field-intelligence with an army, and the bigger the army the greater the constant and monotonous grind. When describing the discovery through a Baden newspaper (examined by an intelligence agent in Switzerland) of the secret of von Hutier's presence at St. Quentin opposite to Gough's Fifth Army in the early months of 1918, I am afraid that I did not accentuate enough the perpetual and monotonous work of examining foreign journals. If that work had not been done conscientiously the important paragraphs on a back page of that obscure provincial paper would have been missed. Instead of receiving six or seven weeks' warning of the great attack which was impending, Gough might then have had only a few hours to prepare, and Amiens might have been lost. Honour and renown are not to be earned by days and nights spent in scanning the columns of foreign journals, but such work may win a battle (or save an army), and all the more credit is due to those who did it conscientiously, both in Switzerland and elsewhere, during the long years of the Great War. The late Sir H. M. Hozier proved that a paragraph in a neutral journal had much to do with the Prussian victory at Königgratz in 1866, and in 1870 the movement of MacMahon to Sedan was disclosed from a similar source.

I mentioned, when describing the intelligence work in Rawlinson's Fourth Army, how information was obtained by examining batches of prisoners. One of the most valuable items in the information was the exact location of headquarters in the hostile commands, some of these being a long way behind the front line. The point will be recalled that Rawlinson had been given a special force of cavalry. As the result of examining many German prisoners during the period of secret preparation and concentration before the great attack, 'Intelligence' of the Fourth Army were able to prepare a number of simple maps showing the exact positions of those German Headquarters, and of the best routes to them. Those maps were issued to the cavalry, with instructions to fight neither with infantry, cavalry nor artillery, but to make for enemy headquarters with all possible speed.

One body of cavalry reached the headquarters of a High German Command. So unexpected was their visit that the occupants only had time to tear up the heaps of documents which had accumulated for many months. The cavalrymen found scraps of paper knee-deep in one room. They made a rough selection before they went on to perform further exploits, and sacks of that torn paper were in course of time dispatched to 'Intelligence' at Army Headquarters. There they were pieced together, and references to the Hindenburg Line were discovered, with maps and plans dating from 1916.

The prospect of even reaching the Hindenburg Line in 1918 was doubtful at the time; to break through it before 1919 was beyond the most hopeful dreams. Over a month was to pass before such an idea dawned in the mind even of Marshal Foch, the most confident of all commanders; so the sacks of torn paper were laid aside for a time. The task of sifting them properly and translating all the German writing thereon was beyond the capacity of the Fourth Army Staff. They were engaged in current work, connected with further battles for which the way had been opened. Soon, however, the services of one 'H', an officer well acquainted with German, became available, and he was lent to the Fourth Army for a month. By piecing the various plans together and examining them, it was then discovered that the German High Command had foreseen, during the heavy fighting on the Somme in 1916, the probability that they would have to fall back to a shorter line which must be carefully chosen for its adaptability to defence. It must fulfil the usual requirements—physical obstacles, field of fire, cover, and so forth. The world-famed Hindenburg Line was carefully reconnoitred, and it was made 'impregnable' by solid and permanent fortifications, obstacles, and shelter from shells and bombs.

The torn paper contained plans showing every detail of the defences; there were reports giving the reasons for the selection of their sites, and describing the strong and the weak points from the aspect of the defenders. For instance, there were detailed plans showing the exact positions of: All headquarters; centres of telephone and telegraph communications; billets for the garrisons of the defences; concrete shelters for men, and deep dug-outs; gun-emplacements, with arcs of fire of the guns, machine-gun posts; refilling places from which to draw ammunition; covered routes for reinforcements to use; dressing-stations and field-hospitals; wireless-telegraphy stations, and, perhaps most important of all, tunnels, of which we will take one as an example.

Experiences on the Western Front had proved over and over again that, however heroic and successful an initial attack might be, a break-through was stopped when an enemy used his reserves for counter-attack. The deeper the penetration, the more effectively these reserves could be used. (Foch's counter-attack with Mangin's reserve Divisions on July 18th, 1918, during the German offensive on both sides of Rheims, had provided a good example.) From a map which was reconstructed from the scraps of paper taken on August 8th it was discovered that there was a tunnel a mile long behind one part of the Hindenburg Line. The tunnel passed through a hill and led to the front line. It was lighted by electricity. It contained large sidings and places for whole battalions to assemble in when waiting to reinforce. There were electric power-stations and communications. Everything was on a colossal scale and heavily reinforced with concrete. Such works could not be moved about, so although the plan dated from 1916 the tunnel would be there in 1918 with all its appurtenances.

There were five entrances to the tunnel, behind the crest of a hill, near the village of Bellenglise. Reserves could thus be poured forward to reinforce the troops in front or to launch counter-attacks from secure assembly-places against triumphant but tired troops who might cross the front lines of defence. The Duke of Wellington has been credited with many wise sayings, some of them —like the one about 'the playing fields of Eton having won the Battle of Waterloo'—being apocryphal. For another saying about Generals in action wondering what there was on the other side of a hill there is better authority. By examining prisoners in July and August, 1918, by thus discovering the positions of the enemy's headquarters by cavalry raids on those headquarters on the 8th of August, and the capture of torn papers, and by laboriously piecing together the scraps, the British Commanders knew for

certain what was behind that particular hill in the Hindenburg Line. The entrances were severely strafed with shell
and bombed, and the result can be imagined. The attacking infantry advanced so fast that they caught an engineer
at work on some mysterious apparatus with which he
confessed that he was just about to blow up the whole
tunnel. He was just too late. That is only one sample of
the intelligence that was collected about the Hindenburg
Line and brought up to date before the attack. The story
of the interview between Foch and Haig which preceded
the attack is worth telling. I had it from an eye-witness.
On September 8th, Foch appealed to the British Empire
Armies (in which some American Divisions were serving)
to attack the 'impregnable' fortress of dug-outs, obstacles,
shelters, batteries and tunnels called the Hindenburg
Line. His interview with Haig lasted only for a few
minutes. After a few words Marshal Foch said: 'You will
do it. There is nothing that the British Army cannot do,'
and Sir Douglas Haig agreed.

It is not for us to follow the epic tale of achievement
that ensued—our object is not to furnish the history of the
great actions, but of the Secret Service that preceded them.
In Mr. Churchill's words: 'By the night of September
30th the Hindenburg Line on a front of 25 miles was
blasted and pierced to an average depth of 7 miles,
and 36,500 prisoners were reported to Sir Douglas
Haig.'

On October 1st Hindenburg demanded, at a conference which had been summoned at Spa on Ludendorff's
initiative as soon as the line was first broken on September
29th, that a request for an Armistice should be made on
the next day. Resistance was prolonged unnecessarily by
an appeal to President Wilson after the outlook for the
German Army was hopeless. Negotiations with the President delayed matters, and the Delegates did not leave the
German Lines until November 6th. The terms of the
Armistice, dictated by the Allies through the mouth of
Foch, were accepted on the 11th of November. Thence-

forward Secret Service was no longer needed for achieving victory.

It may be of interest to add, as an example of the widespread network of organizations of Secret Intelligence, the Chief Naval Censor's account of how he knew, on the Sunday night, that all was over.[1] 'At 9.40 p.m. on Sunday, November 10th, Lieutenant Faudel Phillips rushed into my room with German wireless from the German Supreme Command to the Plenipotentiaries with the Allied Command containing the words 'Your Excellency [Secretary of State Erzberger] is empowered to sign the Armistice. Imperial Chancellor.' A note was added, asking for further negotiations on certain points, and there was also a message from the German Government to the Plenipotentiaries: 'The German Government accepts the Armistice conditions offered on November 8th. Request acknowledgement of receipt. Imperial Chancellor.' Sir Douglas Brownrigg at once informed the First Lord by telephone, and he adds that the Prime Minister must have had a copy of the messages by 11 p.m.

AUTHOR'S NOTE.—Since the above chapter was written, the author has been informed on good authority that armoured cars preceded the cavalry who raided the German headquarters.

[1] *Indiscretions of a Naval Censor*, p. 259.

CHAPTER XXVII

RETROSPECT, AND A FORECAST

IN LOOKING back over a varied experience of British Secret Service in peace and in war extending over nearly forty years, I can recall no single example therein of the use of prevarication in British propaganda, unless spreading misleading reports about intentions for the use of fighting forces in war comes into that category. Nor can I recall an example of a practice, adopted in some foreign countries in the War and in Russia at the present time, of using Secret Services to undermine the authority of foreign governments and to incite internecine strife, class-hatred, and rebellion.

My own personal activities in connection with secret and 'Intelligence' work have been devoted to discovering the naval and military secrets of other countries and to concealing our own, and the second of these objects has sometimes been more difficult to achieve than the first. When plied with questions by the curious, silence sometimes provides them with the sought-for reply, and garrulity, not allowing a questioner to 'get a word in edgeways', provides a defence more efficient than reticence. In extreme cases, to ask an interrogator the question to which he is known to be seeking the answer is as effective as a *riposte* in a fencing-bout. The danger with important naval, military and air secrets in war arises when they become known to gossips likely to air knowledge that seems to them to enhance their own importance. These were so common in London in the summer of 1916 that they gave rise to a skit which was passed round by word of mouth. (I do not think that it ever appeared in print, but it was written by Richard Arkell). It ran :

293

Absolute evidence have I none,
But my Aunt's charwoman's sister's son
Heard a policeman on his beat
Say to a housemaid in *Downing Street*
That he had an uncle who had a friend
Who knew *for a fact* when the War would end.

In war-time deeds dominated the effect of words, but when the War ended the secret influences conveyed by the men of words became all-important. The instruments (navies, armies and air forces) which had been used by the men of deeds were hastily scrapped, some think prematurely.

Amongst the papers that passed through my office at that time there came appeals from various territories, of which the future was in the balance, for Allied troops to act as police and to control the violence of political and racial factions until the new frontiers had been determined. 'British troops preferred' was a proviso that was added to most of these appeals, and one's thoughts naturally recurred to the fleeting effects of secret propaganda in war when it is in direct conflict with the truth.

The most bitter anti-British propaganda, secret and public, emanated from a nominal Ally, Russia, where effective use was made of the word 'Imperialism' as the alleged object behind the British campaigns in Palestine and Syria, in Mesopotamia (now Iraq), and in East and West Africa. Campaigns of conquest in those regions were attributed to an intention to influence the terms of peace and to ensure territorial expansion, rather than to fulfil the proclaimed British war-aim, the expulsion of invading armies from France, from Belgium and from Serbia. The bearing of distant campaigns upon that object was not easily explained.

A Secret Agent from an Allied country came to see me shortly before the end of the struggle. He asked me to tell him in confidence what Britain's war-aims were, in the views of our War Cabinet, and especially what enemies' territories were desired. I told him that I had no power to speak for the Cabinet. I could only give him my own personal opinion, after a year's experience of the Cabinet's decisions, that the British Government sought no territorial aggrandizement whatever. If asked the same question in the light of later events and of further knowledge, I should give the same reply.

When the hostility to Britain of the Lenin régime in Russia became more and more obvious, I remember preparing for the Cabinet a paper, somewhat on the lines of a military 'appreciation' based upon imagination of what is going on in the 'enemy's brain'. The paper attributed to Lenin a desire to wreck the social order and system of government in every country. It assumed that Britain would be looked upon by him as the strongest citadel of established order, and of subjection to laws framed by and in the interests of the community. A further assumption was made that Lenin's plan of campaign would be to work for unrest and rebellion in the outposts of Empire, especially in the East, in order to draw to those the most patriotic law-abiding elements in a war-weary population, and then to work for class-hatred, strikes, riot, and rebellion against constituted authority in the citadel itself, the United Kingdom.

Although an old story, it may be that a tale subsequently told to me by a brother officer who was employed on Secret Service in Transcaucasia after the Armistice still holds some interest, even if only academic. My friend provided me with two accounts, one of which was embodied in an article in the *Fortnightly Review* in 1920. I received the second a few weeks ago, and a few days before his death abroad. For the historical setting of Transcaucasia and the regions round about, the points will be recalled that a Federal Republic embodying Armenia, Georgia, Azerbaijan and Daghestan was proclaimed in September 1917, declared independent in April 1918, and dissolved in May 1918; that General Dunsterville's force reached Enzeli in Persian territory on the southern shore of the Caspian in February 1918; that the independence of Georgia and Azerbaijan as Republics and the control of Armenian affairs by a National Council followed in May 1918; that the sea-command of the Caspian was secured by Britain as the result of a naval action in December 1919; that Baku, after having been in the hands of the Turks from September 1918, was occupied by British troops in November; and that the place was in British hands from the end of December 1918. During the British occupation, Baku contained many Bolshevik propagandists, and my correspondent mentioned their methods, especially that of making personal friends over whom they obtained in due course a strong influence. Of these friends groups were formed which were developed into information companies. The principal Soviet agent in the Caucasus was identified. He was an Armenian, thought to be far above suspicion. In his public capacity he was an advocate of Tsardom, of capitalism and of religion. He was a man of refinement, posing as one of the refugees who had lost all through Bolshevism. His true mission was discovered by intercepted correspondence. His agents were distributed in the factories, in the shipyards and amongst skilled labour in the oilfields. Each agent worked amongst members of his own class in life. Their work was insidious; they held no meetings, and they made no speeches. Private and confidential conversation was their weapon. The noisy gangs who held meetings and followed processions bearing banners were mere tools, providing camouflage for the truly dangerous workers. A similar system was applied in a wider sphere. It was intended, by a method similar to that suggested in the Cabinet paper to which I have referred, to bring about the downfall of the British Empire.

The military situation in the spring of 1919 was that Denikin's White Russians had driven the Red forces from the Crimea to the Volga. British forces dominated the Caucasus, Transcaucasia and Transcaspia. In the East, Koltchak's White Army held Siberia, and hoped to drive the Reds back to Moscow, but the White Russian staff felt that, even if the Central Soviet Government were to be overthrown, the task would only be half accomplished. Bolshevism had moved east, and in Turkestan a focus was being established from which tentacles would stretch out to China, to Persia, to Afghanistan, and to the frontiers of India.

The theory in the Propagandist School in Moscow was that the best agent for spreading Bolshevism in foreign countries would be a man of the race or nationality of the people therein, so the school was opened to Chinese, Persians, Afghans, and Indians, who (according to my correspondent) were at first invited as guests and maintained at Russian expense. In Turkestan a special depot of these propagandists was established, and a mission was detached to accompany every caravan that crossed the Persian and the Afghan frontiers. Two agents formed the minimum for a small caravan. The numbers increased with its size and importance, the idea being to flood Persia with Persian Bolsheviks, Afghanistan with Afghans and India with agitators passing across to British India. The result was first apparent in the Afghan War of 1919. Only our present-day Secret Service can be in a position to tell the remainder of the story. That the British body-politic was too healthy to be seriously affected by foreign secret propaganda was proved in the eyes of the civilized world by the result of the Great Strike of 1926. To the man in the street, it seems that that campaign of secret anti-British propaganda, initiated by Lenin and his agents twelve years ago, is following its predicted course on the outskirts of Empire with partial effectiveness, but that Great Britain still stands four-square to the world as the citadel of established order, with a law-abiding population averse to violence and revolution against constituted authority.

It seems that in peace, as in war, such forms of Secret Service can only be effective in combatant and in non-combatant communities which already contain the seeds of decay; that, in the long run, the spreading of truth is the only efficient form of propaganda; and that concealment of the truth about war-plans is a condition essential to their success.

It has not been possible, in a single book devoted mainly to Secret Services which affected armies and navies, to do justice to the widespread secret system of commercial intelligence which was the necessary outcome of efforts to impose economic pressure upon the Central Powers in the Great War. J. C. Millais (in his *Wanderings and Memoirs*) and other writers have given a few glimpses into the nature of an organization of which the full tale has never yet been told. Mr. Millais mentions an interesting type of volunteer secret agent, a keen sportsman who worked in various disguises as a fish-buyer, or on occasion as a drunken loafer, and succeeded in gaining the confidence of German and pro-German nationals of a certain Scandinavian country. He was successful in marking down German agents, and in the time of the ruthless submarine campaign, he provided valuable information about the movements of German U-boats. He located in one Scandinavian port, up to November 1916, no less than fifteen resident German secret agents, whose business it was to communicate to the German U-boats information about the movements of merchant-shipping, but the most definite case, affecting commercial intelligence, which Mr. Millais quotes is one of the arrival of a Scandinavian vessel at a certain port with a cargo declared by the captain to be 'English'. The captain tried to enlist the help of the British Consul to obtain bunker coal. The Consular service was too well supplied with information from secret sources about the ownership of all cargoes. The ownership of that cargo was German, and the captain did not get his bunker coal. The incident in itself may appear trivial, unless one realizes that the network of such commercial intelligence extended to every neutral harbour in the world.

Another branch of Secret Service, to which it has not

been possible to do justice, is the use of aeroplanes for the purpose, especially in landing spies behind enemy's lines in land warfare, and in picking them up when their missions have been accomplished. Mr. J. M. Spaight has provided in his *Air-Power and War Rights* sufficient information about this interesting subject, with references to many sources which can be recommended to those in quest of 'thrills' connected with Secret Service.

We can, for instance, with his aid, put ourselves in the position and imagine the feelings of a secret agent, flying above the earth for the first time in order to be dropped by parachute behind the enemy's lines on a dark night, hesitating about taking the drop from an unfamiliar machine roaring across the sky and being thrown out by a ruthless pilot.

In connection with the progress that was made in aviation during the course of the War, the point will be recalled that the introduction of the Fokker machine gave the Germans the mastery of the air between October 1915 and April 1916. One of the reasons was that, in the Fokker machine, the pilot used his machine-gun straight ahead, firing through the whirling screw. The passage of the bullets was synchronized with the spinning of the arms of the screw, so as not to strike them. There is a story of a German pilot, a traitor to his country, who landed purposely behind the British lines in a Fokker machine and sold the secrets of its construction. The story reached me through so many sources which I believed to be reliable that I was deceived for a time, but after consultation with experts I attach no credence to it at all. Two or three types of 'synchronized interruptor gear' for enabling machine-gun bullets to pass through the airscrew were used in British machines during the Great War, and I believe the 'constantinesco' gear invented by a Rumanian was the most satisfactory. The system was developed in England, and it had nothing to do with any German invention or discovery. Such are the difficulties which confront writers on Secret Service when dealing

with incidents which have not come within their personal
knowledge. The story has appeared in several 'Spy
Books'.

For the rest, it is hoped that the reader will find in
these pages enough typical examples of the activities of
the British Secret Service, especially of those that affected
the fighting forces in the Great War, to enable him to
form his own judgment of its efficiency or shortcomings.
If, in addition, better knowledge of the information which
our responsible commanders have had at their disposal
should engender more sympathy with them, and fairer
criticism, the purpose of this book will be fulfilled.

APPENDIX

CONVEYING SECRET INFORMATION

EXAMPLES have been furnished in this book of the difficulty that has been experienced by secret agents in conveying to its destination the information which they have obtained, and by statesmen and diplomatists in communicating secretly with their representatives in other countries. These subjects do not lend themselves to brief treatment but, for those whom they interest, it may be desirable to add a few random notes from the author's limited knowledge of methods of dispatching and of intercepting messages, dealing first with ciphers.

I will begin with a simple form of cipher which I will call the 'Schoolgirls' ', as I first heard of its use in a girls' school.

Here is a message in that cipher. It looks very mysterious, but it is only a quotation from *Peter Pan*.

V☐⦿⦿∧ ⅃∨∨

This is the key for solving the cipher (see overleaf), and all that is necessary is to substitute the geometrical figure which encloses the letter in the key for the letter itself, performing the reverse process in deciphering. The use of the dots over the letters in the key is, I hope, obvious.

Then, for the more advanced, there is the 'sliding' alphabet 'cipher', which used to be so popular amongst contributors to agony columns. I believe that its origin is attributed to Julius Caesar, and in its simple form it is so easy to read that when I was a special service officer

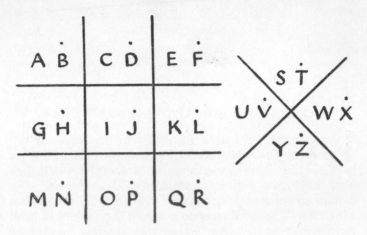

in the Anglo-Boer War of 1899–1902, civilian telegraph clerks used to tell each other the news (sent in that sort of cipher) as the messages were passing through on Morse instruments. The tapping could be heard by any by-stander and understood by hostile secret agents with the same technical skill.

For the 'Sliding Alphabet' system of cipher you put two alphabets together and 'Slide'. If you 'Slide one' this is the result:

A B C D E F G, etc., for message in CIPHER.
  a b c d e f g, etc., for message in CLEAR.

So an 'a' in the clear becomes a 'B' in the cipher, and so on. If you 'slide two' you put a 'C' for an 'a'. Further com-plications can be introduced, but that is the simple form, and it can best be solved by using 'frequency tables', which arrange the letters of the alphabet in their order of common use. For instance: the letter most common in English is E, so if there are more K's than any other letter in the cipher-message, try E's in the place of all the K's in the cipher-message, and so on. I understand that the frequency table in use in America runs thus:

E T A O N I S H R D L C U F M P W G Y B V
K X Q J Z

for ordinary non-technical messages. If a number of surnames occur in the message, I should say that the letter B was put too low in the scale.

The 'Playfair' method of substituting letters is far more difficult to defeat, and it is the one that I have always used myself. 'Frequency tables' are of no use in its solution. It requires no apparatus, only a key-word which can easily be remembered. Say that the key-word is KAISER. If I and J are counted as one, there are 25 letters in the alphabet, so a square divided into five each way will just contain it. Make such a square and fill in the letters of the alphabet, beginning with those in the key-word and adding the others in order, like this:

K	A	I	S	E
R	B	C	D	F
G	H	L	M	N
O	P	Q	T	U
V	W	X	Y	Z

Divide your message into pairs of letters. If the two letters in the pair are at the corners of a rectangle, substitute the letters at the other corners of the rectangle. Thus BY would become DW; HE would become NA; and so on. If the two letters in the pair are in line with each other, for instance, RC, substitute the letters to the right of them, namely, **BD**. If one letter in the pair is above the other, substitute the letter below each. Thus FU would be changed to NZ. With double letters (say OO) you must put dummies between them. The 'frequency' method is of no use at all for solving such cipher-messages. (An N represents an H the first time and an F the second time, in the above explanation.)

Further complications can easily be introduced and even in its simple form the 'Playfair' is not an easy cipher to solve unless you know the key-word. You must burn the diagram as soon as you have used it.

There is so great a demand for letter-puzzles of various sorts in these days that it might amuse some readers to solve the following message, in order to gather some idea of the sort of precautions which secret agents can take to send their reports to the destinations safely. The key-word is KAISER. It is usual to divide the groups of letters in fives; hence the stops:

OVTRX	AAMKE	UPIHG	CKIFS
DKRBT	GPMKI	OUGPC	VXUSV

I am told that experts can solve simple 'Playfair' ciphers without knowing the key-word, so I give them another message without disclosing what the key-word is:

BUFDA	GNPOX	IHOQY	TKVQM
PMBYD	AAEQZ		

I have always imagined myself that 'Playfair' ciphers were insoluble without the key-word. It would be interesting to know whether I have been living in a fool's paradise.

The most objectionable form of cipher for use on active service is in my opinion the 'Dictionary cipher', in which sender and receiver must carry copies of the same edition of the same dictionary (some copies of which are almost certain to fall in the hands of the enemy under active service conditions). The method is to look up the word that you want to send and to note the number of the line on the page where the word occurs. Then you turn over an agreed number of pages, count the same number of lines down the new page, and substitute the word which you find. When you are deciphering a message you go through the same process backwards. Once, at a particularly strenuous time, it took me nearly twenty-four hours to solve a long message sent in that cipher. A conscientious and ingenious colleague used five cipher words to indicate a single regiment such as the Oxfordshire Light Infantry which appeared as Ox. Ford. Light. Infant. Rye. The dictionary, having to be portable, was in minute print and I had only one candle to work by at night.

These examples of ciphers suffice for our purpose. There is a strict rule that no military message is to be sent partly in cipher and partly in clear, because this practice helps the solver.

There is a story of a British General who, at a time when everything secret was sent in cipher, broadcasted his true orders in clear language, thus completely deceiving the enemy, who feared a *ruse de guerre*; and Sir Edward Grey, when he was Foreign Secretary, is said to have upset diplomatic procedure so much by speaking and writing the exact truth that exasperated foreign propagandists protested by calling him 'Liar Grey'.

The British General's trick of abandoning ciphers reminds me of the experience of a Russian naval officer (Semenoff) in the Manchurian War of 1904–5. At Port Arthur certain conditions obtained which were similar all over Russia. Any military secret could be bought at a price, and the more secret a paper was the higher the price. Papers were marked 'confidential'. Their contents leaked out. They were marked 'secret'. The same thing happened. Then 'very secret'. At last it occurred to the authorities to try another plan, only marking unimportant papers in that way and passing secret ones about with no labels at all. The plan succeeded.

From ciphers, and the spreading of news in clear, we can pass on to secret codes. These are usually bulky books containing groups of cipher-numbers with their meanings attached to them and various devices to make changes so as to ensure secrecy. If a code-book or secret cipher is lost, trouble ensues, and the code as previously used is no longer considered safe. In the days when I was intelligence officer to the Mediterranean Fleet the Commander-in-Chief's secret metal dispatch-box, in which such things were kept, was weighted with lead to ensure its sinking. When H.M.S. *Victoria* sank so tragically in 1893 after her collision with H.M.S. *Camperdown*, one of the few things that floated to the surface was that air-tight, heavily-weighted dispatch-box. The makers had forgotten to bore holes both to let the air out and to let the water in.

There is a tale of an heroic expert British diver who succeeded in keeping the Admiralty decipherers up to date with German secret code-books throughout the War by recovering them from sunken German submarines; if necessary, breaking his way in and risking damage to the air-pipe upon which his life depended.

In the old days when I was first connected with naval intelligence, foreign nations who might have been our prospective enemies might have had their intelligence work simplified by the fact that we had distributed a certain confidential code-book to many Vice-Consuls who were not British subjects, but I do not know of any case of leakage through that cause.

One form of code is to use one word to represent another one of different meaning. At the time of the Russian reinforcements hoax at the outbreak of war, someone started the tale that the story originated in some suspicious body who saw a telegram about 100,000 Russian eggs, and thought that 'eggs' must be the code-word for soldiers.

One method, neither a cipher nor a code, for sending a letter secretly is to write on a long narrow strip wound spirally round a rod of a certain gauge. The receiver winds the strip round a similar rod of the same gauge, and so reads the message. The device has been employed in the East from time immemorial.

The ordinary peace-time method of sealing up one's letters so that they cannot be opened by melting the gum in the steam of a kettle can be defeated by experts in the removal and replacement of seals, and it strikes one as humorous when banks and lawyers send confidential documents in long envelopes with enormous seals at one end and the other (gummed down) end left unprotected. Perhaps it is not generally known that even a sealed envelope is not always a protection. A split wire can sometimes be inserted under the flap to catch the corner of the enclosed document, roll it up on the wire, and so extract it. Replacement is done in the same way, and the letter reaches its destination with the seal unbroken.

My first memory of 'invisible inks' dates back to early childhood, an age when knowing 'secrets'—and passing them on—is attractive. In our family we used a very simple form, the nursery milk, and we wrote with quill pens. It was easy to write in milk with a quill pen, if we looked sideways at what we wrote so that the light shone upon it while it was still wet; and quill does not scratch as steel does. Then the milk was allowed to dry and an apparently blank card or sheet of paper changed hands. If the milk writing was held to a hot fire, it became dark brown in colour and could easily be read. Lemon-juice and other familiar liquids made good invisible inks, and it was amazing to hear about the use by Secret Service agents in the Great War of simple expedients familiar in one's nursery days to deceive grown-up people, however unintelligent.

The Germans specialized in invisible inks. They commanded the services of some of the best chemists in the world, and the industry was mobilized to the advantage of the war-party. All sorts of tricks were applied in the War for sending invisible inks, or materials for making them, to agents in neutral and in belligerent countries. Ointments, tooth-paste, soaps, patent medicines, and other innocent-looking goods were carried by people ignorant of their real nature to the proper destinations. Even clothing specially prepared was submitted to soaking in hot water and a good invisible ink resulted from the rinsing. They adopted many other ingenious devices, difficult to detect, but they were all discovered in course of time.

Other devices for passing secret information have been mentioned in the chapters of this book. It used to be said that the only secure method was to report by word of mouth in an empty room with doors and windows closed and no cupboards, recesses or curtains. In these days some 'walls have ears', in the form of microphones. To use an hibernianism, the safest way to deal with secrets is not to know them. But 'Safety First' is a dull maxim for those who are attracted by Secret Service.

INDEX